The struggle for the Cornwall Railway

- Fated decisions

0.2 *The newly opened Cornwall Railway strides across the Cornish landscape on its approach to Truro. An eastbound train crosses the Carvedras Viaduct.* West Briton 6 May 1859

The Struggle for the Cornwall Railway

- *Fated Decisions*

by

Hugh Howes

In memory of my parents with whom I first travelled the Cornwall Railway

TWELVEHEADS PRESS

TRURO 2012

0.1 FRONT COVER: *The Cornwall Railway as originally built with a broad gauge single track and with enough land purchased for a second track. Here the up* FLYING DUTCHMAN *at Black Bridge near Liskeard is hauled by a saddle tank locomotive. The first two carriages were built for easy conversion to standard gauge. The track is laid with bridge rails which are supported on timber throughout their length.* LISKEARD OLD CORNWALL SOCIETY

TWELVEHEADS PRESS

First published 2012 by Twelveheads Press

ISBN 978 0 906294 74 1

British Library Cataloguing-in-Publication Data.

A catalogue record for this book is available from the British Library.

Typeset in Garamond 3

Printed by R. Booth Ltd, Penryn, Cornwall

Contents

List of illustrations

FOREWORD

The railway age began with the opening of the Liverpool & Manchester Railway in 1830. Although many of those who witnessed the occasion realised that it was a momentous event, few would have realised the breadth of its impact. The railways changed everything, from people's dietary and holiday habits, to the banking system and employment patterns, creating such national favourites as fish and chips and league football on the way.

Countless promoters came forward to raise money for railway schemes across the country. The railways were perceived as the money-making enterprise of their day and they did, indeed, create fortunes for those lucky enough to choose the right line in which to invest. The Cornwall Railway, however, was not one of them.

The speed of the growth in the rail network was quite extraordinary, an unprecedented outbreak of capitalism which the world had never seen. By 1840, there was a line which ran through the spine of the country from London to Liverpool and Manchester, the Great Western had almost completed its route to Bristol, and Southampton, too, had a railway to London.

The first major legislation on regulating the railways was not passed until 1844. The government deliberately kept out of the process, allowing the network to build up with no central direction other than through the Parliamentary process to pass the bills required to build these lines.

They were undertaken on the initiative of mainly local citizens and with money raised privately, as this story of the Cornwall Railway shows. Rivalry between companies, rather than cooperation, was the order of the day resulting, at times, in unnecessary duplication. By 1850, there were more than 5,000 miles of railway, a staggering achievement. It relied on the novelty of the technology which contrasted with crude building methods depending almost exclusively on men and horses, with the occasional bit of help from explosives and the odd steam powered pump. Most of that network survives as the backbone of today's railway.

The Great Exhibition, thanks to the railway companies, was able to attract far more people than if it had taken place a decade before. The railway age had truly arrived even if the Cornwall Railway was still struggling to be built, despite having been promoted earlier than many of its now-completed contemporaries.

The Cornwall Railway was unlucky in several respects. Its struggles were legendary but by no means unique. First, it was being built in a remote area of Britain which meant it was always going to struggle to attract investors, especially as the topography was not easy. Secondly, it missed the first wave of investment and the collapse of the railway mania of the 1840s, together with the economic slump, increased these difficulties. Then there was the flirtation with atmospheric traction which proved to be a technological dead end but that was part of the wonder of the Victorian Age – experimenting with ideas. And the difficulties of construction which inevitably led to massive cost increases, a familiar story even today.

This book provides the backcloth to the story of how a particular railway was built, and how its promoters overcame the difficulties of determining a route, raising capital, finding suitable engineers and ensuring the project was kept alive despite economic slumps and topographical obstacles. The Cornwall Railway may only have played a small part in that process, but it was an important one and the decisions made by its promoters still affect the lives of local people and the economy of the region today. The author describes how, despite all the difficulties and, unlike many of its contemporaries, the line was eventually built. It is a compelling account of fortitude and perseverance.

Foreword by Christian Wolmar
Author of *Fire and Steam, how the railways transformed Britain,* 2007 and *Blood, Iron and Gold, how the railways transformed the world,* 2010.

0.3 *The Cornwall Railway began at Millbay and joined the main line, as we know it, at Pennycomequick. Here a steam railmotor crosses the railway's first viaduct.* THE SALTASH HERITAGE COLLECTION

Author's Preface

And west of westward, somewhere, Cornwall lay
John Betjeman: *Summoned by Bells*

Summer meant holidays and holidays meant Cornwall. Like many other children of my generation I was taken year after year on holiday to Cornwall. This was the Cornwall in the age immortalised by Betjeman. A glorious fortnight of freedom ... and it meant getting there, either in the ancient family Humber, which involved, in pre-motorway days, a journey time of 12 or 13 hours, or behind a steam engine. To me the train journey was very much part of the experience. The *Meccano Magazine* had commemorated the 90th anniversary of the Royal Albert Bridge with a powerful image on its front cover and a short article covering the main points of its history and construction. It was sufficient to fire the imagination and enthusiasm of a ten year old and established a lifelong interest in the Cornwall Railway. The Royal Albert Bridge was the highlight of the journey. To cross this bridge was, and still is, an exciting, and above all, for the first time, a memorable experience even though, as a ten year old, I did not understand its technical significance in advancing the science of long span railway bridges.

0.4 Meccano Magazine, August 1949.

Two other things still remain in my mind about the journey. One was the lengthy stop at Newton Abbot. My parents told me that this was to enable an additional engine to be attached to the front of the train. I am not sure that they gave a reason for this but it was something to do with the steepness of the Dartmoor foothills. I do not believe that they knew, any more than I did at the time, about Brunel's flirtation with atmospheric traction and the daunting legacy it left for train operators. The other impression was looking down from the giddy heights of the Cornish viaducts into the narrow valleys far below. I remember feeling, as I still do, that I was spending much of the journey in mid air. At the opening of the railway in 1859 the *Royal Cornwall Gazette*, in a spirit of unbridled exuberance put it this way:

> They add greatly to the effect of the scenery presented to the traveller as he flies like a bird through the air, and commands from above all the beauties of the rich succession of pictures spread out below him.

Looking back on this experience I now see that even at a tender age I had identified the three major problems of building a railway through the West Country namely crossing the Tamar, the 'South Devon Hump' and the heavy engineering works in Cornwall which between them have made the line west of Newton Abbot so costly to construct and operate. As David St John Thomas[1] so succinctly summed up, it had been 'a struggle against economics and geography'. Brunel himself put it this way, 'I do not think any line can be found through Cornwall at any moderate cost without sharp curves and steep gradients'.[2] There was one aspect of the journey to Cornwall that puzzled me which was why when we went there by car (along the A30 long before it was improved) we followed a very different route from that taken by the train. It is only in the course of researching this book that I have discovered the reason for this.

Et in Arcadia sum. EVELYN WAUGH: *BRIDESHEAD REVISITED*

Once across the bridge it was Cornwall at last. Arcadia for us was a primitive and insanitary cottage perched on the cliff edge on the Atlantic coast of Penwith, half a mile from the nearest road and down a steep path. It was, however, set in the glorious coastal landscape of in what is now the Penwith Area of Outstanding Natural Beauty. It enjoyed no services and essentially was little more than a slum. However my father regarded it as a superior kind of camping and essentially this was fine for a sunny fortnight in August. When the mists rolled in off the Atlantic and the Pendeen foghorn sounded it seemed even remoter than it actually was. Whatever its shortcomings half a century ago it provided unlimited scope for adventure. Nowadays the cottage enjoys its own website as a B&B which shows something that was not there in our time, a bathroom.

Many years after my first journey on the Cornwall Railway, I had cause regularly to travel between Derby and Bristol. I had not heard of Captain Moorsom or that he was engineer of this particular line. I observed that, beyond Birmingham, the train passed through mile upon mile of open countryside without touching any of the towns that I knew to be in the general area. On the return journeys I vividly recall that the train, having travelled at speed across Worcestershire, was brought almost to a halt soon after passing Bromsgrove. Just as the Royal Albert Bridge was a critical link in the debate about bridges of long spans, so the Lickey incline was a bench mark in the engineering debate about the acceptability of steeper gradients. Again I had stumbled on the two issues that I subsequently learnt had been key to the building of the Birmingham and Gloucester Railway. Decisions had to be made whether these new trunk routes should concentrate on connecting only the major towns and cities or whether they should connect as many intermediate settlements as possible.

The building of railways involved unprecedentally large civil engineering projects whose construction required a whole range of technical, managerial and financial skills. Railway promoters had to face a rapidly evolving national economic scene and the problems of raising vast amounts of capital, long lead times and uncertain returns. Most of the early railways have been well documented. There are biographies of particular engineers and histories of particular lines. They tend to concentrate on achievements and show the engineer in charge of events. There have also been studies of individual railway lines. However there seemed to be a gap in published literature. The railways were built in a hitherto unrecognised multifaceted culture of the law, finance and local politics. With nothing to guide them railway companies and their engineers had to evolve new working relationships, and management structures. In a small country with a complex geology they were faced with the choice of a high capital initial cost on civil engineering works to obtain as flat a road as possible or whether to economise on first construction and bequeath the operations departments a legacy of higher running costs. Geography and economics were often in direct conflict. This book explains how these problems, with varying degrees of success, were tackled in one corner of the UK.

And all the men ... merely players: They have their exits and entrances
WILLIAM SHAKESPEARE: *AS YOU LIKE IT*

My researches demonstrated that the process of making decisions had a momentum of its own over which the key figures, engineers included, could have only limited influence. Whatever the merits of the particular positions the engineers were to take, the hard realities of economics, power politics and geography would limit their freedom of action.

This is a story about some notable people with strong determination and strong characters. It is about how their interactions brought about the line we know today. I have sought to bring them alive and have provided profiles of some of them. First of all there were the influential landowners, often Members of Parliament who were anxious to use the new technology that railways offered to counteract the remoteness of Cornwall. Then there were the industrialists and mine owners who were keen to exploit the commercial potential of Cornwall. There were also the engineers who provided alternative surveys for the project: And finally, the barristers who had a decisive influence on the shape that the railway actually took.

The story of the Cornwall Railway is about many individuals making decisions in the light of the best information available to them against a fast changing economic and technical background. They included the men of influence in the County. Foremost amongst them were the Earls of Falmouth, Sir Charles Lemon, Joseph Treffry, Michael Williams, William Tweedy and George Smith. They were all men of determination who saw the project through in the face of overwhelming problems. Treffry was described in his obituary in the *West Briton* as having stubborn persistence which (he) pitted against every problem. He had a record of falling out both with his neighbours, with James Rendel who he employed as engineer for the Par Harbour and, in his capacity as Chairman of the Cornwall Railway, with Moorsom because of the latter's lack of attention to the project. However stubborn persistence was exactly the quality needed to get this project off the ground. His successors, Williams and Tweedy, deserve credit for struggling onwards with the construction against almost insuperable financial odds. Lemon and Falmouth, although favouring a central route, both took the decision to support the southern route on the basis that the latter was the only one likely to be built. It was that or nothing.

And their success or failure could be largely determined by the advocacy skills of the barristers who presented their cases to Parliament. They appeared either for the promoters of the Bills or for the petitioners against them. The Queen's Counsel who were involved in the prolonged Parliamentary battles over the Cornwall Railway in 1845 and 1846 emerged as at least as important as the engineers in determining the final form of the railway. Their cross examinations provide a rare insight of the issues over which so much passion was spent.

John Kinglake and William Rowe were the principal advocates. Kinglake's advocacy skills ensured that the line passed its parliamentary hurdles whilst Rowe's persistent cross examination of the Company's witnesses over the detail of Moorsom's plans ensured that the project was subsequently substantially redesigned to remove the shortcomings of the original. On opposite sides, they contrived to have the principle of the line from Plymouth to Falmouth accepted and the details rejected. The resulting decisions by the House of Lords were fundamental to the form that the line was to take.

Lastly were the engineers, Richard Thomas, William Moorsom and Isambard Brunel. Moorsom clearly gave inadequate attention to the job, resulting in several aspects of a survey which were manifestly unacceptable, of which his proposed crossings of Penryn Creek and the Hamoaze were the more extreme examples. Furthermore the uncertainty he exuded over whether atmospheric traction was to be used or not convinced the Committee that the implications of the plans had simply not been thought through. Brunel, too, had built a railway of many shortcomings in South Devon but redeemed himself with the Cornwall Railway. The challenge of the Royal Albert Bridge brought out the best in him and to this day remains an iconic structure which proved that tidal estuaries could be bridged and that deep water foundations could be constructed by using compressed air. It was the misfortune of the Cornwall Railway Company that he did not have the budgetary and implementation skills of his contemporary Joseph Locke. Aspects of work bequeathed maintenance costs on the company out of proportion to the original savings. The timber viaducts, whatever their cheapness at first cost, had very short lives and were being replaced after little more than fifteen years. The maintenance of the sea wall between Dawlish and Teignmouth from marine flooding and landslips was an issue over which the company had no control but on which it critically depended.

Brunel clearly had a talent for choosing people to help him. His exceptionally able team included William Johnson, William Glennie, Robert Brereton and Peter Margery. Johnson's survey is a masterpiece of balancing costs of civil engineering works against gradients and curves, thereby producing an optimal alignment through difficult country. He was a man who gave meticulous attention to detail in his surveys and on whom Brunel could rely absolutely. In this respect he was the very opposite of Moorsom. Brereton was another safe pair of hands, able to take over as Brunel's health began to fail.

Most of the other leading engineers of the time contributed to the debate over the route and form of the railway, notably Robert Stephenson and Joseph Locke. They both became presidents of the Institution of Civil Engineers, Stephenson in 1855-57 and Locke 1857-59. In addition James Rendel, John Hawkshaw, George Bidder and Charles Vignoles fundamentally affected the final form that the railway was to take. None of them were to become household names in the way that Stephenson and Brunel are. But they were all distinguished civil engineers. And between them they were responsible for a very large slice of the railway network which was completed in the second half of the 19th century. Three of them became presidents of the Institution of Civil Engineers, Rendel 1851-3, Hawkshaw 1861-63 and Bidder 1859-61. Their technical advice on the Cornwall Railway had a profound influence on the form of the successful 1846 Bill.

They all struggled with the numerous issues surrounding building a railway with weak economic prospects through a difficult terrain. But they also had to contend with both the unknown potential and the limited technology that was available. Could the atmospheric system be made to work, especially under the adverse conditions of Devon and Cornwall? What gradients and curves could the locomotives of the time be expected to cope with? Could the floating bridge be used to carry trains across the Hamoaze? Was it possible to construct a deep water pier in the Tamar?

As regards the route it was a story of the art of the possible. Despite the overwhelming preference for a central route it was the combination of Treffry and the Great Western Railway that meant that the southern route was the only realistic option. However the greatest weakness under which the company struggled had nothing to do with technical issues. It lay in the absence of proper business and financial techniques, of obtaining reliable estimates and the problem of raising funds.

The final result was a railway which, although it failed to achieve its original purpose, nevertheless stimulated a variety of new industries for Cornwall which helped to see the county through difficult times as traditional industries declined. The railway was fundamental to shaping the Cornwall as we know it today.

I have drawn extensively on the evidence given to the Parliamentary Committees in 1845 and 1846 Parliamentary proceedings because they provide the actual words and arguments of the key players and rival parties, the land owners, capitalists and industrialists of Cornwall together with the leading engineers of the time. There is, therefore, much merit in allowing them to speak for themselves. Their words provide an immediacy without the camouflaging effects of hindsight, and are therefore of especial value which subsequent accounts lack. They provide a dramatic insight into these closely debated issues.

The press were also important players in the long drawn out saga of the Cornwall Railway. The two papers circulating in Cornwall supported not only the opposing political parties but also opposing factions over the choice of route of the railway: They articulated the bitter struggle and perhaps prolonged the arguments.

Until construction actually starts, the engineer is but one of many players. The choices open to these players tend to be constrained and limited with little room for manoeuvre.

Readers may be surprised that there is no profile of Brunel. I have taken the view that his life is well documented already. Chapter eight, however, deals with his approach to financing and contracting which is an aspect with which readers will be less familiar.

My aim has been to show how these key players interacted in an ever changing but generally hostile economic environment. I wanted to explore how decisions were reached on the particular routes, on their particular alignments and how the particular topographical problems were overcome.

Why the Cornwall Railway as opposed to any other? In my initial literature search I discovered that the line had taken twenty years to complete from its initial conception. How could this be? Gradually a tale emerged of inadequate finance, bitter divisions, and unresolved engineering problems which combined to render the project all but impossible to bring to a satisfactory conclusion. The decisions seemed to be fated.

Hugh Howes
Chorleywood
2012

Chapter one
'...A sea of troubles...'
William Shakespeare: *Hamlet*

> No enterprise was ever carried on to success in the face of greater difficulties and impediments, or completed in spite of more frequent disappointments. If success is the more complete in proportion to the obstacles overcome, the Cornwall Railway is one of the greatest successes. The resolution, perseverance and judgement, which enabled the directors and officers to surmount them all, is a pledge that these gentlemen will not be found wanting in whatever may now be required to make it the most available for the interests, whether of the shareholders, or of the County.[1]

So the *Royal Cornwall Gazette* reflected ruefully at the opening of the railway, in 1859, on the long delays, deferred hopes and frustrations that had accompanied the conception, and construction of the Cornwall Railway.

The brief facts are that the Cornwall Railway was conceived in 1833 in response to the threatened and impending loss from Falmouth of the Atlantic packet traffic, which carried mails, goods and passengers to and from the outposts of the empire and other trading nations. A first serious submission was made to Parliament in 1836 but it failed because of lack of financial support. A resolution by a 'County Meeting' to 'progress and complete' the railway was taken in 1839. This marked the real beginning of the project. There then ensued a long and costly disagreement over the route of the proposed railway. There were those who wanted a 'central line' via Bodmin, Launceston and Okehampton and those who favoured the southern route serving St Austell, Liskeard and Plymouth.

The first time that the proposal was fully considered by Parliament was in 1845. Although the concept was approved the scheme failed because of its detailed shortcomings. The company's engineer, Captain William Scarth Moorsom, responsible for these technical problems, was then replaced by Isambard Kingdom Brunel whose scheme eventually gained Parliamentary approval in 1846 for building a southern route via Plymouth. The line was only opened from Plymouth to Truro in 1859 after thirteen years of an intense financial struggle and a major downgrading of its specification. Falmouth was finally connected to London in 1863.

How could it have taken so long? Whereas, for example, the Great Western Railway from conception to completion took eight years to connect the capital to Bristol, the London to Birmingham, eight years, and the Grand Junction four years, it took the Cornwall Railway a full twenty five years to connect Falmouth to Plymouth. The original aim of

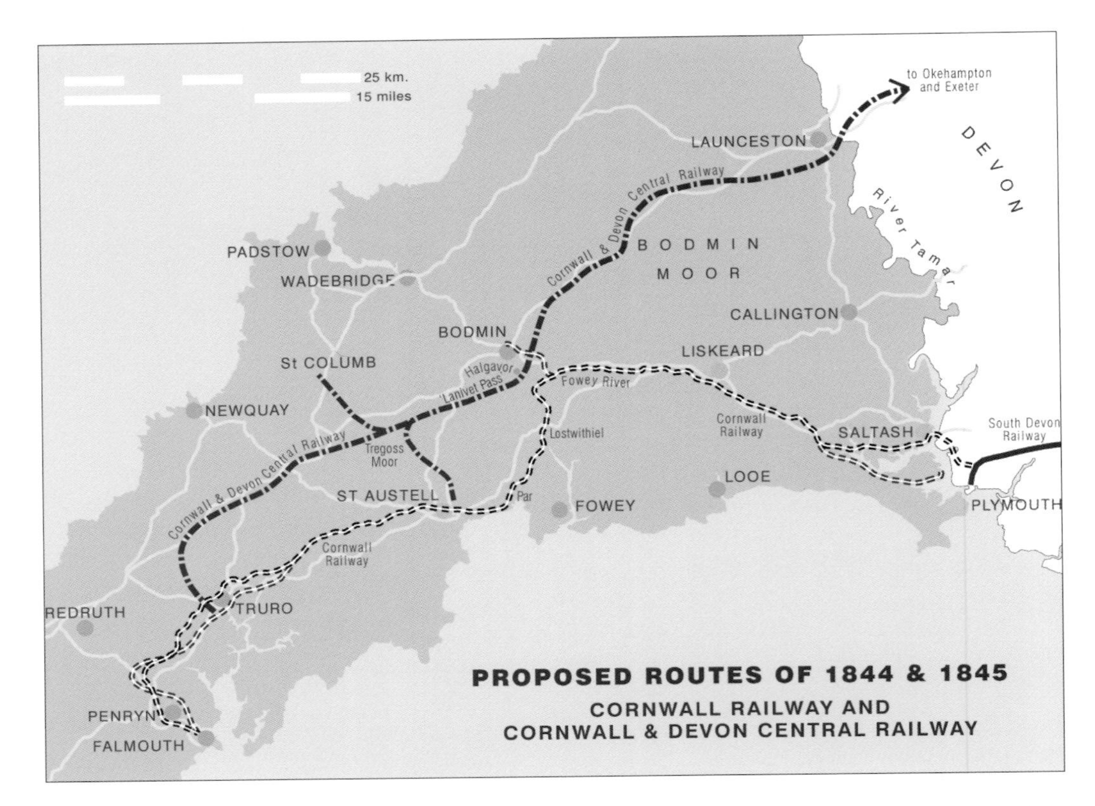

1.1 *Much energy, time and, above all, money was spent by supporters of the Cornwall Railway and the Cornwall and Devon Central Railway on the rival merits of their two routes. The struggle was kept alive until Parliament finally approved the southern route.*

restoring the Atlantic packet traffic to Falmouth was never achieved but the railway was to serve a very different, but valuable, purpose to that for which it was originally conceived.

The philosophy of private enterprise under which the railways of the country were constructed was to be a problem for the promoters of the Cornwall Railway. The *laissez faire* tradition was deeply rooted in the British psyche. Yet the money markets only functioned well where the prospect of a strong economic rate of return could be envisaged. This was never to be the case for the Cornwall Railway where every attempt to promote the railway was handicapped by the inability to raise capital on the open market. The difference between British and continental practice is described by Bourne:

> The railways of the Continent, with very few exceptions, are not indications of the enterprise of the people, but only the will of the sovereign and his Government. English railways, like English charities and hospitals, are supported by the continued untiring energy of the people and are perpetual evidences, the one of that resiliency in our commerce, and the other of that living spring of our moral affections, proclaimed in a manner not to be mistaken, and far beyond the authority of a mere government enactment.

This approach to railway construction had been successful on early railways which connected major centres where healthy revenues could be generated. However it was not so well suited to areas like Cornwall where revenue streams would struggle to cover operational costs, quite apart from repaying capital, or paying a dividend. There were people involved in the Cornwall Railway who would have favoured more of the 'will of the sovereign and his (or in this case her) Government'. In 1839 at the meeting at the Polytechnic Hall in Falmouth into a railway for Cornwall Sir Hussey Vivian[2] was reported as saying:

> It had been said that the Government ought to have taken up the railroads. That was his opinion, and he thought that to put the internal communication into the hands of individuals had been a great mistake. But it would now be very difficult to interfere with these speculations. Yet he was persuaded that the Government would in the end be obliged to take the railroads in the same way as the parties who laid them down took the land.[3]

He had also seen the possibility of 'two classes of capitalist', those with no direct interest in the County who would invest for a fair rate of return and those within the County who 'must be prepared to make some sacrifice'. At the same meeting Sir Robert Rolfe expressed a similar view:

> The learned gentlemen thought that the government should take all rail roads into its own hands, to prevent the monopoly of companies, on the principle *'salus populi suprema lex'* but no one could have so far anticipated the progress of rail roads as to have made a proposition to parliament.

Was this a premonition of the problems that were to assail the Cornwall Railway Company of trying to rely solely on the capital market? The first 'class of capitalist' could see little prospect of 'a fair rate of return' and did not invest. This forced the Company to rely increasingly on the 'Associated Companies' for funds. The second group, 'those within the County', can have had little idea of the scale of financial sacrifice that they would have to make.

The building of the railways was having such a massive impact on the country that the Government was bound, if not to be 'the provider' then to take on the role of regulator of thitherto unfettered private enterprise. William Ewart Gladstone, as President of the Board of Trade, set up a system of central regulation. Our modern system of regulated free enterprise in transport clearly owes a lot to his thinking. Lewin explains the role of Board of Trade:

> Mr Gladstone as President of the Board of Trade in 1844 gave the subject of railways his special attention, recognising that by that date the time had fully come for the state to take some action in order that further developments in the railway system might take place with due regard for the public interest ... In 1844 Gladstone enlarged the Railway Department at the Board of Trade

> whose duties included examination of and reporting to Parliament upon all new Railway Bills to be submitted during the session of 1845.

But the Government did not only have this regulatory role. It could also commission reports into specific issues through the Board of Trade. Two reports were issued in 1845 which were very relevant to the whole subject of the railway through Cornwall. The first was *Report of the Railway Department of the Board of Trade on the Schemes for extending Railway Communication in Cornwall and Devonshire* (see Appendix one). This was published on 4 March 1845 just at the time that the Cornwall Railway Bill 1845 was being considered by the Parliamentary Committee. It reviewed no less than eight proposals for railways in these two counties and produced recommendations in each case. Lewin suggests that the Board of Trade was not wholly impartial in its recommendations:

> The tendency of the Board to recognise existing though somewhat circuitous routes, rather than favour the outlay of new capital in shortening them when the traffic case for the new route appeared doubtful, is well exemplified in their preference for the Great Western route to the West of England as against new schemes in the London and South Western interest.

The report then condemns the 'central line', the route through Launceston and Okehampton, on both topographical, economic and civil engineering grounds. The reader can be left in no doubt about its views:

> Considering, therefore, the unusually expensive nature of the works upon the Central line, the severity of its gradients, implying additional costs of working, and the comparatively small amount of traffic that could be expected to pass over it, we have had no hesitation in arriving at the opinion that it must be considered, under present circumstances, as altogether impracticable as a commercial undertaking.

The second report was *Report from the Select Committee on Atmospheric Railways* which was published on 24 April 1845 (see Appendix two). Even though the system was never used in Cornwall the prospect of it hung heavily over the parliamentary proceedings in 1845 and 1846.

The private bill procedure ensured that an Act of Parliament for a railway was in effect a binding contract on the proposing company to implement the proposal to specification and within a certain time. Any variation would require further Parliamentary approval. The Cornwall Railway Company, for example, was obliged to return to Parliament several times to reduce the specification, to abandon the building of branches and extend the period for completing the project.

The Cornwall Railway was unlucky in many ways. The issues that they faced were particularly intractable. How did the promoters respond and take arms against this 'sea of troubles'? They included:

- A topography which was unfavourable for infrastructure projects and a micro climate difficult for operating a railway,
- Disagreement amongst the promoters themselves over the most appropriate route for the line,
- The tantalising, but illusory, potential of the atmospheric system of traction,
- The dependency on other companies for the major part of the route to London,
- The question of how the great divide , the river Tamar, was to be crossed,
- The question of what gradients would be acceptable in such unfavourable terrain and finding the optimal balance between the expense of earthworks and steeper gradients,
- An unfavourable economic climate for financing, building and running the line.

TOPOGRAPHY AND CLIMATE

> The engineering difficulties on the line are throughout unavoidably great. The character of the Country, everywhere broken into hill and vale, with deep vallies [*sic*] extending from the different granite bosses down to the shore, all crossing the line, required a constant succession of heavy works.[4]

The first major disadvantage that the Cornwall Company had to face was an extremely difficult topography. Cornwall's rivers are essentially short and fast flowing which has resulted in a series of deep valleys which have to be crossed by the southern route. *The Times*[5] described the line as:

> That the whole of the route presents one continued series of engineering difficulties can well be understood from the semi mountainous nature of the country which it crosses. In the short distance of 60 miles there are no less than seven tunnels and 43 viaducts, some of them 150 feet high, besides cuttings almost innumerable.

Bourne neatly sums up this mismatch between economics and geography:

> A road is good in proportion as it is level, or free from hills ...With a view to these perfections, hills are partially cut down or avoided, vallies filled up ...The expense, however in proportion to the advantage of a perfectly level road renders it in most cases impracticable.

Brunel, asked whether the line can be worked efficiently, said:

> It is, as I have before stated, a very rough country, Cornwall: and as between Plymouth and Falmouth, from the direction of the vallies and the roughness of the ground, I do not think it possible to lay down a line of railway through that district with any moderate works, which are likely to be executed by a company, with the gradients – differing, or materially differing; You may

1.2 *'The engineering difficulties on the line are throughout unavoidably great.' The deep valleys along the route made for formidable and expensive engineering works. Here Brunel's original Mooswater viaduct strides across an industrial and agricultural scene.* THE CORNWALL CENTRE

> make a slight alteration from those I have laid down before the committee in this line. Among those gradients will be found a number of 1 in 60. Of course it would be a great deal better if they would be 1 in 100, or better still if they could be flatter gradients, but the nature of the country requires steep gradients and from the experience I have of working steep gradients I do not apprehend any difficulty in carrying traffic upon this railway.[6]

The early railway promoters had so little faith in their locomotives that they had to make their lines as flat as possible at the expense of heavy civil engineering works. In 1835, ten years before the first of the Cornwall Railway Bills, Robert Stephenson's London and Birmingham Railway was built at right angles to the geological grain of the country. It had to cross the chalk and limestone ridges and the river valleys of the Ouse and the Nene and involved extensive cuttings, tunnels and embankments. By means of heavy earthworks Stephenson was able to achieve gradients which, with the exception of the notorious incline out of Euston, seldom exceeded 1 in 134. Similarly Brunel's Great Western Railway, apart from the equally notorious gradient in the Box Tunnel of 1 in 100, was never steeper than 1 in 660. These were completed in 1838 and 1841 respectively. In the few short intervening years before the Cornwall Railway significant improvements in locomotive performance were achieved and steeper gradients, with a consequent saving in earthworks, became acceptable. Furthermore, as engineers started to tackle the Pennine crossings there was no escaping steeper gradients. The subjects of gradients and locomotive power were to occupy much time of the Parliamentary Committees which examined the two Cornwall Railway Bills.

The Cornish weather comes in for several comments in the course of the proceedings concerning the problems of adhesion on greasy rails from Bidder, under examination, confirmed that 'the climate of Cornwall and Devonshire ... is of a humid and foggy character'[7].

THE QUESTION OF THE BEST ROUTE

The second of these issues was the prolonged and largely unresolved disagreement between the members of the Provisional Committee over the route for the proposed railway. Most of the promoters wanted to achieve the shortest and fastest route between Falmouth and London in order to provide a better option for the packet traffic than Southampton, which had, by 1840, been linked to London by the railway engineered by Joseph Locke. The ideal route was seen to go from Falmouth to Truro, Bodmin, Launceston and thence to the north of Dartmoor to Exeter but omitting the growing towns of St Austell (pop 10,320), Liskeard (4,226) and St Germans (6,070), not to mention Plymouth, whose population, combined with adjacent Stonehouse, Devonport and Stoke Damerel, amounted to nearly 120,000 people[8]. This became known as the 'central route' Thence it was to connect to an as yet hypothetical line to be built by the London and South Western Railway from Exeter via Yeovil and Salisbury to London. The difference was set out in the prospectus of the Central Cornwall and Devon Railway. (see Appendix Four)

CENTRAL CORNWALL & DEVON & SOUTH WESTERN LINE		GREAT WESTERN & COAST LINE	
London-Salisbury	81	Paddington-Bristol	118 1/4
Salisbury-Exeter	87	Bristol-Exeter	76
Exeter-Falmouth	98 1/2	Exeter-Plymouth	52
		Plymouth-Falmouth	68
London-Falmouth	266 1/2	London-Falmouth	314 1/2

1.3 *The direct nature of what was to become the London and South Western route, compared with the Great Western and Bristol and Exeter route explains why proponents of the Cornwall and Devon Central Railway favoured it.*

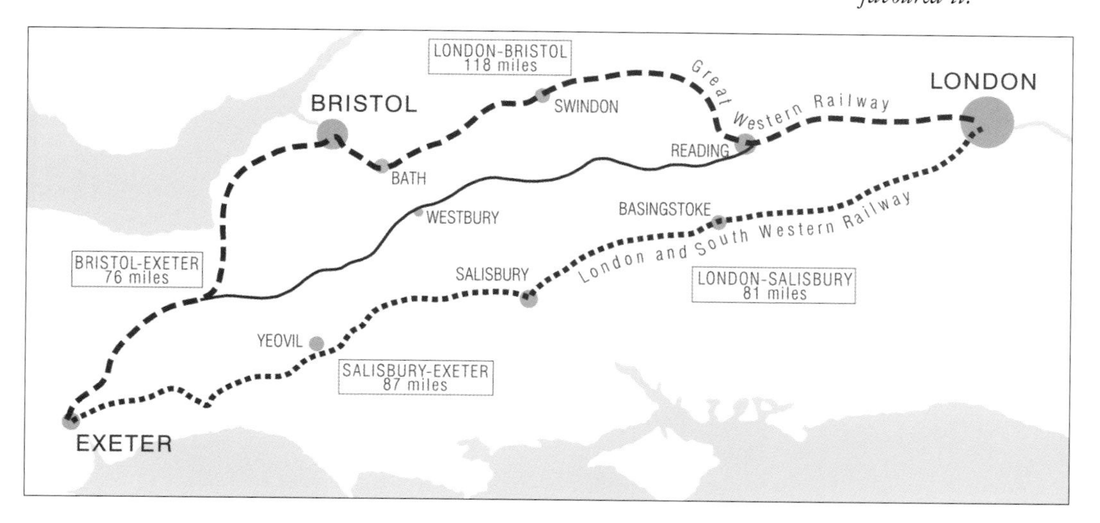

Most promoters quoted the central route as being 44 miles shorter than the southern or 'coast route' which ran to Plymouth and the south of Dartmoor and thence via Bristol and the Great Western main line to London which represented an additional one and a half hours on the journey to London.

A further issue that bedevilled the Cornwall Railway was the question of 'intermediate traffic'. The Company was not alone in facing this problem: Bourne highlights the issue:

> The traffic upon a railway may be divided according to the distance which it travels into two kinds; that going end to end; and that going from station to station, or over a part only and called 'Intermediate traffic'. Different railways often differ materially in this respect. The traffic of the London and Birmingham Railway, for example, is almost entirely end to end. On the Grand Junction, on the other hand, there is intermediate traffic to the manufacturing towns of Wednesbury and Wolverhampton that bears a large proportion of the traffic of the whole line.

This question whether the railway should be seen primarily as a fast route with few stops or whether it should include major centres of population en route had exercised most of the railway pioneers. In planning the GWR, from London to Bristol Brunel had taken the former view. His railway was about connecting Bristol with London without too much regard for intermediate traffic. He was prepared to forego the revenue from towns such as Bradford on Avon, Devizes, Hungerford and Newbury in order to secure a fast run through the upper Thames valley.

In the case of the Cornwall Railway it was a question of whether the project was entirely about Falmouth packet traffic or whether it should serve the then growing and economically important population centres of St Austell, Par and Liskeard, the developing mines of east Cornwall. Those of the former view were prepared to sacrifice these important sources of revenue from these increasingly important population centres. Unfortunately for them this view was to prove less and less tenable as the years wore on. Once the South Devon Railway was under construction in 1845 the southern or coast route started to emerge as a more practical if less appealing alternative.

But the failure of the 1845 Cornwall Railway Bill encouraged the 'centrists' for a final attempt in what was increasingly to prove to be a hopeless case. The issue of the route through Cornwall was ultimately resolved by the passage of the Cornwall Railway Act of 1846. But even after this, right to the end, the 'centrists' were still pressing for their route. During 1843 the provisional Committee for the southern route had started negotiations for financial contributions from the GWR and its Associated Companies. The Cornwall Railway Company[9] as late as 17 November 1846 was seeking their help 'as to the best means to be adopted in opposing the South Western Scheme for the Cornwall and

Devon Central Railway'. These companies were the Great Western, the South Devon and the Bristol and Exeter railways, which had a vested interest in the southern route. They therefore opposed the central route. Influential figures favouring the central route included Sir Francis Rodd, William Pendarves, John Tremayne and William Trelawney, all of whom, in giving evidence in 1846, were urging delay rather than Parliamentary approval for the southern route. Sir Francis Rodd, for example, former High Sheriff of Cornwall, being examined for the petitioners against the bill, confirmed that a line that is 40 miles shorter from one terminus to the other, one terminus being London, would be a line to be very much preferred[10].

Unfortunately for the 'centrists' the London and South Western proved to be a less than enthusiastic suitor. It seems likely that they were reluctant to provide competition for their Southampton route for the packet carriage. The 'tipping point' for the ultimate success of the southern route, was the offer of the GWR in 1842 and associated companies to take up £250,000 of the share capital as preference shares. Once construction had started the Cornwall Railway Company had to rely increasingly on the Associated Companies to complete the project. At the opening of the railway in 1859 the chairman of the company Dr George Smith acknowledged its dependency on them:

> Cornwall would never know the debt of gratitude they owed to the Associated Companies, the Great Western, Bristol and Exeter, and South Devon. When he told them that this company had had more than three quarters of a million guaranteed by the credit of the Associated Companies and realised for the advantage of this company, and they had done all this without anything more than taking measures to secure themselves, leaving every chance to gain with the Cornwall company, he thought he had said enough to prove that they had fallen into good hands, had been honourably treated and had received vast advantage from the Associated Companies[11].

On 26 August 1847 the Cornwall and Devon Central project was rejected by Parliament on Standing Orders. This finally marked the end of the 'centrist' cause.

Dependency on other companies

A problem peculiar to the Cornwall Railway was that, whereas most of the large railway projects involved connecting two or more major centres of population, the Cornwall Railway was dependent on others providing the major part of the connection to London. At its heart was a long standing battle between the GWR and the London and South Western for control of the west of England. Their respective engineers Brunel and Locke took fundamentally different views on railway engineering. These will be examined in Chapter eight but in essence Brunel was an inspired risk taker whereas Locke sought to avoid

1.4 *The Seal of the South Devon Railway Company.*

topographical and engineering problems and had a much better reputation for delivering projects on budget and on time.

The two fundamental problems of the South Devon line became readily apparent all to soon after the opening and have affected accessibility to Cornwall ever since; to the east of Newton Abbot it is vulnerable to the sea and to landslips; to the west the formidable gradients and sharp curves have been major operational problems. The steep gradients resulted in several instances of burst boilers and the coastal section would soon be damaged by storms with the resultant interruption of the link between Cornwall and the capital. In 1873[12] a letter suggested abandoning the sea wall and diverting the line through Chudleigh and the Teign Valley: 'An alternative line past the dangerous point has become an absolute necessity...'

The re-examination of Brunel during the passage of the South Devon Railway Bill in April 1844[13], makes it clear that the initial capital costs determined the choice of route:

Q One of the first questions you were asked was as to your having in the first instance in 1836 taken a line which was more inland than the present, but since that time, upon consideration, you had adopted what you call the coast line or line of the beech [*sic*]. Give the reasons, according to your judgement, why the line you have adopted upon the beech is preferable to the line that was more inland.

A The more inland line was a very costly line, heavy cutting and embankment and considerable tunnelling. It would, in my opinion, be very much more costly. The amount of severance and interference with property would have been greater than the present line. The levels would

1.5 *The weakest link between Cornwall and London has always been the sea wall between Dawlish and Teignmouth where services have often been disrupted either through landslips or breaches of the coastal defences by rough seas.* COLIN J MARSDEN

> not have been so good and it would not have given so good an access to the towns where we wish to have stations and traffic from.

The South Devon line demonstrates how a series of well-meant but short-sighted decisions resulted in a line which was difficult and expensive to work. If only the money, wasted on the atmospheric system and the subsequent cost of maintaining the sea wall, could have been channelled into a shorter, albeit more expensive, route along the line of the A38 through Chudleigh and on lower ground than over the Dartmoor fringes at South Brent and Ivybridge. These ill-fated decisions had lessons which were not lost on the various parties in Cornwall. For the supporters of the southern line excessive curves and gradients had to be avoided. For supporters of the central route there were good reasons for an alternative to the South Devon Railway.

THE ATMOSPHERIC SYSTEM

The other major technical issue which bedevilled the promoters was that of atmospheric traction. Its tantalising potential was very much alive at the time of the Parliamentary Committee into the Cornwall Railway Bill in 1845 and 1846. Its perceived (if not actual) advantages, in terms of the potential for tighter curves and steeper gradients with a less costly civil engineering works, were particularly alluring. It had been installed on the London and Croydon Railway and the engineering profession avidly studied its progress. Its application to the South Devon Railway between Exeter and Newton (Abbott) was still nearly two years away.

The prospect of using the system had induced Moorsom to propose a line which, whatever its defects in terms of gradients and curves, did nevertheless have the one, and not inconsiderable, advantage of cheapness in initial construction. So at the time that the Cornwall Railway Bill was before Parliament in 1845 the use of the atmospheric system was a real possibility which occupied a significant amount of Parliamentary time just as its operational shortcomings on the London and Croydon Railway were becoming apparent. The Select Committee Report on the atmospheric system failed to provide the ringing endorsement that the promoters and patentees of the system had hoped. Nevertheless the report did not condemn the system out of hand:

> While Your Committee have thus expressed a strong opinion in favour of the general merits of the Atmospheric principle, they feel that experience can alone determine under what circumstances of traffic or of country the preference to either system should be given.

At the 1846 Parliamentary Committee Brunel was subject to a rigorous cross examination on the atmospheric system on the London to Croydon Railway. This particular application was clearly the subject of what might euphemistically be called 'teething troubles'. Brunel is decidedly evasive under cross examination about the everyday operational problems on the Croydon line:[14]

Q Have you taken the trouble to ascertain the number of times in which the atmospheric has stopped and the locomotive has been obliged to be had recourse to?

A Not exactly the number of times, but I know the causes of most of these stoppages and they had nothing to do with the atmospheric.

More ominously:

Q Do you know in numerous instances the passengers have had to get out and shove the train along themselves?

A No, not very numerous instances

Q The train has been obliged to be pulled up with ropes and the passengers have helped pull it up?

A Not numerous instances. If the Committee wish to know in consequence of that question what that stoppage on hauling up was, it was this: On one part of the line, I think imprudently on a line which was nearly on the level they in one part put a gradient of 1 in 50 over a bridge with a station at the bottom.

As the possibility of steeper gradients was one of the claimed advantages of the atmospheric system this was a damaging admission.

CROSSING THE TAMAR

Unlike the hypothetical issue of whether to adopt the atmospheric system or not, the question of how to cross the Tamar was a very real and formidable one which provided the source of much Parliamentary debate. The 'central route' neatly avoided the issue but the southern route meant that the Hamoaze had to be crossed, and the original intention was that trains should be taken across by placing them on James Rendel's steam ferry between Torpoint, on the Cornwall side, and New Passage at Devonport, on the Plymouth side. There were several estimates as to how long this process would take. Robert Stephenson was of the view that it would have taken the time equivalent of an additional 12 to 15 miles[15]. So he considered that there would be the equivalent of an effective difference of 60 miles between the two alternative routes to London. This is one reason why those favouring the 'central route' fought so long and hard for it even after the case had been lost.

1.6 *James Meadows Rendel 1799-1856* INSTITUTION OF CIVIL ENGINEERS

Rendel's steam floating bridge had been operating very successfully for some 13 years. Moorsom had seen no difficulty in running the railway carriages onto the ferry which, with its engine house in the centre, would have allowed room for three carriages on either side. It would have provided a cheap, if hazardous, crossing for rail passengers in their

carriages. But it would also have involved negotiating steep ramps at times of low tide and a steep gradient of up to 1 in 30 from New Passage up to Eldad, which was the then planned terminus of the South Devon Railway. Varying views were expressed not only about the self evident dangers of such an arrangement but also about the cost in time. Eldad was never used as a terminus because the line to serve Rendel's Millbay Pier had been completed in 1844. Millbay formed the terminus of the South Devon Railway from April 1849 until the present station at North Road was opened in 1877. The name 'North Road' was dropped in 1958. Millbay Station became a goods depot following the Blitz in 1941 when the original station was destroyed.

It was only during the 1845 Parliamentary debate that the possibility of an alternative to the ferry began to emerge. Gradually the case for a bridge became compelling despite the potentially very high cost for an impecunious company.

1.7 *The only realistic crossing of the Tamar was to be the Royal Albert Bridge. This view, at the time of its completion, shows the impact of the bridge on the Tamar valley. Also visible is the floating bridge crossing between New Passage and Saltash with its chains clearly visible in the foreground. Tall masted ships upstream demonstrate the need for 100 foot clearance under the bridge.*
WEST BRITON 6 MAY 1859

GRADIENTS

A significant theme that was well aired at the two hearings was what gradients were acceptable. Hawkshaw and Locke endorsed the enhanced capabilities of the latest locomotives and were enthusiastic exponents of steeper gradients. They gave evidence to the Parliamentary Committees of the Cornwall Railway Bill in 1846 which was trying to achieve an optimum balance between costly earthworks and steeper gradients. This was clearly an issue very relevant to Cornwall. The argument was neatly summed up by this comment by Locke on the revised line ...

Q If it were thought indispensable to construct a line, a coast line from Falmouth to Plymouth, do you think one could be constructed with better gradients than this one?

A Yes, my Lord, I think it could but I must say at the same time that I cannot say whether you ought, as a commercial question or not, to spend so much money in order to obtain those better gradients.[16]

... and by Hawkshaw:

Q Looking to the fact that Cornwall and that part over which this line passes is a rough County and intersected with the valleys does it appear to you from the sections that it is judiciously laid out with reference to the gradients?

A There can be no doubt about it. The country is a very rough country and to seek gradients flatter than those proposed would involve an enormous cost without any corresponding advantages in my opinion.

Q In your judgement can this line, if constructed, be conveniently and sufficiently worked for all concerned and [for] public purposes?

A It can, in fact it is not a question of what can be; it is no longer a problem to solve.[17]

A DETERIORATING ECONOMIC CLIMATE

So far the difficulties facing the promoters of the Cornwall Railway were essentially internal matters. Cornwall had been as important in the forefront of the industrial revolution as any other part of Britain until the 1850s. However the mining industries were particularly susceptible to booms and slumps. The output of both copper and tin peaked in 1856 and 1884 respectively. Production declined thereafter to be overtaken by workings in Malaysia, Australia and Chile. The migration of the skilled miners accelerated in the late 1860s. Added to this was the decline of the pilchard industry and falling demand for other Cornish minerals. However this could not have come at a worse time in terms of national events which were to impinge on the already strained resources of the Company.

The late 1840s were notable for the repeal of the Corn Laws and by the aftermath of the 'railway mania' events which, between them, resulted in an acute shortage of capital for railway building. The Corn Laws had originally been introduced to protect land owners and farmers in the aftermath of the Napoleonic wars. 1816 had been 'the year without a summer' in Europe because of the clouds of volcanic ash from the eruption of Mount Tambora in Indonesia. Their repeal, whilst succeeding in the aim of providing cheap food for the expanding urban cities, caused disruption amongst the landed estates on which investment in railways depended. They had prospered under the protection against cheap imported grain that the Corn Laws had provided. With that protection gone they found themselves in more straightened circumstances without the surpluses that they had previously been able to invest in railway projects. A significant agricultural depression followed and did not lift until the mid 1850s. The recovery was due to improved methods of cultivation and a downward adjustment of farm rentals. The latter added to the problems of the estate owners and further reduced their ability to invest in modern infrastructure[18].

Agriculture was not the only sector to suffer from the withdrawal of tariffs on imports: The 1840s saw the reduction and eventual removal of duties on foreign tin and copper. In 1847 there were riots in the mining and quarrying areas against diminished wages and the price and scarcity of wheat. Lobbying for the removal of tariffs on grain in the west of Cornwall and for their retention in the east meant that there was no coherent Cornish view on this issue. The removal of tariffs on agriculture hit the east of the county whilst the removal of those on tin and copper hit the west. The economic conditions were significantly worse for the capital investment in a railway than they had been when the Act for its construction had been passed.

There had been gross over-optimism in railways as an investment. In 1842 the *Royal Cornwall Gazette* referred to 'The abundance of unemployed money (which) has recently given an extraordinary impulse to Railway investment and induced a very general disposition to seek them'. Now there was a crash in railway shares. After 1845 it became increasingly difficult to induce shareholders to honour calls for capital payments. Inflation reached a peak of 12% in 1847 followed by a deflation of a similar amount in 1848 creating a lack of confidence for investors[19].

The massively inflated market in railway shares collapsed and, as the effects spread through the economy, companies failed. Lewin identifies two causes of the collapse of finances for railway building of 1847:

> ... that the failure of the potato crop in 1846, and the consequent repeal of the Corn Laws, immediately altered the financial position of the country. The abundance of money awaiting investment prior to 1846 gave place to a shortage in 1847. Several financial houses of established reputation had to admit inability to meet their liabilities and the increasing gravity of the situation culminated about the month of October in a financial panic for which unusual remedies had to be applied to ease the situation. Under these circumstances railway construction was stopped automatically through the inability of shareholders to meet their calls.

All this was enough to bring construction of the Cornwall Railway to a halt for nearly four years. It was only after 1850 that confidence gradually returned and the directors were able slowly to proceed with construction to a much reduced specification. The Cornwall Railway

1.8 *Ringwell viaduct on the Falmouth line represented the final refinement of the timber viaducts. It was replaced by an embankment.* STEAM MUSEUM OF THE GWR

Company struggled for a further nine years to open a cut price single track version of the line simply to have some revenue coming in. This involved installing the timber viaducts which, however much they demonstrated Brunel's creative genius, were to prove costly to maintain and even more costly to replace.

Devey puts the situation quaintly:

> Immediately after followed the smash, leaving the fancied possessor of thousands, like Lear on the wild heath, with no covering but his mantle between himself and heaven.

But the *Manchester Guardian* of 25 October 1848 deals with the situation more soberly:

> The Railway market continues its downward course. Great Western shares [have been sold] at £67, being a discount of £23 on £90; Midland Counties at £66, or a discount of £34; Lancashire and Yorkshire at £51, or £35 discount; and North British, on which £25 has been paid, are worth £11 5s. Such are the facts in relation to the choicest lines in the kingdom. The lamentable facts disclosed in these few lines are producing consequences of the most painful and dangerous character; and to what extent derangements and disorganisation of property will go, if the causes of the root of the evil are not rapidly stayed it is impossible to say.

Then the report spells out the implications for those potentially less profitable lines such as the Cornwall Railway:

> Too much has already been done to suit the pockets of railway proprietors. The proprietors say to themselves– 'There are still "calls" of one hundred and thirty millions to be made. What we have already done at such enormous sacrifices, was to (build) the choicest lines. What we have yet to do is to construct works which will never pay for themselves, but which hang like an incubus upon the work we have already done'.
> This is the language every one talks (in private). No arrangement that does not contemplate the entire abandonment of a great majority of (future lines), will afford any true and permanent relief to railway property.
> They must guarantee that 'calls' are at an end – that the expenditure of capital, which has been so much more than the country could spare, shall cease. Then, and not till then, will they have found a remedy commensurate with the disease.
> And they may now rest assured on this subject, inasmuch as recent discussions have shown the inextricable ruin into which they will plunge by persevering in their present course and completing the works for which they have parliamentary sanction.

The Cornwall Railway Company was already sensible to the worsening economic climate. In August 1847 the Chairman, Joseph Treffry, had reported to the shareholders:

> The difficulties in which the financial affairs of the Country generally have been involved since your Directors last met you are well known and the paralysing effects of them have pressed with particular severity on Railway Companies in all parts of the Kingdom inducing many well established Companies to contract their operations.
> Your Directors feel assured that under such circumstances you will give them credit for having exercised a sound discretion in not having so pressed forward the works on your line as to render heavy calls requisite; and in the future prosecution of them you may rely on their endeavour being diverted to the construction of the line, the importance of which is clearly becoming more manifest, with as little delay and due regard to the interests of the shareholders will permit.[20]

The economics of the Cornwall line have always been very tight with a low revenue base and high maintenance costs. Any traveller on a through train from Paddington to Penzance will have noted that, after leaving Plymouth the train is significantly emptier and that the numbers getting off at Penzance are but a fraction of those joining at Paddington. Added to this the line, with its viaducts, tunnels and, above all, the Royal Albert Bridge is expensive to maintain. In the 1960s there was even talk of closing the line west of Plymouth altogether.

Little did the promoters of the line know just how difficult the financing of the line was to be. As it was they had to start construction in the aftermath of the railway mania. The discrediting of George Hudson (1800-71) had just given investment in railways a bad name as is reflected in the *Manchester Guardian*:

> In many cases the shares in railways that were at a premium before the bill was obtained in 1845 were now at a discount. Was it not time for the Government to interfere to prevent if possible a financial disaster ...
> The monetary difficulty continued to increase in intensity, failures in the corn trade amounting to £1,300,000 being announced during the week ending August 12th.

Hudson's fall also undermined the confidence in investing in railways. He was revealed to have falsified accounts and paid dividends out of borrowed capital rather than out of profits. By the beginning of 1849 the full scale of his fraud was coming to light and this further contributed to the general deterrent of investing in railways. The collapse of the mania for speculation resulted in debts and litigation and the railways never quite recovered their reputation with the public[21]. By 1853, as confidence was beginning to return, inflation was again on the rise, reaching a peak of 15% in 1854. This contributed to the bankruptcy of two key contractors on the Cornwall Railway, and to an additional difficulty in raising further finance.

These then were the unfavourable circumstances with which the promoters of the Cornwall Railway had to contend. The topographical challenges were always going to require resourcefulness to overcome. However the self destructive tendencies over the choice of route compounded their problems and led to unnecessary delays. The West Cornwall Railway Company had gained Parliamentary approval at the same time as the Cornwall Railway and was able to complete their line in four years. It opened in 1852 whereas the Cornwall Railway did not open until 1859 and even then it did not include the section from Truro to Falmouth. This was far too late to wrest the packet traffic back from Southampton. Falmouth was never to be the terminus of the Cornwall Railway as Penzance had already gained that status because of the earlier completion of the West Cornwall Railway.

The story of the Cornwall Railway raises so many 'if onlys'. If only the promoters had succeeded with their first bill in 1836 the line could have been completed when capital was plentiful and before the financial aftermath of the 'railway mania' had set in. They might have saved at any rate some of the packet traffic. If only they had been able to complete the line with a double track and permanent viaducts they would have been saved the subsequent costs of widening and replacement of timber viaducts.

Dr Smith, chairman of the company, made all too clear the strain and stress that the railway had caused:

> We have struggled for years as you have been told, with numerous difficulties – years of labour and trouble, and very painful anxiety. Early in our career our finances were crippled, under the pressure of circumstances that arose in England immediately on the commencement of the works ... all these arrangements for carrying out all this work were not full-grown and ready-made. They were laboured out by a long and tedious course of very severe labour, by untiring effort, by anxious hours; we have been on the verge of despair; again and again we have been brought to a deadlock. I have been in town with my friend Mr Tweedy, when we have talked over the whole matter for an evening, and have retired to bed as dark as midnight as to the future and not known what steps to take. No, gentlemen, you ll never know – for no words can tell you – a tithe of the amount of labour, effort and painful wearisome anxiety your Directors have experienced in carrying out this work. Here you find us so far successful that we have brought the railway from Plymouth to Truro.[22]

These then were the difficulties encountered by the promoters of the Cornwall Railway right through to its eventual absorption into the Great Western in 1889. The story starts with a group of eminent landowners and members of Parliament trying, in vain, to save one of Falmouth's industries, the nation's packet traffic.

2.1 *A westbound broad gauge passenger train leaves the newly completed Moorswater replacement viaduct with an 0-4-2 saddle tank locomotive and a rake of original broad gauge coaches.*
The Liskeard Old Cornwall Society

CHAPTER TWO
CONNECTING THE CAPITAL

> To the Right Honourable the Lords Commissioners of Her Majesty's Treasury:-
> The Memorial of the Mayor, Aldermen, and Burgesses of the Borough of Falmouth, and the inhabitants of Falmouth and its vicinity in public meeting assembled:
> Sheweth - That your Memorialists have heard, that it is in contemplation to contract for the conveyance of her Majesty's Mails to the West Indies by steam vessel, and that Southampton or some other port may be selected for their embarkation and return, which measure, if carried into effect, they are convinced, will not only be detrimental to the public services, but will seriously injure the interests of the town, and the county at large.[1]

Such was the concern in Falmouth about the potential loss of the packet traffic and its economic consequences that, in 1839, the Mayor organised this 'memorial' to be sent to the Government. Although the Cornish economy showed healthy growth during the 25 years from first conception to completion of the railway, that of Falmouth was in decline.

At the time of the accession of Queen Victoria in 1837, Cornwall had powered ahead on the basis of advances in mining technology. The output of tin more than doubled between 1800 and 1840 and the output of copper more than tripled over the same period. The demand for mining engines resulted in successful local foundries being set up which contributed to the prosperity of the county. The prosperity of Cornwall led to the building of country houses, the strengthening of the position of the landed classes and the emergence of a 'Jane Austen' society. Essentially they formed an entrepreneurial class with capital for investment in the county's infrastructure. The names of the owners of these houses were the leading guarantors for the railway project.

The evidence of Sir Charles Lemon for the second Cornwall Railway Bill, gives a good idea of the wealth of Cornwall at that time in a 'statistical account' of the mines in 1838. It shows the increasing importance of mines in and around Liskeard. He outlines the chief mining areas as:

> There are three principal and one rising into consequence. One is rather to the west of Penzance, the other in the neighbourhood of Redruth, a third at St Austell, (and) a district of growing importance at Liskeard.[2]

It was this 'district of growing importance at Liskeard' that was to prove crucial in the debate over which route the railway was to follow and would weigh heavily in favour of the southern route.

2.2
Sir Charles Lemon 1784-1868.
ROYAL INSTITUTION OF CORNWALL

Combined with neighbouring Penryn, Falmouth was the largest centre in Cornwall with a population of over 12,000. Its decline was due in part to reduced naval victualling and provisioning of merchant ships, which faded away following the end of the Napoleonic Wars, and partly because of the loss of packet traffic to ports, particularly Southampton, which enjoyed better connections to London than Falmouth. The Government had given assurances as early as 1822 about the merits of Falmouth as a packet station serving the West Indies, the Iberian Peninsular, the Orient and the Americas. However during the 1830s there was a growing sense of unease in Falmouth that this could change. The railway from London to Southampton was completed in 1840. Sure enough the Government announced on 29 May 1842 the transfer from Falmouth to Southampton of all but the South American traffic and that, too, had ended by 1850. In order to attempt to reverse this decision the county gentlemen consisting of landowners, Members of Parliament and industrialists got together and adopted a two point plan: to improve the port of Falmouth and connect it to London by railway. These two elements had a symbiotic relationship. They both gained parliamentary approval in the mid 1840s, both then were delayed for nearly twenty years through lack of investment capital and both came to fruition at the same time. The harbour improvements only started in 1860 and the final link in the railway was finished in 1863. And neither succeeded in the original objective of restoring the packet traffic to Falmouth.

Foremost amongst the hotels serving the packet traffic was Selley's Hotel on Greenbank Quay. This was a significant location, adjacent to the quay used by the packet steamers and influenced where the terminus of the railway was originally to be located in the plans submitted to Parliament in 1845 and 1846. When the line was finally built the proposed terminus was changed to the Western Dock, (See Chapter 10). Falmouth lacked a modern harbour and docks, suffered from shoals and was therefore unsuited to the larger steam ships that were coming into use. As early as 1834 it was recorded that:

Mr Price, an engineer, has (been) for some time employed in surveying Falmouth harbour, in order to form an estimate the expense of clearing the accumulations in that part of it where the packets lie, and where the depth of water has considerably decreased within twenty years.[3]

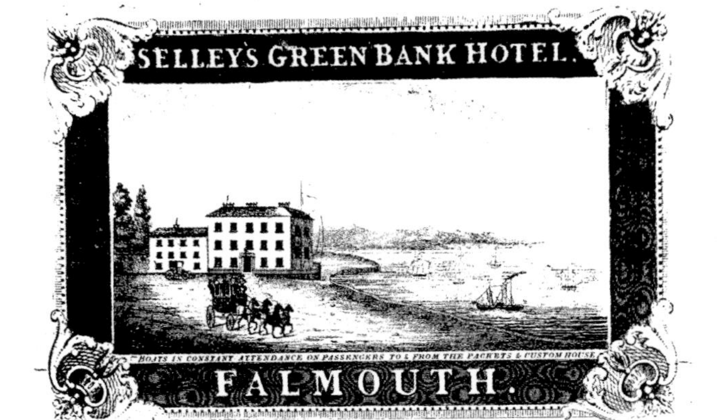

2.3 *Selley's Hotel at Greenbank Quay in 1835 close to the original proposed site for the Falmouth terminus of the Cornwall Railway. Captains and passengers of packet ships stayed there. It was also an important stop for coaches leaving for Plymouth, Exeter and London.*

SUPPLIED BY THE GREENBANK HOTEL

Although communications to London had been improved by turnpike roads, Falmouth still suffered from its remoteness from London. First attempts to regenerate the fortunes of Falmouth appeared to get off to a good start. In April 1840 operations were in progress to deepen the inner harbour 'thereby facilitating the access of steamers of the largest size at all times of the tide'. The first Bill for comprehensively improving Falmouth harbour was deposited in 1845. Amongst other things, it proposed to enclose Penryn Creek with an embankment between Falmouth and Flushing and to develop a floating dock in the creek. It included:

> ... all necessary piers, jetties, locks, waterways, quays, buttresses and other works for admitting, penning up or letting out the water from Penryn Creek. It is intended ... to light the said Dock or Docks with gas and to construct and maintain a footpath and carriageway along the said embankment to Flushing...

The preamble of the Bill was proven but the improvements were never carried out. The reason becomes all too obvious. It was an over-elaborate and unaffordable scheme. The full amount estimated by James Rendel, the engineer:

> was £220,000 but that £150,000 would be sufficient for such works as were at present contemplated and that they expected that a guarantee of at least one half of that sum would be furnished by the Railway Company ... to report to the Board how far, if at all, this Company is under by any promise either expressed or implied to afford pecuniary assistance to the said Commissioners.[4]

The chances of the Cornwall Railway Company contributing £75,000 were remote and nothing further happened for a further 12 years.

Despite increasing evidence to the contrary the hope remained that the lost packet traffic could one day be restored. Captain Beaufort, for example, hydrographer to the Admiralty, when examined before the Parliamentary Committee for the first bill for improving Falmouth, expressed the hope that it would become 'a port of far greater consequence than it has yet been'. And Captain Edward Holland, Commander in Her Majesty's Royal Navy Harbour stressed the hazardous nature of sailing to Southampton:

> 'It is dangerous for steamers and the danger is increasing constantly on account of the increase of trade and on account of the increase of steamers, the risk of collision is considerable in the Channel especially from the number of steamers running: accidents happen'.[5]

From this it is easy to understand why the Falmouth Harbour Commission clung to the hope that the packet traffic would return and that, if only a modern deep water port could be constructed and a railway built, then Falmouth could still have offered an advantage over

Southampton. There would be a saving in sailing time and risks of collision in the increasingly crowded English Channel would be avoided.

Although the battle for the packet traffic can now be seen to have been lost by 1840, Lord Falmouth under cross examination[6] during the passage of the second Cornwall Railway Bill of 1846 had to agree that success of the port 'must depend upon the security, speed and economy of your railway communication'.

In 1859 a bill, for improving Falmouth Harbour, but not Penryn Creek, did succeed and the foundation stone for the new docks was laid in 1860. Writing to William Bond, Secretary to the Cornwall Railway Company, in May 1860 Robert Brereton, who was Brunel's right hand man and successor in his practice, describes the works as:

> They consist of a graving dock and gridiron for repairing vessels and the construction of the Eastern and Seaward Breakwater, inside of which the harbour is to be dredged to 18 feet below low water spring tides, enabling vessels to lie afloat at all times of the tide.[7]

Early Bills for the Central Route

There were four serious attempts to obtain Parliamentary approval for the central route connecting Cornwall and the capital, in 1836, 1837, 1841[8] and 1846. All failed through the poor take up of shares. Looking back in 1859 the *Royal Cornwall Gazette* recorded:

> In 1835, a Company in London announced a Line of Railway to connect London, Salisbury and Exeter, thence to proceed to Plymouth and Devonport to Falmouth, and to be called "the London, Salisbury, Exeter, Plymouth and Falmouth Railway." Col. Landmann was announced as the Engineer, and Mr Dean of Exeter, the Surveyor. The published plan showed a line running straight as an arrow from London through Basingstoke to Exeter, thence following the course of the present south Devon, crossing the Tamar at Saltash, and running along the South Coast of Cornwall to St Just Pool, in Falmouth Harbour. Suggestions made to the promoters led them to issue a second prospectus with a different plan in which the Western portion of the Line ran from Exeter to Okehampton and there divided into three, one North to Bideford, one by Tavistock to Plymouth, while a third ran straight on through Launceston, Bodmin, Truro and Falmouth

However, despite its failure, the initial proposal sparked off the whole controversy over the route which was to cause so much trouble for the next thirteen years. The rival arguments were first aired in an anonymous and acrimonious correspondence in the *Royal Cornwall Gazette* between 'A Friend of Trade' and 'The Labourer's Friend'[9] . The former represented the interests of the mineral industry around St Austell and Par whilst the latter represented the Falmouth interest concerned with, in the short term, saving the packet traffic and in the longer term the regeneration of the county's economy.

In its editorial in May 1859 the *Royal Cornwall Gazette* looked back on the events of 1836:

> But whatever the motives of the promoters, they did the good service of rousing the Western Counties to the importance of securing railway accommodation. Public meetings were held in May 1836, at Launceston, Bodmin, Truro and Falmouth, at which a Mr Andrews[10] attended as a deputation from the committee, and such interest was excited, that at Truro and its neighbourhood 1,730 shares were subscribed for. Three of the county members, Mr Pendarves, Sir Charles Lemon, and Sir W Trelawney, gave their names and support and the late Mr Richard Thomas of Falmouth, was employed to make a survey through Cornwall

A series of meetings to discuss the railway had taken place in 1836, just at the time that the port of Falmouth enjoyed some temporary fame from the return of the *Beagle* from its epic voyage with Charles Darwin on 2 October. The first public meeting took place in the Guildhall in Bodmin on 19 May 1836. The main resolution was;

> That this Meeting, having heard with great satisfaction the proposition made by William Andrews, Esq. as representative of the London Exeter and Falmouth Railway Company, for constructing a Central Line of Railway from London to Exeter, and thence through this county to Falmouth forming, if practicable, a junction with the Bodmin and Wadebridge Railway near this place, (i.e. Bodmin) are of the opinion that the Undertaking calls for and deserves the zealous co-operation of the Borough and its Neighbourhood.[11]

The accompanying plan showed the route to Exeter and choice north or south of Dartmoor. It approaches Falmouth from St Mawes. It was 'Resolved to unite with the London and Southampton Railway near Basingstoke with capital of £2,500,000'. The project went through preliminary Parliamentary stages but consideration was eventually postponed in part because of 'insuperable engineering difficulties' and partly because of lack of financial support. The meeting set up a committee and an invitation was issued for the purchase of shares which, once again, was to prove unsuccessful.

The proposal was nevertheless submitted a year later for the 1837 session of Parliament by the London, Salisbury, Exeter and Falmouth Railway Company. The plans showed a line from Reading and Basingstoke to Taunton. It was to connect with the Bristol and Exeter at Lyng which is close to the current Cogload junction. So the promoters presumably had in mind to reach Exeter over the Bristol and Exeter line. Tantalisingly there are no details of what was intended west of Exeter. It would seem that the company was primarily seeking to establish a route independent of the Great Western to London.

This was closely followed by another public meeting, chaired by the

2.4
Joseph Treffry
1782-1850
THE CHINA CLAY HISTORY SOCIETY

Mayor of Truro, Edmund Turner, who was to be one of the most persistent advocates of the central route. Meanwhile Joseph Treffry (then Austen) wrote to the press urging caution about proposals for a central route. Under the heading 'Look before you leap' he advises potential shareholders

> ... to hesitate a little longer before you borrow money on a speculation which, if the Railroad be made from London to Falmouth, will never pay an interest of one per cent[12].

Colonel George Landmann (1779-1854) was of a military background he had, early in his career, worked on the docks at Plymouth. His best known railway work is the London to Greenwich Railway with its lengthy brick viaduct. He placed the survey of the Cornwall Railway in the hands of Richard Thomas (1779-1858) who had been the engineer for previous proposals for a central route and was to fulfil this role again in the final attempt of 1845. Thomas was a civil engineer whose work was mostly in western Cornwall. He had carried out work for the Truro Turnpike Trustees and had been responsible for the Hayle Railway which opened in Dec 1837. His in-depth local knowledge gave added force to his subsequent comments on Moorsom's survey. He was also opposed to the broad gauge, something that may have weighed against him with the Committee.

Thomas subsequently petitioned against the 1845 Bill on the grounds of its tight curves, steep gradients and the perceived errors in the plans and deposited documents.

Thomas and Stephenson had reason on their side as it is difficult to imagine a line less suited to the broad gauge (which was specifically designed for the fast, straight GWR main line from Paddington to Bristol) than the line Moorsom planned for the Cornwall Railway with its

2.5 *A rare broad gauge survival. A turntable, thought to have been manufactured for the Cornwall Railway in circa 1868 as originally installed within the South Yard of the Devonport Royal Dockyards. It has now been restored and relocated at the Didcot Railway Centre.*
PAUL BURKHALTER

succession of sharp curves. Robert Stephenson, an opponent of the broad gauge and apparently unaware that it was to be used, confirmed the point and seems to have responded with relish:[13]

A I did not know that this was on the broad gauge. Then it is still more objectionable than I thought they were – I have no hesitation saying that.

Q Why so?

A Because in bringing round the curve, the wheels will all be fixed on the axles, and being of the same size, of course the outside has to go over more ground than the inside and therefore the outside ones slide upon the turn, and consequently, as you see in the Bristol stations, you will see such wheels grind in their operation.

The design of the locomotives used on the Cornwall Railway in broad gauge days reflected the particular conditions. The saddle tank layout optimised adhesion on the often slippery gradients. However the short wheelbase, which suited the curved nature of the track, combined with a wide wheel base meant that they lacked stability.
Thomas described his role as follows:

> I was first engaged in the survey of this line in June 1836, at which time nothing had been done towards ascertaining the general direction of the road, and it took up the time of myself and assistants until the middle of September trying the levels of the country so as to determine where the line ought to pass, and after that it became a hard race against time as to our being ready with plans, sections, descriptions, and lists of owners and occupiers of the grounds together with all other information required to complete the needful particulars, so as to lodge them with the clerks of the peace in due time and there was never an opportunity of ascertaining by further examination how far the line might be improved by partial deviations either as to gradient or the saving of cost.[14]

From these remarks it seems that the survey could have benefited from more work. Thomas addressed the Provisional Committee in a report dated 27 September 1839. He, perhaps unwittingly, reveals one fundamental weakness of the Central Route, north of Dartmoor, that it had little chance of success without support from Plymouth:

> Our first aim was if possible, to get a line along the Northern scarp of Dartmoor, through Okehampton Park: and westward of that, of Sourton Down, to branch into two, one of which passes along by Tavistock to Devonport and Plymouth and the other to go to Falmouth. But as the inhabitants of Plymouth and its neighbourhood contemplated being able to bring a line from Exeter on the South East side of Dartmoor, I understand that they would not support our proposed junction line from Exeter to Okehampton ... But, if Cornwall is to be disappointed of the assistance of Plymouth, we must recollect that the railway will give to the harbours of this

> county that facility of communication, and consequently of trading, with the interior and northern parts of Cornwall and Devon which Plymouth will not possess.

However he suggests that the economics and speed would be favourable.

> The line as above mentioned, through the lower grounds on the north of Okehampton, is a direction adopted for the railway, which would connect itself with the Bristol and Exeter line at Cowley Bridge, in the vale of the Exe River, near Exeter ...
>
> One of the accompanying papers shows the whole of the gradients throughout, together with a calculation of the time it would require to travel over the lines; and it appears that supposing the velocity made good, after allowing for stoppages, to be twenty miles an hour on the level, it would require five hours and forty eight minutes from Exeter to Falmouth and from Falmouth to Exeter five hours and forty minutes.
>
> My estimate of the cost of making the road, amounted to £1,700,000. It will be seen that nearly thirty per cent on the cost is added for contingencies, although about ten per cent considered as a fair average amount for this particular ...

Thirty percent does seem a very liberal figure for contingencies and may have counted against him when comparing it with Moorsom's figure of 6% in an estimate of £1,000,000 which he included in the 1845 Cornwall Railway Bill. Thomas continued:

> The plans and needful particulars were deposited with the clerks of the peace on 30th November 1836, after which, for the purpose of reducing the cost of forming the road. I had to revise the whole of the work, and make such small deviations as the survey would admit of, in the direction of the line as well as the gradients; and corresponding plans were deposited on 1st March 1837 ...
>
> It ought also to be clearly understood whether local interests along the line are to be attended to in preference to the saving of cost, or the general improvement of the road with the towns and other localities that may require it by branches, for in my humble opinion this railway should be regarded as the great highway from the centre of the population and from the several railways and roads of Great Britain, to the south-western harbour of the country, which might then be considered as the great station for the ferry boats to cross the Atlantic to the several southern and western countries by the shortest, safest and best line of water carriage. And, if the projected harbour at Mount's Bay should be formed and take away from Falmouth its present superior advantages, this line of railway will be what is wanted for that locality as it can easily be extended to Penzance and that neighbourhood; and, without waiting for the new harbour there, it might be desirable so to extend the railway; but, the first object is, of course, to carry it to Falmouth Harbour.

Mentioning the rivalry with Penzance cannot have endeared him to the Committee.

The failure of these Bills for the improvement of the harbour and building the railway induced a state of paralysis which was only overcome when the threat of removal of the packet traffic became a reality. The growing anxiety over the future of the packet traffic came to a head in 1839 triggering a series of activities which galvanised support for the projects. As the size and volume of the mails increased it became increasingly clear that a railway was essential to Falmouth's future as a packet station. The first major event was a public meeting convened by J. Ellis, the Mayor of Falmouth, on Wednesday 17 July 'for the purpose of considering the propriety of presenting a Memorial to the Lords of Her Majesty's Treasury on the subject of Steam Packet Communication'. It concerned the threat to Falmouth of its status of a packet station by the increasing superiority of Southampton. The Memorial then sets out the perceived advantages that Falmouth could offer for the packet traffic, not least that transferring it to Southampton would involve an additional 160/170 miles sailing through increasingly busy and hazardous waters:

> That Falmouth Harbour, for its great safety, facility of access at all times, and under all circumstances and from its extreme south western position, possesses advantages over every other port in the Channel, as an outlet to the southward and westward; and all vessels from and to any other port to the eastward, must necessarily on their outward and homeward voyage pass near the entrance of Falmouth Harbour, the English side of the Channel being considerably less dangerous than the French side, and invariably preferred by all navigators, who consider it of the utmost importance to make either the Scilly or the Lizard, from the latter of which Falmouth is distant by about two hours sail ...

Seen from the Southampton point of view the case against Falmouth and in favour of Southampton as the preferred port for the packet traffic, as soon as its railway to London had been completed, was convincing:

> More coaches were proved to run upon that route (London to Southampton) than formerly had run between Liverpool and Manchester and more goods waggons [*sic*] than between London and Birmingham. Then there were the Torbay fisheries, the produce of which was often found rotting in Southampton for want of a speedy communication with London; and the merchant vessels, instead of discharging their cargos at an opportune harbour, were obliged to pass round the North Foreland, and proceed at a snail's pace up the blockaded Thames. By a railway from Southampton their freights would reach town in five hours, while the transit up the river, even with a clear passage, would take up to twenty- eight hours [15] .

Meanwhile on 16 September 1839 a further meeting took place.

Under the heading of 'Cornwall Central Railway', it sought an open 'union with the South Western Railway' and spurred the project into action.[16] This was followed on 9 October by a 'Railroad Meeting' which was held at the Polytechnic Hall in Falmouth at the initiative of the Mayor, who was seeking to build on the success of the 'Memorial' he had promoted two months earlier. He was able to report that a deputation had just returned from London with an assurance 'that if a Railway was constructed from Exeter to Falmouth, nothing would induce the government to remove the Packets'. Thus encouraged, the Royal Cornwall Polytechnic Society passed the following resolution:

> That the Sheriff be requested to convene a County Meeting, for the purpose of taking into consideration how far it may be desirable to take measures with a view to bringing a Rail Road into the County; and if it be desirable what measures it will be advisable to take [17] .

The meeting was duly called for 29 October. It was a 'County Railway Meeting', at Shire Hall, Bodmin convened by Francis Rodd, High Sheriff of Cornwall, in compliance with a requisition signed by 1,600 noblemen, landowners, magistrates, yeomen and traders.

> 'This is a requisition for the purpose of taking into consideration the most effectual means of insuring for this County and its various important interests a most direct and available railway communication between Penzance, Falmouth and Exeter'.

The *Royal Cornwall Gazette* summarised the meeting[18]:

> 'The character of the meeting, and the tone of its proceedings, fully accorded with the imposing appearance of the Requisition and with the energetic and determined though cautious spirit which had been manifest through all the preceding stages of the laudable effect now making for the introduction of a measure of vital importance to the County'.

There was euphoria about the project which reflected the commercial advantages in terms of marketing fish and vegetables on the London market. There was, however, concern about the adverse topography and the difficulty of raising capital; 'I will not deceive you into any expectation that you will raise in this County the sum required. '(Pendarves). The view was expressed that cheap land could be offset against costly civil engineering works (Sir Hussey Vivian). The meeting resolved to set up a provisional committee 'with power to call the best engineers'.

There was an increasing sense of concern that the Government might indeed be moving away from its endorsement of Falmouth especially as the completion of the London to Southampton Railway could be envisaged. The Earl of Falmouth remarked that 'even if the Railway to

2.6 *Broccoli being loaded on to railway trucks at Marazion goods yard on a wet day in 1959. The transport of Cornish vegetables, flowers, meat and fish provided a much needed revenue for the Cornwall Railway both in its early days and for many years afterwards.*
P. Q. TRELOAR

Southampton be completed, Falmouth would still be by land on the same footing, as to time, as Southampton'. Using a delicacy of phrase concerning the 1837 bill for the central line, Lemon stressed that 'the last did fail almost entirely for want of means'. Clearly the problem of 'means' or lack of them, was well appreciated at the time although whether anyone could have appreciated that it would dog the entire project for the next twenty years and more, can only be guessed. The lack of 'means' was to be a recurring theme. As the *West Briton* put it in the vernacular of the day:

> The directors were cramped in their operations to an unusual extent owing to the want of pecuniary support which was required for the successful prosecution of the undertaking[19] .

The key players on the Provisional Committee of the Cornwall Railway were split. The Conservative group had opposed Parliamentary reform, and was set to oppose the Repeal of the Corn Laws. Much of their support came from the east of the county where agriculture prevailed. Hence they favoured the southern route. The radical group of Whigs and Liberals had supported the Reform Bill and the repeal of the Corn Laws. Their support derived from the mining industries predominantly in the west. They favoured the more direct central route avoiding the towns in the east of the County.
The Conservative group included:
THE EARLS OF FALMOUTH OF TREGOTHNAN:

a) Lord Edward Boscawen Rose 1787-1841 who succeeded to the title in 1808 at the age of 21. He asserted conservative principles strenuously in the House of Lords and throughout his career as a public man. Described by the *Royal Cornwall Gazette* as 'able and energetic' he 'took his accustomed lead' in promoting the railway at the time of the withdrawal of the packet services.

b) George Henry Boscawen Rose 1811-52. He was a member of the House of Commons for the western Division of the County. His elevation in 1841 created a vacancy.

JOSEPH TREFFRY (1782-1850) was chairman of the Cornwall Railway Provisional Committee from 1844 until his death in January 1850. He was instrumental in securing the southern route, in driving the Bills through Parliament, in replacing Moorsom with Brunel and in initiating the project in the face of almost insuperable financial difficulties. Ostler describes him 'from the first and through all the vicissitudes of the undertaking, [he] had been one of the most energetic, prudent and valuable of promoters'.

According to the *West Briton* he was 'endowed with great talents and much indomitable perseverance'. Clearly these were qualities very much needed to drive the Cornwall Railway project forward. Keast confirms this view. He had 'a stubborn persistence which [he] pitted against every problem'. Described as the great entrepreneur, he was one of the leading industrialists of his day. Of the directors of the Provisional Committee he had taken out significantly the largest number of shares. The leading holders were:

Joseph Thomas Treffry	Place	£12,000
Rt Hon Earl of Falmouth	Tregothnan	£ 7,500
Sir Charles Lemon	Carclew	£ 3,000
Charles Russell*	27 Charles St, St James	£ 1,125
Thomas Gill *	Buckland Abbey	£ 6,250
Robert Cateworth	St Helens Place London	£13,375
Thomas James Agar Robartes	Lanhydrock	£ 2,000

*Charles Russell was Chairman of the GWR and Thomas Gill, Chairman of the South Devon Railway

In 1829 Treffry had constructed a new harbour at Par which was a vital outlet for minerals particularly the expanding china clay industry and a rival to Fowey, Pentewan and Charlestown. His Fowey Consols mine was reaching its peak production in the late 1830s at 15,000 tons. The output at Par Consols mine peaked a little later at nearly 8,500 tons. They were producing profitable amounts of copper at that time but the price declined steadily thereafter.

He had brought industrial success firstly with the copper mines in Tywardreath and St Blazey, then with the granite workings at Luxulyan, and finally with china clay extraction to serve the fast developing ceramics industry in the Potteries. It followed that he was adamant about the Cornwall Railway serving Par and hinterland and was resolutely opposed to a central route which would have bypassed the area. It is only through appreciating Treffry's interests that one can understand the route that the Cornwall Railway now takes. When serious planning of the railway began after 1839, the harbour, quarries and mines were established facts which were to prove pivotal in the planning of the route.[20]

SIR CHARLES LEMON BARONET 1784-1868

The name, Lemon, is remembered today by Lemon Street in Truro which is named after Sir William Lemon, father of Sir Charles. Charles was returned as MP for Penryn as a Whig for Cornwall until the 1832 Reform Act and as Liberal MP for West Cornwall from 1832 to 1857. He took an active interest in social and political matters particularly in the workings of the various Cornish institutions as a means of promoting social change and industrial progress. He was described by the *West Briton* as 'a Reformer, but rather one of the moderate Whig School, than of the more advanced politicians who are to be found in the Liberal ranks at the present time'. (Clearly he was not sufficiently radical for the tastes of the *West Briton*!) He had a number of interests which were of direct interest to the regeneration of Falmouth and the Cornwall Railway. He was Chairman of the Falmouth Board of Guardians and in 1836, headed the petition to the Admiralty concerning the packet station. He financed the forerunners of the Camborne School of Mines and was president of the Royal Geological Society of Cornwall; hence his knowledge of mining and its significance for the economy of Cornwall. '... [He] had been of eminent service as a country gentleman, and conspicuously so in political affairs, and in connection with scientific institutions of Cornwall'. He was President of the Royal Cornwall Polytechnic Society which was a Quaker-founded organisation whose aim was to promote scientific ideas and inventions.

He served on the Committee of Management of the South Western Railway. This explains his passionate initial support for the 'Central Route' and the arguments surrounding it. However, unlike other supporters of that route he took a pragmatic view and came to realise that the southern route was the only realistic possibility.

He also served on the Parliamentary Select Committee on Atmospheric Railways in 1845 and was therefore anxious to see what its prospects were before deciding whether it was appropriate for the Cornwall Railway. He lived at Carclew, a notable Palladian mansion overlooking the Restronguet Creek which was destroyed by fire in 1934.[21]

All the following took the view that postponement of the project, in

2.7
John Hearle Tremayne
1780-1851
The Tremayne Family Archive

the increasingly vain hope of securing the central route, was the preferred option.[22]

John Hearle Tremayne, 1780-1851 (The H is mute as the Parliamentary clerks record it as 'Erle). He was a Tory MP from 1806 to 1826, a magistrate and owner of Heligan (of Lost Garden fame) and Sydenham in Devon. He was married to the sister of Sir Charles Lemon.

William Trelawney, 1781-1856, was educated at Westminster School and Christchurch, Oxford and rose to become Lord Lieutenant of the County. He represented the Eastern division from 1832 to 1837. A passionate fighter for the Reform Bill he lost his seat on the Corn Law issue ironically because; 'he being the only man among the candidates who most nearly agreed with the farmers who excluded him. He was described: such was the singular modesty of his character that few but those who really knew him were aware of the shrewd observation and real knowledge of the affairs of the world that were concealed under an apparent bluntness of manner, and were let out in a few strong sentences or pertinent remarks.'[23]

Edward William Wynne Pendarves, 1776-1853, was educated at Harrow and Oxford and was MP from 1826 and for the Western Division from 1832 to 1853. He had served on the Management Committee of the South Western Railway in 1836; hence his support to the end for the central route. However he was mainly known as a staunch reformer and messianic pursuer of civil and religious freedoms and a passionate advocate of Parliamentary reform. He was described as the father of liberal opinion in Cornwall. The *West Briton* clearly empathised with his views and considered that he 'would so fully represent the wants and opinions of the industrious classes of society'.[24]

The Provisional Committee lost little time and met on 20 November 1839 at Pearce's Hotel, Truro where they resolved to appoint a sub-committee:

> to obtain information as to the progress of the railroad now in the course of formation between Bristol and Exeter and the probable period at which it may be expected to arrive at that city, and also any proposed Railway intended to connect the metropolis directly with the city of Exeter.[25]

They were clearly aware of potential alternatives. The sub-committee was instructed to obtain information 'as to the traffic that may be expected on a railway between Exeter and Falmouth distinguishing a direct line from one connected with a railway from Exeter to Plymouth ...' The sub-committee was also to look into 'the state of preparation for carrying into effect a line from Exeter to Plymouth'. Within a few short

weeks the sub-committee had reported back that the Bristol & Exeter were determined to open their line 'at the earliest possible date'. (It was opened in 1844). On the other hand the Directors of the South Western Railway delayed extending their line west of Salisbury at that time. Even at this early stage the South Western route to London was looking like a weak partner.
Meanwhile the Sub-Committee had received from Moorsom:

> some very valuable communication containing suggestions and advice of the greatest use to the Committee. Capt Moorsom's known ability and experience in railways renders every communication from him important and the handsome manner in which he has preferred us and in carrying out the great object of a Devon–Cornish Railroad deserves the warmest thanks of the Committee.

Moorsom's reputation was still undamaged at that stage. The Committee had to decide whether to engage him or Richard Thomas:

> Captain Moorsom then attended and explained his arrangements respecting the Survey and delivered a written plan of those arrangements and a declaration of his willingness to undertake it for a sum not exceeding £1,542 and to complete it by the first of March next.
>
> Mr Rich Thomas was subsequently asked to state his views but the Committee ascertained that Mr Thomas only desired making use of the line formerly surveyed and to adopt such improvements as a more careful investigation would enable him to make.

This was the survey for the 1837 Bill on which Thomas had indicated that improvements might be made. However on this basis the Committee decided to enter into a contract with Moorsom to complete:

> A comprehensive survey with a view to ascertaining the most advantageous line for a Railway from Exeter to Falmouth so as to enable the Committee to lay their plans before Parliament on the first of March next, it being understood that every expence [*sic*] is to be covered by the sum mentioned and they be at liberty to submit the plans to any other engineer the Committee may choose ... [26]

When the harbour works at Falmouth and railway connection were completed Southampton was far too well established to be challenged in the confident tones of the 'memorial' of 1839. Ironically it was the South Western Railway, which had won the first round of the battle for the alternative routes for the Cornwall railway although in the end they were not to win the war. The failure of successive attempts to secure the central route prompted Lord Falmouth and Sir Charles Lemon to see whether, even if it meant abandoning the cherished central route, a potentially more successful alternative might be found.

Meanwhile a similar debate on the choice of route was being debated across the county boundary. For on 28 October 1840 a meeting had been held in Plymouth, chaired by Dr Cookworthy, the Mayor. It had speedily resolved to promote a railway from Exeter to Plymouth but was then presented with a choice of three potential routes by Rendel the Engineer:

> The South Hams line would be fifty miles long and cost two millions. The line on the north of Dartmoor would be longer and cost more. The line over Dartmoor would be forty miles long only and cost £800,000 ... The great objection to this line was the inclined planes ... which were to be worked by fixed water power.[27]

Unsurprisingly nothing more was heard of this third alternative. However much more was to be heard of something else raised by a member of the meeting who prophetically ' ... recommended the atmospheric scheme for consideration of the railway proprietors'.

Making the decision to build a railway into Cornwall was comparatively simple compared with the prolonged, and above all expensive, battle over the choice of route which was to follow.

Chapter Three
'... A Civil War between Gentlemen'.

Can you at all estimate the amount of money which may have been spent in the civil war between gentlemen? I suppose if we said £100,000 or £200,000 should be within the mark?[1]

Bearing in mind that no self respecting barrister asks a question to which he does not already know the answer, these sums are likely to be of the right order and do represent a very large proportion of the ultimate cost of the railway. If only this could have been made available for the construction how much easier the task of the Cornwall Railway Company would have been! Plans for a railway through Cornwall were the subject of an increasingly severe schism between opposing parties whose only common point was the need for a railway to connect Falmouth to the capital. There were those who wanted to attach the railway to the South Western and those who wanted to go with the GWR. Ostler is of the view that there were only two routes through central Cornwall, the Lanivet pass or the valley of the Fowey. The central route was to use the former and the southern route, the latter. The Cornwall railway project became embroiled in a bitterly contested battle between the GWR and L&SWR for control of the west.

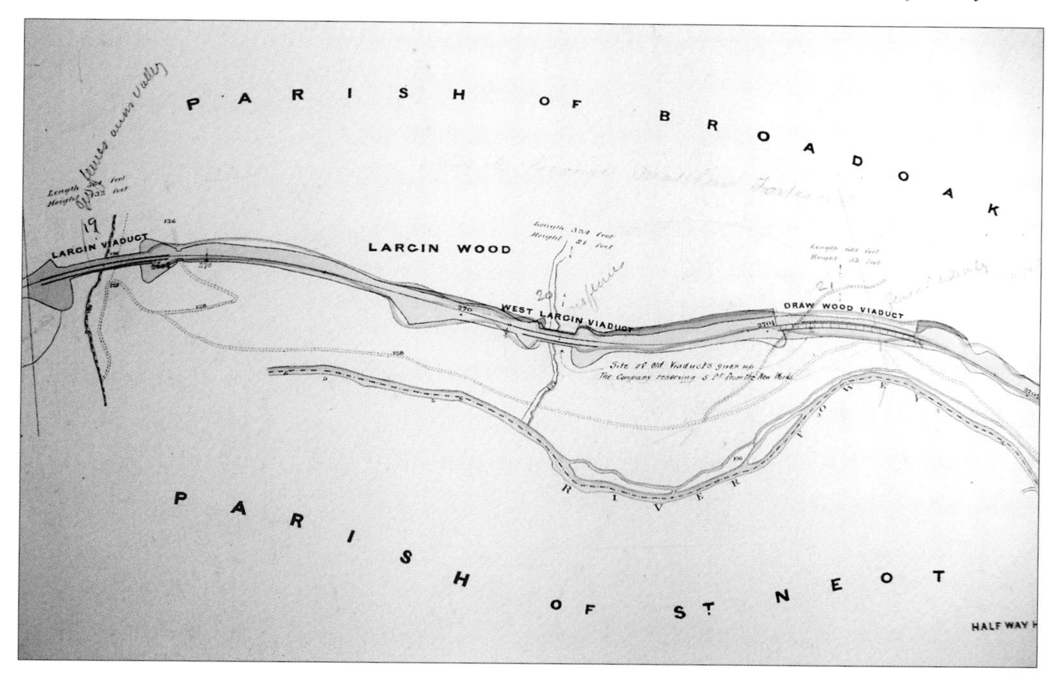

3.1 *The greatest concentration of viaducts is in the Fowey Valley.*

On the face of it the central route seemed to have everything going for it in terms of providing the fastest route to London. It also avoided the topographical disadvantages of crossing the Hamoaze and the steep valleys of south east Cornwall. However it had the disadvantages of not serving the two growing population centres of Liskeard and Plymouth.

Gradually the balance began to swing in favour of the southern route. The GWR with its associated companies was in a much stronger position than the SWR. The Bristol and Exeter Railway had just been opened in 1844. The South Devon had secured its Act of Parliament in 1844 and had started construction right away. The line was opened to Newton Abbot in 1846 and, despite the wasted time, money and effort on atmospheric traction, had reached Plymouth in 1849. In contrast the South Western was way behind, only reaching Salisbury in 1857 and Exeter in 1860. It followed that, if the Cornwall Railway was to proceed within a reasonable time frame, connecting it to the South Devon at Plymouth made overwhelming sense even if the route was less direct. The Cornwall Railway Company, despite having surveyed the central line in 1842, switched to the southern route. The support of the GWR depended on this. Feelings were still running high for the central route and it had become a head to head race with both parties vying to secure an act of Parliament first. Victory finally went to the Cornwall Railway Company in 1846.

The 'Civil War' had started in 1839 when the Provisional Committee had realised that the central line had twice come to grief in Parliament and had failed to attract funds. They therefore started to investigate the alternative of connecting to other lines associated with the GWR. The war only ended in 1847 when the final attempt at a central route suffered an ignominious defeat before the Standing Orders Committee.

By 1839 the 'coast' or 'southern' route began to emerge as a serious alternative. Although inferior in terms of mileage and gradients it nevertheless did have a better chance of commercial success. A full survey was carried out by Moorsom and a bill deposited before Parliament for the 1845 session. The rejection of this Bill led to a final flurry of activity by both factions during the autumn of 1845 to procure a successful Act of Parliament. Once Parliamentary approval had been secured for the South Devon Railway in 1844 the odds were stacked even further against the central route. Ultimately it came down to expediency of connecting to the South Devon Railway at Plymouth versus the more direct central route which had, however, failed to pass the Parliamentary hurdle. The issue was neatly summed up by Lord Falmouth in reply to Rowe.

> Q I don't know whether I should carry your judgement so far as this my Lord: If the matter were, as we lawyers say *res integra* if we were dealing with a virgin country, without the South Devon, that in your judgement

the best communication to the eastward would be the line to go from Falmouth to Exeter and also to Plymouth?

A *A priori*, I should say certainly, without having tried the surveys and found them abortive, that the most direct line was the best. Allow me to explain. On finding now that four schemes have failed on that line I am confirmed in the other line as the only one that can succeed.[2]

The Board of Trade took a similar view; that it was less a question of what was preferable as to what was practicable:

The question, however, assumes a very different aspect when we consider that the Legislature has already sanctioned the South Devon line from Exeter to Plymouth, by which a large proportion of the traffic which was calculated upon to support a central line is irrevocably diverted into another channel; and such an advance is made towards Falmouth that the construction of 66 miles of new Railway as compared to 100$^1/_2$ by the Central line will be sufficient to complete the communication.

THE CIVIL WAR IN THE PRESS [3]

During the nineteenth century Cornwall was the setting for a prolonged battle between the two rival newspapers, the well established *Royal Cornwall Gazette* and the upstart newcomer the *West Briton* which described itself as a 'dissenting' newspaper. The *West Briton* clearly was out of sympathy with the Tories, less than totally enamoured with the Whigs and only fully at home with the radical Liberals. The two papers also demonstrated the split between church and chapel.

The 'war' only ended when the papers merged in 1951. It had originated in the campaign in the 1820s for the reform of the parliamentary franchise which had culminated in the Reform Bill of 1832. As a radical paper the *West Briton* actively supported the campaign and became its organ whilst the *Gazette*, a pragmatic Tory paper, opposed it. There were other national issues on which the papers took opposing views during the 1820s, notably Catholic emancipation, the abolition of slavery and the reform of corrupt municipal corporations. However, as the 1830s progressed the papers focussed their battle on a local issue, the route of the railway. These papers reflected the political views of the time: the Whigs, or Liberals, advocated the central route whilst the Tories favoured the southern route.

The editors of the two papers were men of radically different views. The editor of the *Gazette* was Edward Ostler. A local man who, despite a Baptist upbringing, had become a staunch member of the Church of England which he saw as supporting traditional values. He saw its congregation, in terms of the 18th century epithet, as 'the Tory party at prayer'. He also wrote *History of the Cornwall Railway* in 1846 which was reprinted from the *Gazette* and reflected his strong preference for the southern route.

The policy of the *West Briton* was determined by its proprietor, Joseph Thomas, ably aided by its chief reporter Isaac Latimer. Thomas had been editor of *The Welshman* and continued his radical, nonconformist views in the *West Briton*. He became a Weslyan minister at Liskeard.

This rivalry also reflected the political division in Cornwall: Liberal support was strongest in the mining communities in west Cornwall whilst the Tories enjoyed more support in the agricultural and less traditionally mining communities in the east. It was little wonder that the Tories wanted to see the railway serve the fertile agricultural area south of Bodmin Moor and their developing mines around Fowey and Liskeard whilst the Liberals favoured a faster more direct route avoiding these areas. When the 1845 Cornwall Railway Bill failed, the *West Briton*, on 5 September 1845, took a prematurely triumphalist line essentially saying that as the Bill was lost, that was the end of the southern route and that the way was clear for the central route to go ahead without further opposition.

When the line was opened in 1859 both papers gave it extensive coverage. To commemorate the occasion the *West Briton* published a special 4 page broadsheet supplement, an *Illustrated Railway Supplement*. This covered the history of the company, a description of the line, the

3.2 *Engraving of Moorswater Viaduct:* WEST BRITON 6 MAY 1859

opening of the railway, the Royal Albert Bridge and the scenery, topography and antiquities as well as coverage of the opening ceremony. The *Royal Cornwall Gazette* covered a similar range of topics. The *West Briton* took an essentially low key attitude to the failure of its campaign for the central route which it had long espoused. It was to provide a rare victory for the *Gazette* over its rival. in alluding to the battle over the route the *West Briton* alluded to its previous stance:

> '... an active and determined contest ensued between the supporters of the rival schemes both in and out of Parliament. We have no wish to revive any of the acrimonious feeling which was then evoked upon the subject, and which we trust has long since passed away...'

The severity and costliness of the 'civil war' can be illustrated by the further details of Tremayne's cross-examination by Merevale which demonstrates the depth of feeling on the rival routes and the lengths to which the opposing factions are prepared to go:

> Q The county still I am afraid is pretty much divided as ever it was?
> A Yes, it appears so.
> Q Now remembering all that, Mr Tremayne, do you persist in the opinion that it would be better that this civil war should be prolonged?
> A The object was always to avoid any civil war and to push it off so that we may come together.

Moorsom's plans for a central route were ready by January 1841. On the rival merits of the two routes his view was that:

> To carry any line westwards into Cornwall would be far more difficult through the districts lying South of the parallels of Tavistock and Liskeard, than to take a course to the North of those parallels; a southern line would cut all those streams and ridges at right angles ... in such a manner as to involve very expensive and difficult works, including a very doubtful passage across the Hamoaze on the lower part of the river Tamar.[4]

He reported that he had:

> Found that a good practical working line of Railway, of a generally very easy character, may be obtained from the Bristol and Exeter Terminus to the town of Falmouth.

The plans were reported to a public meeting held on 5 January 1841. The reporter of *The Falmouth Packet* managed to describe the whole route in a single sentence![5]

> The route which Captain Moorsom lays down as the most preferable, starts from Falmouth, goes near Chacewater to Truro, along the vale of Ladock to St Austell, by Lanivet, a little to the north of Bodmin, by Blisland, within three miles of Camelford, to Altarnun and Launceston, from thence along the valley

> of the Lyd to Lidford, and parallel with the Tavistock to Okehampton Road to Okehampton, and crossing the road at Zeal takes the course of the Hollacomb and Spreyton waters into the valley of the Creedy, and passing within a mile of Crediton, joins the Bristol and Exeter Railway two miles on the London side of Exeter.

Having, no doubt, paused for breath, he then alludes to the problem of balancing the cost of initial capital works against subsequent running costs.

> Capt Moorsom next proceeds to consider the manner in which the line may be most advantageously graded, formed and worked. He urges the importance of keeping the cost of construction as low as possible which may be best done by not endeavouring to form the railway theoretically perfect in the first instance. The question of successful result is involved, not in the absolute returns of traffic, but in comparison of the gross outlay with those returns. As applied to Devon and Cornwall, if a railway were completed and set to work between Falmouth and Exeter, upon a total outlay of £1,000,000, the returns under ordinary management, would produce a net revenue as high as any of the first-class railways (except perhaps the Grand Junction) now at work: but if the outlay were made to double that sum, it seems equally improbable that the fair interest of money would for many years accrue to the proprietors. It is clear, therefore, that to be a successful line to the proprietors, the Devon and Cornwall Railway must be a cheap line.

The Committee should have been worried by the concept of '... not endeavouring to form the railway theoretically perfect in the first instance'. Furthermore Moorsom's estimate of £1m for 100 miles is significantly less than Thomas's. Only three years later he quoted the same sum for the 63 miles from Plymouth to Falmouth. His figure suggests a capital cost of under £10,000 per mile which does seem improbably low.

The report then goes into the question of the speed required upon the railway and recommended that the fast trains should not exceed 20 miles per hour. Thus the total time consumed in the journey between Falmouth and Exeter would be less than 5½ hours. Moorsom adopted a quarter of a mile as the minimum radius of curves, with a maximum grade of one in sixty. Again these figures contrast favourably with his subsequent gradients and curves for the southern route.

Clearly Moorsom had impressed the Committee for the reporter concludes:

> The committee were highly gratified with Captain Moorsom's statements, and acknowledged the diligence and ability which that gentleman had shown in fulfilling the duty that had been assigned to him. They were also fully impressed with the conviction that the railway was both necessary and practicable. We understand that Captain Moorsom, in the course of the

> proceedings, stated to the committee, that the South Devon Company would save fully £500,000, or half their proposed capital, in adopting the line from Exeter to Plymouth via Lidford and Tavistock, in junction with the West Devon and Cornish Trunk, independent of that being the most if not the only practicable route. This is, however, the concern of the Plymouth committee, and not ours.

This last remark does seem complacent bearing in mind the size and importance of Plymouth and the interest of the GWR in it. Nevertheless the Committee were 'well satisfied' by Moorsom.

At this stage everything looked favourable but the intervention of, a no doubt disgruntled, Richard Thomas suggests that this was about to change. Thomas, clearly incensed by Moorsom's report, published a detailed critique. Although he does not raise any fundamental engineering issues there are a whole range of inaccuracies which would seem to be symptomatic of Moorsom's lack of attention to detail:[6]

> I have read in your last paper 'Capt Moorsom's Report' on the proposed line of Railway. Some of the statements contained in it, appear to me to require explanation, in order that the comparative merits of the line proposed by him, and that which was surveyed by me in 1836 be better understood.
>
> I will take the several parts that I shall speak of, in the order in which they appear in the report. And first, in speaking of the connexion of the Cornwall line with a line to Plymouth it is said:
>
> 'It would appear that this connexion did not form a prominent point of consideration in the year 1837, when the latest survey was made by Mr Thomas, under direction of Colonel Landmann, &c'
>
> This survey was made in 1836, and, in the first place, was intended for a line both to Plymouth and into Cornwall, and the trial levels were accordingly made over the line of country in which Capt. M. proposes to carry his line; but on finding that the people of Plymouth would not adopt any line that should pass round the north of Dartmoor, the committee very properly immediately abandoned the idea of carrying the line in that direction, and a very much better line was tried and adopted. If Capt M had referred to the committee of management who had employed him, he might have been better informed on this point, as they had been previously furnished with a report from me, a copy of which, I subjoin.
>
> It may be proper now to mention that the survey was first undertaken under the direction of Col Landmann, who retired shortly after the line was surveyed, on which the company employed me as their engineer for the line from Exeter to Falmouth. This will explain the reason of the plans and sections lodged in 1836 being in the Colonel's name. I afterwards lodged other plans and sections on 1st March, 1837 in order to be prepared for the next session of Parliament in case of being disappointed of obtaining the act in the then existing session.

Thomas concludes by pointing out that his line had been shorter than Moorsom's:

> It now only remains for me to state, that the line which I surveyed is about seven miles shorter in its length from Exeter to Falmouth, than that adopted by Capt. M. and if the gradients of the two lines be made to correspond, will be a saving of about one fourteenth, both in time and expenses of conveyance of goods and passengers; that the merits of the two lines must be compared by reference to the gradients as well as to the lengths; and if the amount of inclinations be made the same in both lines, that the line, as surveyed in 1836, will not cost so much as that which has recently been surveyed, by nearly two hundred thousand pounds .

The Committee was not insensitive to these points which may have resulted in some reservation over Moorsom. However once again 'means' were lacking and the company needed help from the Great Western which would only support a connection to the South Devon Railway at Plymouth. The minutes of the Provisional Committee show all too clearly how little scope the members enjoyed over the choice of route. They are more concerned about what was going on outside the county and how such happenings would determine what they are able to achieve.

Packet traffic

The long-dreaded announcement, officially made on 29 May 1842, that the packets would shortly be removed from Falmouth led to renewed exertions. A private preliminary meeting was held at Truro on 7 July, and a large meeting shortly after at Redruth, at which Tweedy and Bond were appointed to confer with the Great Western directors seeking their immediate support. They obtained the assurance that as soon as the South Devon should be completed, the directors would be prepared to support 'an extension through Cornwall'.

The removal of the packet traffic fundamentally undermined the revenue assumptions on which the central route had been based. Its promoters had allowed a figure of £123,913 out of a total of £160,548 for 'passengers, mails, parcels etc' from the packet steamers. As Tweedy put it:[7]

> I will state that some sources of traffic included in this estimate which have no longer any existence.

In August 1843 Tweedy and Bond reported that they had met directors of the GWR, Bristol and Exeter and the South Devon Railway Companies who were 'decidedly favourable to the Southern Line'. The Cornwall Company could expect no support to a separate, and in some respects competing, line. Indeed the associated companies interpose every possible obstacle to any project for a Northern line. At a further public meeting held in Bodmin at the beginning of 1842 with the High Sheriff in the Chair, Tremayne reports on a letter from Charles Saunders, Chairman of the GWR, which sets out that company's position. It assures the Committee of 'the very favourable position in which the South Devon line stands with reference to obtaining their bill in the ensuing session of Parliament'. It urges the Cornish interests to decide on their course of action regarding the proposed South Devon line and to form a company and sub-committee: He explained the situation tactfully 'stating the disinclination of the Company to dictate in any way to the Cornwall Committee but explicitly stating that they could receive no proposals for assistance to a North Line'[8]

This provided plenty for the Provisional Committee to think about. It had become clear that a northern, or central, route would not succeed and that the Committee should concentrate on securing a line connecting Plymouth and Falmouth. Having just spent a considerable sum on Moorsom's central line they were going to have to write this off.

The examination of Tremayne by Rowe[9] clarifies not only the GWR's attitude but also the deep-seated antipathy towards the central route in general and to the South Western Railway company in particular:

A I attended the meeting at Paddington that was the first meeting of the Great Western Railway I ever attended ... I did beg correctly to impress upon the directors the expediency of their not giving encouragement to any other scheme which might be proposed and which would interfere with any measure hereafter to be proposed for carrying the communication by railway through the centre of Cornwall and Devon. Mr Russell's answer was to this effect as well as I recollect that ... he would not deceive me for one moment, but he would not hold out any hope of attempting any communication with Cornwall except by the coast route ...

Q I believe you thought and do think, the course of that Cornwall Railway from Falmouth to Plymouth by Par and the valley of the Fowey is on many accounts objectionable?

A Oh yes, I have also said so and maintain that opinion.

1844, a critical year for the Cornwall Railway

This was to be a crucial year for the proposers of both routes. It proved to be the year in which the advantage swung decisively in favour of the southern route and marked the beginning of the end of the central route. The year began with a firm, if not unanimous, decision that the southern route was the only realistic option.

The whole issue is vividly set out in the acrimonious correspondence between Bond, Secretary of the Cornwall Railway's provisional committee, and Edmund Turner MP in October and November 1844. It demonstrates the clash between idealism and pragmatism. Bond set the tone that the question was about economics:

> ...to ascertain the capabilities of the two counties of Devon and Cornwall for supporting such an expensive mode of transit.

Their letters cogently summarise the difference of opinion on the two routes. Bond saw the need to set out how the provisional committee had been obliged to change its support to the southern route by facing the reality of the situation, even after going to the expense of commissioning Moorsom to survey the central line.[10] His letter of 12 November 1844 (Appendix five) sets out cogently the logic of the change of mind. In summary he explains that the Parliamentary approval of the South Devon Railway was a recently established fact, that the GWR would only give support for a southern line, that there would not be enough traffic to support the central railway, that it could not generate a reasonable rate of return and that it could never be carried out.

A County meeting of shareholders and 'others interested in the construction of a Railway through Cornwall' was convened on 25 January, 'not to talk merely, but to act'.[11]. This set up a Provisional Committee, 'consisting of the Noblemen and Gentlemen resident in the County', and authorised the issue of £50 shares. £1 was to be paid immediately and 10% on 31 December with a further call of 10% as soon as an Act had been obtained. Subscriptions amounted to £70,000. For a short while it seemed that 'means', or lack of them, might not be a problem. On the question of the route Bond summarised the position:

> The committee have kept in view these two grand principles; that it is our place if possible to go the shortest route, but rather than not go at all, we will go by way of Plymouth. Your object being to have a line which is possible. To have one that is impossible, I suppose you would hardly expect!

The meeting sought to clarify the basis of future relations with the Associated Companies:

1. That it is most important to ascertain whether the capital required for the construction of a direct line to Exeter can be obtained and therefore to ascertain the plans of the Board of Trade and on what terms they will be prepared to render assistance to the Cornwall Railway.
2. That it is desirable also to ascertain to what extent and on what terms the assistance of the Great Western Railway and its associated companies will be given to a Cornwall line and, should their support be refused to a direct line, whether the South Devon Company will carry their line to the waters edge and what further assistance they will render.

Moorsom was meanwhile instructed to draw up plans for the southern route. The Committee had effectively changed sides in the 'Civil War' but several members resolved to fight on for the central route. There was a resolution, conspicuous for the formal withdrawal of support for the southern route by Pendarves and Edmund Turner, MP for the Western Division of Cornwall, and former member of the Provisional Committee

As the year progressed the *Royal Cornwall Gazette*, only a few days before the deadline for submitting railway projects to Parliament for the 1845 session, showed the 'Civil War' still being fought out in adjacent columns[12]. There were no less than fourteen notices, letters, reports of meetings, and statements of the merits or demerits of both proposals. One letter starts: 'There is nothing talked of just now but Railways...', a sentiment with which the readers must have wholeheartedly agreed! There were the formal notices of the intention to apply to Parliament for the construction of the southern route from Eldad to Falmouth and for the Central Route, together with a list of its provisional Committee and an application to buy shares. This contains, sequentially in the same column, an unattributed statement of the merits of the southern route followed by a report of a meeting in Penzance which resolved that the central route was the only one calculated to meet the requirements of the town and neighbourhood (Appendix six). In brief the supporters of the central line blandly assert its superiority. And, with justification, criticised the alternative for its 'dependence on the doubtful passage of the Hamoaze'.

The *Royal Cornwall Gazette*[13] commented on this renewed flurry of correspondence:

> The construction of a line through Cornwall still continues to excite interest, and, so far, we are well pleased to find the Cornish spirit aroused. 'One and All' is their motto, but we now find them divided: yet, for the interests of, 'One and All', we feel satisfied the present excitement to be well calculated to effect the object all have in view - that of the formation of a line, whether north, south or central - so that the line be. The South line has the start; it holds out advantages peculiar in themselves, and more especially in a pecuniary point of view to which we apprehend the Central Line will not lay claim.

Allowing for the bias of the paper against the central route, the stress on the 'peculiar pecuniary advantages' of the southern route was an acute observation: The central line was doomed never to enjoy such benefits.

REACTION TO THE FAILURE OF THE 1845 CORNWALL RAILWAY BILL

The rival factions interpreted the decision in different ways. Both promptly called meetings: shareholders of the Cornwall Railway met on 26 August when they decided to rectify the shortcomings of their failed

Bill and resubmit in time for the 1846 session (See Ch six). Meanwhile the supporters of the Central route met on 28th when they jumped to the premature conclusion that the southern route was dead. They saw the decision as a final vindication of the inherent shortcomings of the southern route. Their meeting appears to have been enthusiastic with numerous instances of loud cheers as the various resolutions were passed unanimously. Clearly the recent rejection of the Cornwall Railway Bill had created a euphoric atmosphere. The dynamic force behind the meeting was Tremayne. In proposing one of the motions he gave a lengthy address reported as;

> He would not enter now into the engineering questions; but his own opinion was that they should leave Penryn on the right (not cross the estuary), leave Truro on the right, leave St Columb on the left, come to Roche, and he thought it necessary it should come to Halgavor, about two miles south of Bodmin.
>
> Now how were they to make this railway? It was impossible from local funds or any money they could bring forward in this county. They must look without – they must go round and see whether they could get support from associated companies, or large capitalists from the city of London, who were accustomed to invest large sums of money in profitable undertakings. It struck him very early that they must come to that, and he had no hesitation in saying, although many might think he had been acting in a hostile spirit, that he had thought it his duty, as a shareholder of the Great Western Company, to go to one of their meetings at Paddington and ask of the chairman, that if any accident should happen to the Cornwall bill, would they pledge themselves not to give any opposition to the central line? Mr Russell gave him a very honest answer, for he said he could give him no encouragement.
>
> The sun now shone brightly upon them, in all their undertakings...
>
> If he was to have a railway through Cornwall he would rather wait ten years than sanction a coast line over the estuaries, over the valley of the Fowey, and over the Hamoaze.[14]

The meeting received very full coverage in the *West Briton* which enjoyed a short lived triumph. Under the heading 'Important County Railway meeting ...' whose purpose was to take:

> 'into consideration the most effectual means of insuring for this county and its various important interests, the most direct and available railway communication between Penzance, Falmouth and Exeter'.

It concluded:

> There is now before the public a plan for direct communication with the metropolis, giving a line of road without the extraordinary engineering difficulties and supported by the leading gentlemen of

this county, and also of Devon, Somerset, Dorset and Wilts, backed by eminent capitalists. With this combination there seems every probability of carrying into effect that line of railway which has always been admitted to be the one which for the general advantage of the county ought to have been adopted; and which was laid aside and the coast line substituted for it, only because in the then state of the money market it was thought impossible to procure funds for carrying it into execution. There never has been, there never can be, any doubt as to the fact of the Central line the true one to be adopted here, both in a local and national point of view ...[15]

Later, in 1845, the Provisional Committee of Management of the Direct London and Exeter Railway Company issued a prospectus for £3,000,000 with a terminus in central London and eventually managed to submit their bill at the end of 1846. Lewin comments

> In the meanwhile a new Cornwall and Devon Central Ry. had been initiated at Bodmin, as the G.W. had refused to help the central portions of the counties. It was strongly supported along the line of route, and allied itself with the two narrow gauge projects east of Exeter, ultimately obtaining the approval of the L.& S.W., as we have seen before. The scheme was a very ambitious one, consisting of a main line from Exeter to Truro, via Okehampton, Launceston, and Bodmin, with a branch to St Austell and an extension to Penzance and St Ives.

THE END FOR THE CORNWALL & DEVON CENTRAL RAILWAY

The much revised Cornwall Railway Bill for the southern route was duly submitted in time for the 1846 Parliamentary session and the choice of route occupied an appreciable amount of time. Despite attempts by the Parliamentary Committee to restrict discussion to the project in hand the respective merits of the two lines were once again given a comprehensive airing. It must have been clear that if the bill succeeded the consequence would be the effective end of the central route. Hence the tactic employed was to urge postponement and delay. There were repeated attempts, notably by Mr Sergeant Kinglake, not entirely successfully, to have such discussion excluded. The 'gentlemen of the county' were still split. Falmouth, Lemon and Treffry were prepared to support the southern route for reasons of expediency, to get back packet traffic and to gain traffic from the increasing commerce in the neighbourhood of Par. But Rodd, Trelawney, Pendarves and Tremayne favoured further delay to try to secure the central route.

The 1846 Parliamentary hearing was to be the forum for the last act in the drama over the route. Rowe realised that the only chance of saving the central route was to press for a postponement of a decision on the southern route. There was a lengthy argument about whether it was permissible to discuss the issue of the central line and the contingent question of the actual existence of the South Devon Railway. The chairman generally allowed it. But it did not affect the outcome. The proposal in the bill was determined on its merits alone[16]:

THOSE WHO STUCK OUT FOR THE CENTRAL LINE

On a single day a formidable group then gave evidence for delay on the southern route so that it would not prejudice the ultimate success of the central line. First Francis Rodd made the case for the central line [17]. Then Pendarves explains that if the southern route went ahead it would rule out any possibility of achieving the direct central line[18].

Q Allow me to ask you this. Do you concur in the opinions that have been expressed in this room to day that it would be desirable that this great question should be postponed in order to obtain the best line?

A I certainly do.

Trelawney took the view that the optimal route had yet to be found and that hence delay was to be preferred to approval of the southern route:

Q Allow me to ask you whether since the bill for the central line has been thrown out upon the standing orders, you think it is still advisable that Parliament should postpone granting a railway in Cornwall until another Parliament?

A Yes I do. That is my firm belief and opinion - that a better line may be found than the present one - than the Cornwall line a considerably better line – and that the difficulty of crossing the river is almost insurmountable.

Q You mean to say a better line might be found than either of those already projected?

A Yes I believe the very best has not been discovered yet. We have had a great many engineers seem to differ very much.

Q Where is it your opinion the best line would come?

A I think the best line would be very nearly the line that has been checked out by the central, but that line may still be improved. I think that the lines that have been checked out would be better than the present Cornwall line, but I have no doubt a better line may be discovered and as good as we could wish to have.[19]

Finally Tremayne urged postponement in the interest that the two routes could be directly compared:

Q Allow me to put this question to you – That being your strong opinion do you think it a matter of vital importance to the interests, I will not say of Cornwall only, but the western peninsular, that this question should not be predominantly decided in this year: but that it would be wise to wait to have the

3.3 *'An area of growing importance around Liskeard ...' A busy scene at Liskeard Station in broad gauge days with a lengthy double headed train. The leading engine is an Armstrong 0-6-0 designed to be converted to standard gauge. The train engine is an 0-4-4 side tank. The siding in the foreground has already been converted to standard gauge. The signal is of the slotted post variety.*
LISKEARD OLD CORNWALL SOCIETY

best line to Exeter and so to communicate with the best line to London. Is that your opinion?

A My creed has always been delay and, I may be laughed at, but I say now that perhaps, I think, the best line has not yet been found. A great benefit will arise from delay and the matter receiving further consideration and I think that this benefit may also arise from that course, that there may be a better chance of bringing interests together and not wasting any more money in this way.[20]

The objectors were clearly determined to put up a good fight. However, they were handicapped by events outside their control, and outside the county; namely the economic consequences of the loss of the packet traffic and the support of the GWR for the southern route.

THOSE WHO WERE PREPARED TO COMPROMISE

Their opponents, despite their change of heart over the route, were able to mount a more cogent case. Two of the original promoters, the Earl of Falmouth and Sir Charles Lemon, had reluctantly come to the conclusion that the southern route was the only one likely to succeed. The Earl of Falmouth examined by Kinglake:[21]

Q Do you know that in 1844 a bill was obtained which had the sanction of the legislature for making a railway which is now called the proposed South Devon?

A It was the probability of the passing of that bill which in a great measure influenced me in coming to the decision which I did that that would be the best line for the County of Cornwall.

Q On that bill obtaining the sanction of the legislature did that influence your judgement as to the expediency of adopting the line of railway now proposed to Plymouth?

A Certainly, very considerably.

Q Is that judgement which your Lordship has formed from deliberate consideration of all the bearings of the question?

A Yes, after addressing my attention to the subject after having seen over and over again that the attempts to establish a central line have always proved abortive.

Q Was there a report drawn up by the persons to whom the task was entrusted?

A There was such a report.

Q Do you recollect what was the effect of it?

A It was generally to this effect, that they found it was so important to have the Great Western and the South Devon Company for their friends, that they thought, it was much better to direct their attention to form a communication with Plymouth than to form a direct connection with Exeter, which had before been attempted and failed.

And Lemon makes much the same case:[22]

Q I believe that central project fell through in consequence of their not being able to raise the capital?

A Yes, just so.

Q You said, I believe, that a change came over your Councils [*sic*] in consequence of the impossibility of getting funds and you then applied I believe to the Great Western Railway Company, and the Great Western Railway Company accorded you its aid provided you came and met them at Plymouth?

A No the scheme was given up altogether in despair. We tried to get capital and it was found impossible. A public meeting was held, I think in the beginning of 1844, and I protested my own feeling so strongly that we had no chance of getting capital that I opposed the progress of the scheme at that time. It afterwards turned out the Great Western were willing to advance capital and that set it on foot again

3.4 *Truro Station in broad gauge days. The train shed was lost when the station was rebuilt by the GWR in 1897.* STEPHEN ROWSON COLLECTION

This gives a flavour of the intensity of the debate. Pendarves voiced his concern in a letter dated 27 August 1845[23]:

> I am more than ever convinced that the best interests of the County will be sacrificed unless we all pull together, promptly and decisively to support a direct central and continuous communication by Yeovil and Salisbury to London.

In contrast the *Royal Cornwall Gazette* in 1859, predictably, reflected on the merits of the southern route:

> The Cornwall Railway laid down a line which they thought the best and cheapest for the county – from Truro to Liskeard and thence to Plymouth. They were blamed for this – it was said to be out of the direct line. But let gentlemen who talk in that way draw a line on any map from Truro to Exeter, and they will find it passes by Liskeard not many yards from where it actually exists. So you see they have not gone so very much out of the direct line. They have carried the line from Liskeard through the very best road they could choose.[24]

Ostler summarises the difference between the routes:

> Considered as a commercial undertaking, no lines can present a greater contrast than the Cornwall and Central Railways. The Central Line has no advantage. From Falmouth to Exeter it is 13 miles shorter than the Cornwall and South Devon, and two miles shorter than the Cornwall and Launceston. It obtains this saving in distance by crossing worthless moors, while the Cornwall brings nearly all the wealth, trade and population of the county upon the main line. Measuring by time, the Broad Guage [*sic*] Railway of

> 102, or even 113 miles, is practically shorter than the Narrow Guage Railway of 100.

The Board of Trade, too, had been much more favourable to the southern route.

> We are of the opinion, therefore, that the extension of the Coast line from Plymouth to Falmouth may fairly be sanctioned as a commercial speculation, and that, in this point of view, it affords the only practicable means present of extending the Railway communication to the County of Cornwall.

The views of the Board of Trade did not however have the effect of killing off the central route. In 1845 the stakes were raised. In January the Provisional Cornwall Railway committee declined the proposal of the Central Cornwall Company[25] and authorised he sum of £4,000 to oppose it.

Undeterred, the provisional committee of the Central Railway pressed on. The prospectus of the Cornwall and Devon Central Railway of 1845 concentrates on putting an unfavourable perspective on the rejection by the House of Lords of the Cornwall Railway Bill of 1845 (Appendix four). It stresses the benefits of the central route as against the *'waste of capital and time involved in the circuitous route round BRISTOL.'* It claims that its route is *'no less than 30 miles shorter than the devious course of the Great Western Railway.'* It also claims that *'the saving in actual distance amounts to more than 50 miles; whilst the time also saved by avoiding the passage of the Hamoaze ... was estimated ... as equal to a saving of 15 or 20 miles more'*. However it plays down the fact that the construction of the route between Salisbury and Exeter is several years behind the South Devon. Just how significant a consideration this was is shown by Devey.

> It had, since the undertaking of the South-Western, been one of the pet schemes of Mr Locke to continue the line from Salisbury to the junction, at Yeovil, of the Great Western, as also to Bristol and Exeter. In 1847 he bought the manor of Honiton, one of the towns through which the projected railway was to run, and was shortly after sent to Parliament by that borough. Owing however to the strenuous opposition of the Great Western Company, it was not until 1854 that he could get the Act for the projected line incorporated by Parliament. The capital of half a million had been for some time raised for its execution. But that was a very small portion of the difficulty, as more than thirty times this amount had been spent by the South Western in struggling against the Great Western for a parliamentary sanction. The difficulties which natural obstacles and human timidity threw in the engineers' path were a mere flea bite in comparison with those presented by legal casuistry and parliamentary interference. The time guaranteed for the completion of the works expired in 1858. But the full extent of the line was not opened until June 1860, a few months before Mr Locke's death.

At the opening in 1859 the *Royal Cornwall Gazette* reflected on the battleground, not without it seems, a touch of *schadenfreude*:

> At the following half yearly Meeting of the Great Western the intention to support the Cornwall Railway was officially announced, and in August 1844 the same intention was announced by the Bristol and Exeter, and South Devon Companies also. In this month, the South Western Railway began their policy to prevent a Line from being carried to Falmouth, by promoting an agitation for the object, now impracticable, of carrying one over the Moors to the North. By their deceptive promises of support to this project many were deceived, and a very severe and costly struggle was carried on between the friends of the Cornwall Railway, and the promoters of the so-called Central Line. The popular cry was most decidedly in favour of the latter, and this paper stood alone in the Western press in exposing and resisting the delusion. Though the Cornwall Railway had thus received the sanction of both Houses of Parliament, the South Western made one more attempt to prevent a Railway from being carried through Cornwall. They revived the agitation for a Central project, and the railway mania which prevailed in 1846 enabled them to obtain large support for a plausible scheme, and to compel a desperate and costly contest. The plans they deposited were filled with so many and astounding blunders that it is impossible to suppose they were serious in promoting the Central Line. Three thousand errors were detected in them, some of them enormous and inexcusable blunders. The Lords Committee on Standing Orders flung out the Bill after a scrutiny of half an hour, and the expenses incurred on this miserable project were no less than £96,000! To the Cornwall Railway plans 95 objections on standing orders were taken, which all broke down except two. One of these was the omission to figure a pump let into a wall – the other the failure to specify a small cabbage plot in the corner of a field. The Bill passed the Lords on the 30th of July, and on the 3rd August received the Royal assent. The expenses of this successful contest were just one half of those incurred for the central scheme.

This was to all intents and purposes the end of the central line. On 26 August 1847 it was reported that the Cornwall and Devon Central Project was rejected on Standing Orders. (See Ch 5) It had been a long and painful fight. In the end expediency triumphed over idealism.

Unfortunately the choice of route and the question of with which company to align themselves for connection to London was not the only irresolvable problem with which the Provisional Committee had to wrestle: They also had to face the question of whether or not to use atmospheric traction.

4.1 *An atmospheric train.*

CHAPTER FOUR

'PERCHANCE TO DREAM ...'

WILLIAM SHAKESPEARE: *HAMLET*

> On this system of working railways, the moving power is communicated by means of a continuous pipe or main, laid between the rails and divided by separating valves, into suitable lengths for exhaustion; a partial vacuum is formed in this pipe, by air pumps, worked by steam engines, fixed at intervals along the line or by water-power, if the nature of the country be such as to afford it. These valves are opened by the train as it advances, without stoppage or reduction of its speed. A piston which is made to fit nearly air tight, by means of leather packing, is introduced into the pipe, and is connected to the leading carriage of each train, by an iron plate which travels through a longitudinal groove or continuous aperture, the whole length of the pipe.

This is how Jacob Samuda, the prime mover of this revolutionary 'atmospheric' system, described it in his paper to the Institution of Civil Engineers[1] . His brother Joseph set out its advantages in his evidence to the Parliamentary Select Committee on Atmospheric Railways:

> Under our system we have no engine travelling with the train, and consequently any derangement or any accident, which is likely to arise from the presence of the engine, is by that means entirely avoided. We have the leading carriage on our line propelled by the power applied to the piston, and inside the tube: and as this power is constantly applied by drawing out of the air in the direction of the piston's motion, we have a directing influence exerted upon the train by the piston inside the tube, instead of a disturbing influence by the action of the wheels of the crank axles of a locomotive. That enables us to make a circuit round sharp curves with a greater amount of security than we could do on the locomotive system. It also prevents our being so easily disturbed from our right course; and as the power is to be given by a stationary engine, it can only be given in one direction at the same time as the same section; it is impossible that we can have trains travelling in opposite directions upon the same length of tube. This renders any chance of collision impossible...

Asked about ascending steep gradients he replied:

> We have a great advantage in that respect; the reason we have that advantage is, because the locomotive engine has to apply its power first to move itself, and then gives the balance of its power to move the train. Now when the locomotive engine is drawing a load upon a level, the traction per ton is of course considerably less than when it is drawing it up a steep incline; but at the time of drawing it up a steep incline, the locomotive engine necessarily requires an additional power to overcome its own gravity, and is consequently

not prepared to give the train even the same amount of power it had been able to afford it on the level, at the very time when the train requires a greater amount of power.

So much for the theory: The attractive prospect of using the system was understandably very powerful and blinded many people to its shortcomings. It split the engineering profession. Those in favour included Brunel, Cubitt and Vignoles. They pointed to no loss of power through locomotives having to pull their own weight, stationary engines subject to less wear and tear than locomotives, reduced infrastructure costs because atmospheric trains are lighter and allegedly had better hill climbing ability, and (fallaciously) that stationary engines cost less to run. Those unconvinced included Robert Stephenson, Bidder and Locke. They believed that the atmospheric system was less economical than the conventional locomotive, speed would be no greater, and lines would be no cheaper to build. The evidence of the engineers at the Cornwall Railway hearings was to throw up these differences all too clearly and much time was spent on a fruitless debate.

The system had been quite successfully applied on the Kingstown and Dalkey line near Dublin. It operated, using the system, from 1844 until 1854. This line was short, steep and with sharp bends, characteristics which persuaded visiting engineers, particularly Moorsom and Brunel, that the system would enable substantial savings to be made on civil engineering works in Devon and Cornwall. So promising did it sound that the Cornwall Railway Company's provisional committee resolved on 6 Aug 1844 to send Moorsom to Ireland to report on the results of the experiment. The demonstration of the atmospheric train took place in September 1844. Moorsom returned greatly impressed, and recommended its adoption as peculiarly suitable for a railway through Cornwall[2] . On Brunel's recommendation the South Devon Company took up Samuda and Clegg's patent. Brunel was evasive as to what the fee actually was and the Parliamentary Committee prevented an answer to the question put to him under cross examination by Rowe who suggested that the figure might be £400 to £500[3]. However, as the question was ruled out of order, the exact figure was not revealed.

The South Devon Railway Act received the Royal Assent on 7 July 1844 and at the Company's first meeting in August, despite the problems emerging from the installation of the system on the London and Croydon Railway, it was resolved to use atmospheric traction. This proved to be a costly mistake and the final demise of the system came in September1848 when the South Devon Company was obliged to suspend atmospheric working. After this no-one attempted to develop the system any further.

The Cornwall Railway was one of a small group of companies that obtained an Act to build lines that could have had atmospheric traction. It was seen as an extension of the South Devon and, as such, an obvious candidate. Moorsom perceived that he could save the Company much expense in overcoming Cornwall's difficult terrain by using steep gradients and sharp curves. Accordingly the possibility of using the atmospheric system hung over the Parliamentary hearings into the Cornwall Railway Bills in 1845 and 1846. By the time of the 1846 hearing the South Devon Railway had been partially opened but the atmospheric system was not yet operating. Clearly however financial alarm bells were already sounding:

> ...that it (The Cornwall Railway) was projected as an Extension of the South Devon Railway which the Petitioners were advised was in an embarrassed state in its Finances, was unable to procure Loans, and that, if the Atmospheric Principle failed, the Company would be unable to raise funds for its Completion.[4]

4.2 *The only known surviving sections of atmospheric pipe are now installed on a section of broad gauge track at the Didcot Railway Centre. This 22inch pipe had been made for the Dainton bank west of Newton Abbot.*
THE GREAT WESTERN TRUST

Locke, under examination, was not totally hostile to the technical aspects of the system but he said that the economics were worse than for locomotives.

Q I believe you entertained doubts of its success from the commencement?

A Not a doubt of its success as a mechanical problem but always a doubt of its success as a commercial speculation in regard to its economy.

Q I ask you whether the result of the experiment of the last several months during which it has been in operation has tended to increase your confidence in it or still further to diminish your expectation of it ever becoming successful?

A It has perfectly convinced me and the first view I took of it that it is not so cheap as locomotive power and that it is very far short of being anything like as cheap as locomotive power, that is in reference to its economy; that is my first view. Now I am much taken in its success as a mechanical problem but I am not one of those who will say it is impossible: it can work. I will not say so but I do not believe they will make it cheaper than the locomotive power and therefore it will not be introduced.

Q Or as certain in its operation?

A Nor as certain as with locomotives.

Q Judging from the numerous failures which have taken place within the last twelve months you cannot calculate with any degree of confidence on the certainty of its working?

A I could not.

Q I will ask you whether you would think of recommending to any company or body of shareholders who might employ you as their engineer the adoption of the atmospheric principle as a means of laying down and working any line of Railway on the results of experiments which have been made up to the present moment?

A I would not.[5]

However it was the practical objections, rather than economic ones contained in Robert Stephenson's report to the Directors of the Chester and Holyhead Railway Company that was to deter many railway promoters. During March 1844 the Committee had been seeking information from Robert Stephenson on whether the system was to be adopted on the Chester to Holyhead line. The sceptical Stephenson advised against it on the basis 'that on that line especially as the works are not heavy, the adoption of the atmospheric system was not calculated to produce any particular economy in the first construction, and that it would be more expensive in working'. Stephenson criticised the system as 'not an economical mode of transmitting power,' that it would be no quicker, that it would result in high installation costs, be more expensive to operate, be inflexible and most tellingly:

> The efficient operation of the whole depends so completely upon the perfect performance of each individual section of machinery. Each train, in moving between London and Birmingham, would be passed, as it were, through thirty-eight distinct systems of mechanism, and it cannot be deemed unreasonable to suppose that in such a vast series of machinery as would be required in this instance, casualties occasioning delay must not infrequently occur. If the consequences were confined to one train, such casualties would be of small moment, but the perfect operation of the whole is dependent on each individual part, and when the casualties extend themselves not only throughout the whole line of railway but to every succeeding train which has to pass the locality of the mishap, until it is rectified, whether this occupies one hour or one week, the irregularity must be admitted to be very great.[6]

Jacob (1811-1844) and Joseph (1813-1885) d Aguiler Samuda

For the railway historian the Samuda brothers merit little more than a footnote and then only in the context of patentees of an unsuccessful experiment in a potentially revolutionary form of railway traction. Yet they were significant engineers in their own right particular in the field of marine engineering. The atmospheric system was a departure from their core business and occupied them for the best part of ten years from the preparations for a demonstration at Wormwood Scrubs in 1840 until after the abandonment of the South Devon system in September 1848. The Samudas had put a great deal of energy into developing the system and both brothers had published learned papers on the subject. Furthermore they assiduously pursued the cause of atmospheric traction both in its advocacy and in its practical application. Joseph remained involved right up to the bitter end, receiving the brickbats of the shareholders of the South Devon Railway Company for his troubles.

The brothers came from a family who were prominent members of the 19th century Anglo-Jewish community which was noted for its advancement in the sciences. The brothers were unusual in the community in pursuing mechanical engineering. They had set up in business as marine and general engineers with premises initially at Bow Creek in East London and subsequently at Cubitt Town in the Isle of Dogs. (The site is now occupied by a Greater London Council housing estate built in the 1960s which commemorates the Samuda name.) They specialised in improvements to marine engines and sadly Jacob was scalded when a marine engine exploded whilst on trial on 12 November 1844. The *Gypsy Queen* had just returned to Blackwall. Samuda raised the boiler pressure to its full operational level when an expansion joint gave way filling the engine room with 'scalding vapours' killing Samuda and six others. The inquest found that the cause of the accident was the giving way of joints of a large steam pipe connecting the boilers with the cylinders. These joints were known as 'spigot and faucets'. To modern eyes they appear incredibly dangerous. One end of the pipe was inserted a few inches into the end of the other without any fastening except for hemp packing to keep it tight. A witness stated that '...the pressure of steam lifted the spigot out of the socket, and caused the steam to escape.'[7] His death came at a critical time for the atmospheric project and robbed it of its most enthusiastic and able exponents. Hadfield[8] concludes:

> His was the best brain and the finest mechanical engineering ability behind the atmospheric system and if he had lived, it is just conceivable that the story might have ended differently.

The marine engineering business pioneered ships incorporating the latest technological advantages. Soon after the failure of the atmospheric system the Crimean War brought orders for several small warships of advanced design. Joseph went on to achieve great distinction in establishing the Institution of Naval Architects, as a member of the Metropolitan Board of Works and as a Liberal MP, first for Tavistock and latterly for Tower Hamlets. His obituary in *The Times* makes no reference to the atmospheric system.[9]

4.3 *Joseph Samuda 1811-85.* INSTITUTION OF CIVIL ENGINEERS

Great strides in developing the steam locomotive had been made in the preceding 15 years particularly in their hill climbing ability. Yet they remained dirty and had to carry their own coal and water which had to be frequently replenished. J. M.W. Turner's picture 'Rain, Steam and Speed' shows the lot of those who had to travel in third class trains exposed not only to the weather but also liable to be showered with cinders, soot and steam,[10]. In contrast the atmospheric system offered fast clean silent travel, where gradients would present little problem and where the risk of collision was eliminated. It presented a tantalising vision of a potentially superior form of traction to the steam locomotive. No wonder that there was so much hope that the system could be made to work.

In his paper to the Institution of Civil Engineers Jacob Samuda sets out a vision of advantages to both the railway companies and public alike. The one phrase in his paper that identifies the Achilles heel of the system is 'when all the present drawbacks are removed'. Brunel too confirms that 'the mere mechanical difficulties can be overcome'. With hindsight one can see that they never were going to be removed, and proved to be too formidable to be overcome. Jacob Samuda goes into detail on attempts to deal with the 'continuous aperture' before summarising with presumably unconscious irony:

> The failure of these, as also of some subsequent attempts, is clearly traceable to the want of a valve, which would close sufficiently air tight, to allow a useful degree of vacuum, after the valve has been opened and closed again, by the passage of the train.

He addresses the subject of the economics with some caution but reaches his conclusion with a degree of assurance:

> The next point treated, is the cost of working, and the author is fully aware, that on this head, it is more difficult to convince than on any other. The following detail is given, in order to show that many items of very heavy expense, which are indispensable on the present system of locomotion, are avoided on the atmospheric system. The weight of the locomotive engine, is of course dispensed with, and in quick trains, this forms no inconsiderable portion of the weight to be moved. Coal is substituted for the more costly fuel, coke, and besides the saving in value from this substitution, its quantity is reduced, by the facility afforded by stationary power, of introducing all the means of obtaining the best effect from the fuel consumed;- condensation, expansion, and a more perfect absorption by the boilers generated by combustion, are among the advantages.

When the Provisional Committee for the Cornwall Railway was preparing to submit its Bill to Parliament during 1844 for consideration during the1845 Parliamentary session the prospects of using atmospheric traction looked bright. The Wormwood Scrubs trials had been successful and the Dalkey line had been working for nine months. The patentees had asserted that 'the Atmospheric Railway can be constructed at less cost, and worked at one third the expense of a locomotive line, whilst the speed of 50 miles an hour can be obtained over gradients of 1 in 40, with 35 Tons of Passengers or other traffic'. They reached the conclusion that 'there is ample evidence which would justify the adoption of an Atmospheric line at the present time'. During much of 1844 the Committee had tried to come to grips with the atmospheric system and whether to use it or not. Just how seriously they took the possibility is shown in both the Committee minutes and in the debate in the Parliamentary Select Committee. The report in the press[11] reveals the anxiety to take advantage of the new system against the advisability of waiting to see how it worked out in practice in Croydon and South Devon. A spirit of cautious optimism prevailed. In March the Provisional Committee concluded:

> That it appears probable that within the next two months such an amount of information may be obtained respecting the atmospheric principle as will render it easy for the Provisional Committee to decide on its adoption or rejection.[12]

Treffry too was impressed:

> ... I think I shall be able to show how the atmospheric Railway may be of very great importance in this county, and that it will be well worth our attention to obtain more information on that important subject. But I shall show by and by that if we adopt the atmospheric principle, we can do with much less weight of iron than that ... little or no tunnelling with the atmospheric...

He is clearly convinced by the advice he is getting:

> As to the atmospheric principle of Railways, the last letter I wrote to the committee was in consequence of having some information from Ireland which Lord Eliot got for me. On considering that information, I wrote to the Committee that we ought no longer to postpone our survey, in order that we may be able to make up our minds whether the survey shall be on the atmospheric principle or not. I am so satisfied that the line of the country will be so very much different for the atmospheric principle from what it would be for any other, that it is at present impossible to say what country we shall have to go through. The fact that we can go by the atmospheric principle with a gradient of 40, at a speed of double what we can with any other, with a gradient of 80 must be sufficient to satisfy the committee that every inquiry should be made.

By August 1844 the Cornwall Committee had come down in favour of adopting the atmospheric system. However equivocal Moorsom was to be before the Parliamentary Committee the following year it seems quite clear that his alignments were based on the assumption that the atmospheric system would be used:

> That it appears to this Committee from Captain Moorsom's report that a good and practicable line of Railway with passing places every three miles, to be worked on the atmospheric principle can be made from Falmouth to Plymouth at an expense not exceeding £900,000.[13]

At the same time they concluded that a single locomotive line with similar passing places might be made for £700,000.

Some members felt it advisable to defer submitting the Bill until there was more convincing proof available. However the Committee felt it best to proceed, partly in view of the long delay in getting that far, and partly because of the ever present threat that the promoters of the central route would get their bill to Parliament first. Accordingly they went ahead and submitted Moorsom's line with its excessive curves and gradients without any real assurance of whether atmospheric traction would be used or not. This was to prove to be a major reason for the rejection of the Bill.

There is nevertheless conflicting evidence about whether the 1845 Bill assumed that atmospheric traction would be used. On the face of it Moorsom confirmed that the system was to be used:

> Q Will you give me the inch tube you propose to use?
>
> A I think a 16 inch tube will be sufficient upon that railway.
>
> Q Now, before we go onto the engines, will you tell me what you calculate a 16 inch tube will cost per mile?
>
> A I have allowed £4,000 per mile including apparatus.
>
> Q When you say including the apparatus, is that the piston and so forth?
>
> A The piston is a mere fractional expence. It forms part of the tube. I mean including the valves and so on.
>
> Q Does that include the price of laying the tube and so on?
>
> A Yes.[14]

It seems obvious from this that the Cornwall Railway was to have had atmospheric traction but Moorsom is strangely equivocal when being examined. He also can hardly have endeared himself to the Committee by trying to postpone the decision to 'two or three years hence'. It is also inconsistent to say that the cost of the earthworks will be the same whichever system is used. Despite Moorsom's apparent uncertainty over the mode of traction other contemporary sources are quite clear about it. Ostler for example:

> There was also a feeling, which none entertained more strongly than the Friends of the Line, that his gradients and other works were more unfavourable than the difficulties of the County required. His error in this respect was mainly owing to his confidence in atmospheric traction, which, its advocates then imagined, would enable a train to surmount any moderate gradient.

The Board of Trade report confirmed the point:

> The promoters state that the line has been laid out with a view to the adoption of the atmospheric system, upon which system the gradients and curves might not be objectionable.

Stephenson's cross examination by Kinglake, however, suggests that Moorsom's intentions on the use of atmospheric were not clear. It does show that even Stephenson, an arch sceptic of the atmospheric, did see that its perceived facility for dealing with gradients may have had some applications. Kinglake asks whether Stephenson was saying that atmospheric trains could not ascend gradients as well as locomotives:

> A I do not think the atmospheric system will supersede locomotives. But I have said that there are many cases in which the atmospheric may operate where the locomotive is not applicable.
>
> Q Is that the case where gradients are too bad for the locomotive system?
>
> A Just so.
>
> Q You have said I think that in your opinion Captain Moorsom must have intended to lay this out as a locomotive line?
>
> A That is my belief.
>
> Q Don t you know that Captain Moorsom, a gentleman of respectability, has stated before this Committee the contrary?
>
> A I am not aware of it – Of course I am bound to believe Captain Moorsom – But to say, on the face of Captain Moorsom's sections and knowing also the opinion of Engineers just about that time when the atmospheric system was being considered and seeing the nature of the country and that he had not cut down into the vallies or filled them up I certainly was of the opinion that Captain Moorsom did intend to work this by locomotives.[15]

Whilst the Bill was being scrutinised a more dispassionate paper was presented to the Institution of Civil Engineers by Peter Barlow in Feb 1845[16] . He reached some useful conclusions about where the atmospheric system would work best. He concluded that the system was best suited to situations where there were frequent light trains particularly in urban situations where the lack of noise would be an advantage. He applied his findings to the two lines 'on which the atmospheric system is in course of execution, viz., the London and Croydon, and the South Devon'. Barlow was prescient. The London to Croydon was abandoned for the two reasons, that it formed a portion of a trunk line and that using the atmospheric system would have necessitated two changes of motive power for each trunk train movement. And secondly the New Cross incline proved to be too much thereby negating one of its major selling points, its hill climbing abilities. Barlow concluded that 'The South Devon line is a case, to which it would appear from the above results, that the atmospheric system is not adapted'. This must have caused the directors of the South Devon much concern as, by this stage they were already committed to installing the system between Exeter and Teignmouth. Equally Barlow's words must have caused the promoters of the Cornwall Railway to reconsider very carefully the wisdom of adopting the atmospheric system. If it was ill-suited to South Devon then it followed that it must be just as unsuitable in Cornwall. However even Barlow had an over-optimistic view of the reliability of the valve:

> In the application of stationary power to traction on a railway, by means of the exhaustion of air in a pipe, several of the inconveniencies of the present mode of traction by a rope, are avoided, and the great difficulty of rendering the pipe air-tight, has been in a great measure overcome by the ingenuity and mechanical skill of the inventors. It is but fair to assume, in comparing the atmospheric system with traction by locomotive power, that still further improvements will be made in those features of the invention which relate to the mechanical construction.

Hot on the heels of Barlow's paper came the official *Report of the Select Committee on Atmospheric Railways* (Appendix two) which was published on 24 April 1845. This Committee was clearly in a dilemma. The Parliamentary year 1845 was the busiest for railway bills. Many schemes were open to the possibilities of atmospheric traction. The Committee had been under pressure to produce the report to provide guidance to railway companies on whether to adopt this system. However they found that the absence of practical examples placed them at a considerable disadvantage. Neither the Croydon line nor the South Devon was up and running and the Committee could only reach qualified conclusions. However they were clear that the system would be best suited to running frequent light trains in urban areas whilst locomotives were better suited to a smaller number of heavier trains. The report concluded with the not altogether helpful comment:

> While Your Committee have thus expressed a strong opinion in favour of the general merits of the Atmospheric principle they feel that experience alone will determine under what circumstances of traffic or of country the preference to either system should be given.

Both Barlow and the Select Committee had come to the same conclusion; that the South Devon was not a suitable application and by inference neither was the Cornwall Railway.

A year later, when the 1846 Cornwall Railway Bill was at the committee stage, the London and Croydon had been operating for several weeks over 5 miles and the South Devon was being constructed as an atmospheric line. There was a significant amount of evidence about the working of the London and Croydon which was keenly raked over by the engineering profession and the defects of the system were becoming all too readily apparent. However the final debacle of the South Devon was still two years away.

Although the possibility of using atmospheric traction was still open during the 1846 hearings, there was never to be any real likelihood of its being used in Cornwall. Indeed the question arises whether Brunel was delaying work on the South Devon until lessons from Croydon had been learned:

Q Did you not say you had waited to have the benefit of the experiments at the expence of the Croydon Company?

A I did not say I waited for that – I do not remember exactly my words but I meant to say then exactly what I mean now. The object of the question was the same that the delays which have occurred in the Croydon have arisen from the mechanical difficulties and that I have intentionally waited and I have delayed completion of the line – I have intentionally waited as long as I possibly could until the Croydon had made these experiments but if our engines and engine houses and pipes had been ready I should not have delayed longer than that moment. I kept all the details back until the engines and the pipes were ready.[17]

Clearly the messages coming from Croydon after five months working were not reassuring. Locke, for example, reported his observations:

Q You are aware I believe I do not want to go into the general history of the atmospheric but you are aware failures have been constant upon the atmospheric line – the experience of the atmospheric between London and Croydon?

A Yes I know they have been frequent.

Q And they have been obliged to have recourse for weeks together or for many days together to locomotives?

A Yes and latterly I believe have entirely given up the use of the atmospheric they are now working it by locomotives.

Q It has been suspended for as many as ten days at a time?

A At this moment it has been suspended for more than ten days I believe. I am speaking from recollection.

Q I believe you have watched the experiments very carefully?

A I have.

Q And have had people on the line?

A Yes.[18]

Under a tetchy cross examination Brunel had some difficulty explaining the use of both methods of traction:

Q How long has your pipe been laid down on your South Devon line?

A It has been laying for the last 4 or 5 months as fast as we can get the pipes.

Q Are your engines made?

A The engines are fixed at present.
Q Are they made?
A Yes all made long ago.
Q How long have they been made?
A Six of them have been made or finished three or four months.
Q How many are there to be to Teignmouth?
A Teignmouth there will be 8 there as the rest are not finished. They are in the manufacturers shop and quite finished.
Q They have been quite finished for a month or two have they?
A Oh yes.
Q The rails are laid down and pipes laid down and the engines are complete for the most part of two months. There remains nothing but the engine houses?
A No the engine houses the fixing and finishing of the pipe. When I say the pipes are laid they are not all finished – the valve is not finished.
Q How long have they been ordered?
A A long time – the valve is not fixed – there is not a mile of valve fixed.
Q You have adopted the locomotive instead.... Have you not opened the line with locomotives?
A That is not adopting it instead .
Q You are using the locomotive there?
A Yes.
Q Why have you stated your line that was to be an atmospheric line is worked with a locomotive? Having got your pipes and all that – why not proceed with it as an atmospheric line?
A Now you have asked me a strait [*sic*] forward question I will give you a strait forward answer – for no other reason than that from the delays of finishing the engine houses and getting the engines and casting and pipe and making the valve we have not got it ready and I am not sorry for it.[19]

Brunel became defensive about the problems on the Croydon line. He offered rational explanations for all the failures, or 'difficulties' as he described them

Q Are you prepared to say in March there were not stoppages on upwards of 60 occasions when they had had to have recourse to the locomotive?
A I do not know how you count 80 or 60. If you mean there were have been 60 trains run that would not be many considering there are 40 a day at present are there not?
Q There were not in March?
A There are now. There were upwards of 20 a day
Q Do you know there have consistently stopped for two three four and five days together?
A No they have not – there have been several stoppages owing to the breaking of the beams and cranks of the engine. The cranks of three

engines were made of cast iron which they ought never to have been ...

Q Independent of the breaking of the cranks which you have just referred to do you not know they have from the imperfections of the valves been obliged to stop and that they are stopping now and they have not for the last ten days been running the atmospheric train?

A I do not think they are stopping now.

Q Up to this morning?

A Up to last night.

Q Was not that in consequence of the imperfection of the valves and not connected with the crank?

A It was in consequence certainly but they need not have stopped two days or one day if it were not then having, as I said before, half the line working locomotives. It was much simpler for them to run on the locomotive than take their time (with an) alternative ...

Q Have they not taken up the whole of the valves and been obliged to lay it down afresh?

A They might not have taken up the valve there was no necessity for it

Q Then they have gone to that expence quite unnecessarily in your opinion?

A That is the twisting of my words I never said quite unnecessary .

Q Unnecessary?

A If you mean unnecessary in the sense I used it as unnecessary I should say it.

Q Inexpediently?

A That is quite another thing ...

In South Devon, in March 1848, Brunel reported that more than 20 miles from Exeter to Newton (Abbot) were worked solely by atmospheric. However it was decided not to extend the atmospheric system beyond Totnes:

> at present the engines were kept constantly at work, but the boilers being insufficient for such a supply of steam the fires are obliged to be forced and the consumption of fuel is irregular and excessive[20]

Meanwhile he reported that the five timber viaducts in South Devon were 'strengthened about seven months since, when larger and more powerful locomotives were expected to be put on'.

The strengthening of the Devon viaducts was, at the same time, both an admission that Atmospheric traction would not reach Plymouth, and also that the viaducts would be a ready-made and cheap solution to the problem of crossing the Cornish valleys (Chapter 10).

At the next meeting of the South Devon Committee on 29 August the secretary reported that:

> Great disadvantage was occasioned to the line by working it part atmospherically and part locomotively [*sic*]. The cost of the first named mode

> had excited the serious attention of the board, who from their body had nominated a committee to whom was referred the consideration of this momentous subject. The directors, without pronouncing any opinion on the utility of the atmospheric, had arrived at the conclusion, with the advice of Mr Brunel, to suspend the use of that principle until Mr Samuda and the patentees could put the South Devon machinery into a state of profitable working ...[21]

Events were soon to rule out any chance of this happening. As regards costs, working with locomotives had been 2s 6d per mile and that worked by atmospheric 3s 10d per mile. Unconsciously Thomas Gill, Chairman of the South Devon Company was arriving at the same conclusion as Barlow:

> It was due to the locomotive to say that it had been worked on short distances, with double banked engines at a great disadvantage. The atmospheric had also had disadvantages in the small number of trains; its greatest economy was in working a large number of trains.

Atmospheric traction was suspended on the Croydon line in May 1847 and on the South Devon in September 1848. Yet its ghost refused to lie down. Gill still wished to pursue it further and used the word 'suspended' rather than 'abandoned'. Initially everything to do with the atmospheric was left in place presumably in the hope that the technical problems might still be overcome[22] . Gill held six propositions:

- That owing to the sharp curves throughout the line, and steep gradients on that part of it between Newton and Plymouth, the atmospheric system of traction is peculiarly applicable to the line.
- That the working cost of the two systems is decidedly in favour of the atmospheric.
- That the abandonment of the atmospheric system would necessarily involve a loss of nearly £300,000., and thereby entail a perpetual unproductive charge for interest of £15,000 per annum.
- That all the engines for working the line to Plymouth as well as those on the Torquay branch were on the eve of completion it was essentially important that a trial should be given to the system over steep gradients.
- That the offer of Mr Samuda to effect the repairs and improvements in the longitudinal valves and to keep the same in good working condition at a moderate and fixed charge for a period of 12 months would make it highly desirable to continue the system at least for that period.
- That if the locomotive power be substituted a double line of rails should be laid throughout.[23]

The issue was finally settled at a large meeting of shareholders at Exeter on 6 January 1849, when it was overwhelmingly resolved not to pursue atmospheric traction any further. The voting was 2,275 to 6,900.[24]

One has to conclude that, by that time, the climate was not good for experiments of this nature. The collapse of the 'mania' meant that promoting companies were less keen to try out revolutionary ideas. They preferred to go for the evolution of tried and tested methods. No doubt if there had not been so many teething troubles the system would not have suffered such a bad reputation and been quite so vulnerable to the rapidly deteriorating economic conditions. However the litany of inadequate tube size, untested stationary engines and the inability to achieve an adequate vacuum were to prove fatal. Many companies were prepared to try it. Moorsom, Samuda, Brunel and Vignoles staked their reputations on making it work. St Jude, patron saint of lost causes, would have been proud of them all!

Could the atmospheric system have succeeded? It would have stood a better chance if Jacob Samuda had been alive to deal with the technical problems as they arose. And if only the London and Croydon Company had persisted with their system where there were frequent light trains and if it had not been applied in South Devon, to which both Barlow and the Board of Trade had indicated it was unsuited. Even then the economics were against it. Under no circumstances was it suitable for the Cornwall Railway and the Cornwall Committee must have regretted spending so much time and energy on it. However the company was spared the expense of actually trying it. Moorsom might have produced a very much better alignment if he had designed the line unequivocally for locomotives and just might have remained the engineer for the Company. As far as the Cornwall Company was concerned atmospheric traction ceased to be an issue. This was just as well as they had quite enough other difficulties to contend with in building their line.

CHAPTER FIVE

THE PARLIAMENTARY LABYRINTH

A hundred years ago our Victorian ancestors could build 400 miles of railway in a year; in twelve years since the post-war plan for motorways was announced in 1947 we have contrived to build eighty miles of new motor road. Legal difficulties in obtaining land, often given as an excuse, are not a convincing explanation; Victorian railway promoters had more formidable difficulties. They had to get acts of Parliament to authorise routes, and they had to negotiate with landowners in days when rights of private property were more jealously guarded than now. When they had got their land, they had to depend on men with picks and shovels to lay out the track.

The Guardian report on the opening of Britain's first motorway, the Preston bypass, on 2 November 1959 suggests that the Victorian railway pioneers were more successful than their modern equivalents. Today proposals for the provision of infrastructure are usually dealt with under Public Works legislation often involving a lengthy public inquiry. These are usually promoted by local authorities and statutory undertakers. However the system of public inquiries has been developed in order to make it easier for ordinary members of the public to express their views.

Under the Victorian system of private bills objection to infrastructure projects was a more complex matter. It involved the mobilisation of petitions which aggregated and articulated local objections to projects of greater than local impact. Its merit was that the system did deliver clear-cut decisions within a manageable time frame. This tricky question of balance between providing adequate time for objectors and streamlined decision making has never been wholly resolved. It is still a topical issue as demonstrated by the recent and short-lived Infrastructure Planning Commission whose aim was primarily about establishing the need for infrastructure projects. The process of turning a private bill into a private act was a complex one as befits the tricky interactions of private and public interests involving some interference with the rights of property which were highly respected in Victorian times. Local landowners were going to be subject to compulsory purchase for the greater public good. Williams explains:

> The most important fact is, however, that the expansion of railways for the first time brought more clearly than before into the consciousness of Parliament the conception that in private legislation there was an aspect of public, as well as one of private, interest, to which no Government could be indifferent; and that the function of Parliament was, not merely to act justly as between parties, but also to consider and promote the interests of the public as a whole.[1]

Once the proponents had completed the initial surveys, the next stage was to seek Parliamentary approval through the process of the private bill. This was a long, complicated and above all expensive procedure. Devey suggests that a quarter of the cost of railway construction was swallowed up by Parliamentary expenses. The GWR, for example, spent £88,710 in legal and parliamentary fees. Ostler quotes the cost of the survey and the Parliamentary expenses for the 1845 Cornwall Railway Bill as being £48,000. Assuming that the cost of the 1846 Bill was similar, one can begin to appreciate the burden that this represented for an impoverished company. In addition the promoters of the central route will have spent similar sums without anything to show for it.

The two rival factions, in promoting their alternative routes for the railway, had to negotiate the following procedural labyrinth: Forming a provisional committee and garnering support, issuing a prospectus, attracting potential investors, drawing up a bill and guiding it through Parliament, meeting the requirement of the Committee on Standing Orders, proving the preamble, presenting evidence to the Committee on Bills and rebutting evidence from petitioners. This is a formidable process where success could by no means be guaranteed.

The procedure for private bills is semi-judicial. The case for the bill, if opposed, is opened by promoter's counsel. A preamble must explain, however shortly, the reasons why legislation is expedient on each of the more important subjects dealt with and must also show that promoters have complied with Standing Orders.[2] The preamble to the Cornwall Railway Bill of 1845 read:

> 'An Act for making a Railway to connect the Towns of Plymouth and Falmouth with a branch to the town of Bodmin to be called the Cornwall Railway'.

If the bill passed Standing Orders it would then go to a Select Committee on Railway Bills. Promoters would open with a statement of their case. They were required to submit plans and cross sections of the proposed line. These had to be accompanied by Books of Reference giving the proprietors, occupiers, and descriptions of each plot of land or building numbered on the plans. Petitioners followed, both for and against. Those opposed to the proposals might include landowners or turnpike trusts or carriers along parallel roads who could object by means of a petition to Parliament. Although bills had to be passed by both Houses the detailed work was done by Select Committees on Railway Bills. The process was largely technical needing professionals, engineers and barristers.[3] Consideration of the Cornwall Railway Bill began in May 1845 and lasted for two months. On 23 June it had passed the Commons and consideration in the Lords started the same day but was rejected by Parliament on 22 July.

The Cornwall Railway Bills of 1845 and 1846 coincided with the busiest period for railway promotion at the height of the so-called 'Railway Mania'. In 1836 some eight years before the speculative boom some 57 railway bills were introduced. In contrast in the 1845 session 248 plans were submitted, and 118 sanctioned by Parliament, for 2,700 miles of railway with powers to raise capital of £56,000,000. Before the 1846 session opened, plans for 816 new lines had been lodged involving the construction of 20,687 miles of railway with a capital value of no less than £350,000,000.[4]

A private Act of Parliament incorporated the company. It included the rights not only to construct a railway but also to purchase the land, compulsorily, over which the line was to run. It also imposed the obligation to carry out the scheme in full and within a specified period of time. There remained the question of establishing the price of the land, a matter which could involve prolonged negotiations.

The Provisional Committee

The Provisional Committee for the Cornwall Railway comprised some 84 names including all the significant shareholders. It included six members of the Privy Council, seven MPs, the Chairmen and Directors of the GWR, South Devon and Bristol and Exeter Railways, ten members of the provisional committee of the North Devon Railway Company together with the Mayors of Truro, Bideford and Devonport.[5]

There was a Management Committee of 16. Joseph Treffry was the chairman, W.M. Tweedy, the Treasurer. It included Thomas Gill, chairman of the South Devon Railway. There were directors of the South Devon Railway, Clement Carlyon, Mayor of Truro, George Smith and Michael Williams, both future Chairmen of the Cornwall Railway and Thomas Agar Robartes of Lanhydrock. Captain Moorsom was the Engineer, Messrs Smith and Roberts, Solicitors, and William Bond the Secretary. (Appendix three)

Sir Charles Lemon[6] reflected on the composition of the Committee.

> I think it contains a large majority of the chief landowners and the miners and Capitalists and also the merchants.

Lined up against them was the breakaway provisional Committee of the Cornwall and Devon Central Railway. It contained 90 names including Sir W. J. Salisbury Trelawney, Lord Lieutenant Francis Rodd, E. W. W. Pendarves, Hanway Plumridge, J. H. Tremayne, the Mayors of Exeter, Launceston and Bodmin, members of the Salisbury and Yeovil Railway Co, the Dartmouth Torbay and Exeter Railway Co and the Exeter Yeovil and Dorchester Railway Company[7].

THE STANDING ORDERS COMMITTEE

Examination of a bill by the Standing Orders Committee gave opponents an opportunity to kill it at the outset if they could persuade the members that it contained inaccuracies or violations of orders and many were rejected on pure technicalities[8]. The committee was required to report, to each House, on a wide range of matters which meant that promoters were required to submit detailed technical, economic and financial information. Likewise the House would not proceed to consider the report on any bill, until it had received specific replies from the Standing Orders Committee. The passage of the Cornwall Railway Bills and the Cornwall & Devon Central Railway Bill throws up several instances of potential non-compliance. It was open to any party to submit a memorial, specifically stating the subject at issue and complaining of non-compliance with Standing Orders.

Much time was spent at the 1845 hearing into the Cornwall Railway Bill over the question of what Standing Order No 6 meant. It was concerned with whether any competing lines existed or were contemplated. This was relevant to the central route for which, at the time of the hearings, there was no formal submission. Indeed the provisional committee of the Cornwall and Devon Central Railway was not in a position to proceed with a bill. However they had submitted a petition against the Cornwall Railway Bill. The Parliamentary Committee reached a compromise view that the petitioners might be allowed to show that the line contained in the Cornwall Railway Bill was not the best but they were not to go into detail about any other specific line. In 1846 the position was somewhat different in that the promoters of the central line were almost in a position to deposit a bill and were accordingly allowed to put their case.

The 1845 Cornwall Railway Bill was found to have a great number of inaccuracies with gradients being incorrectly recorded. These were subsequently corrected by the permission of the House of Commons in the plan deposited in the office of the Clerk of Parliaments.[9]

Petitions against the Cornwall Railway Bill of 1845 pointed to the, not inconsiderable, errors …

> A certain stream numbered 194 upon the plans in the parish of Kenwyn is shown on the sections as 14 feet or thereabouts higher than the true level of the bed thereof and that the greatest height of embankment is shown to be 34 feet whereas it should be 48 feet or thereabouts.

The Cornwall Railway Bill 1845 throws up an instance where the Committee is unsure whether Standing Orders have been complied with on grounds of 'fitness from an engineering point of view'.

> The Committee Room was cleared. After a short time the parties were again called in and informed that the Committee had cleared the room for the

> purpose of considering the course which they should take with reference to the examination of witnesses and they had come to the following Resolution:That under the peculiar circumstances of this case the Committee will be ready to examine persons upon any point upon which the Committee have a doubt as to whether Standing Orders have been complied with.
> The Chairman further stated that the Committee considered it would be productive of great inconvenience if every person who pleased were allowed to come forward and give evidence but that the Committee were bound to exercise the power which they possessed for the purpose of satisfying their own minds whether the Standing Orders had been complied with or not and that themselves were the sole judges of the importance of any suggestion or information which might be communicated to them upon the subject.
> The Chairman further stated that the Committee had fully gone into the examination of Captain Moorsom upon the engineering points of non-compliance alleged in the Petition and they had also themselves examined the plans and sections and that as far as they were at present advised they did not require any further information upon those points ...

In the case of the Cornwall and Devon Central Railway Bill of 1846 the main complaint was that a sheet containing about ten miles of the line had been omitted. Counsel for the Bill stated that

> The plan deposited for public inspection contains three sheets more than the plan deposited therewith and sealed up as directed by the Standing Order and that the sealed up plan contains two sheets in duplicate.

Under the circumstances the Standing Orders Committee concluded that Standing Orders had not been complied with and the House of Lords decreed that the bill should not be allowed to proceed.[10] By such basic administrative errors an expensive bill could be brought to nought. This was the last that was heard of the Cornwall and Devon Central Railway. It was a humiliating and ignominious end for a bravely fought campaign. Bearing in mind Ostler's views on the central route his account is quite graphic:

> Errors in the levels were established, in one instance amounting to 50 feet. After a short examination of the engineering defects, the Committee desired that another class of objection should be considered. On this, the opponents cited the defective lodgement of the plans at Exeter, where sheet No. 9 was wanting. To meet this, two witnesses were produced who declared that they had examined and compared the plans, sheet by sheet, previous to their deposit, and found them correct, and it was insinuated that the missing sheet had been abstracted by agents of the Cornwall Railway. On this, the Committee directed the sealed Plans be opened and compared, when it was found that the sealed copy was defective, not one but *four* sheets! The chairman exclaimed - 'that's fatal!', threw the plans from him, and ordered

the room to be cleared; and when the decision of the Committee had been formally come to, it was announced by the doorkeeper, with a waggish allusion to the merciless lopping the project had previously sustained - 'their lordships have thrown it out *root* and *branch*!'.

Standing Orders required an indication that finances were in place. The promoters of the Cornwall Railway were at an advantage over the promoters of the central line in that they were able to point to substantial subscriptions from the Associated Companies. In 1845 this amounted to £250,000 and in 1846 to £337,500. They were also able to demonstrate the take up of shares by the directors amounting to £35,250 and shares subscribed for of £133,610.[11]

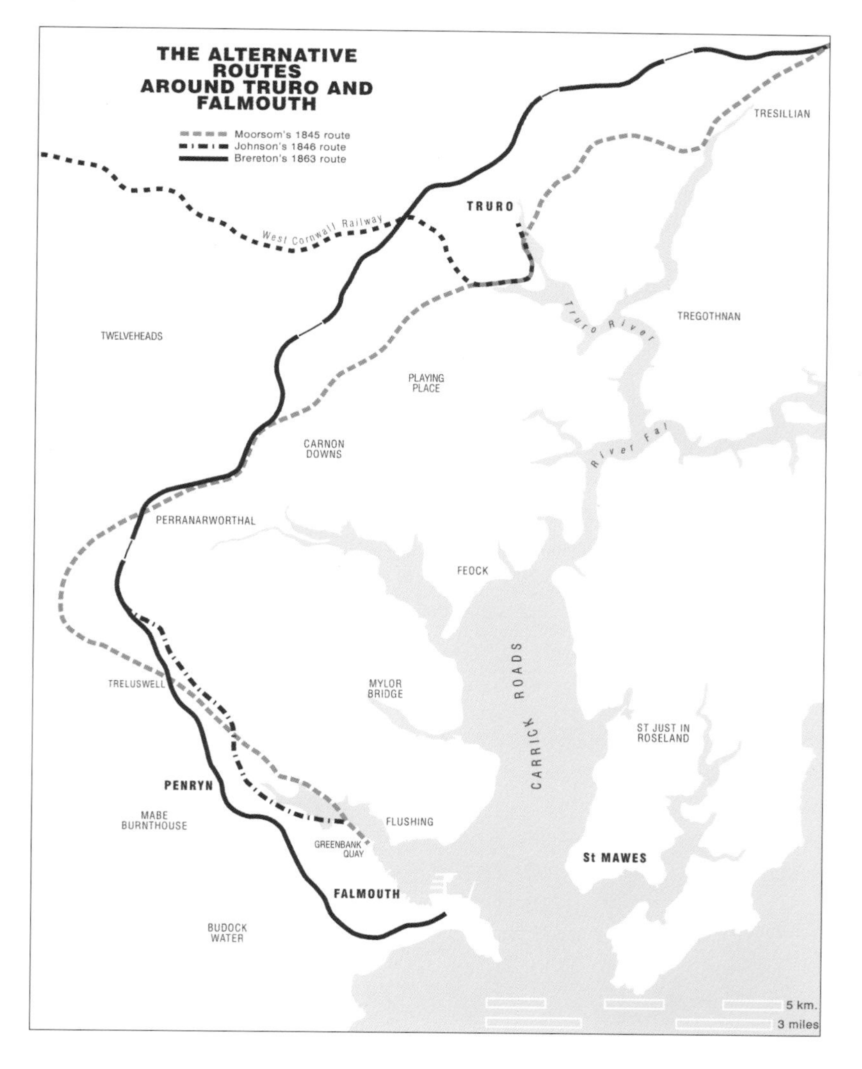

5.1 *Moorsom's original route involved a crossing of Penryn Creek and a viaduct over the River Fal south of Truro; features which doomed the Cornwall Railway Bill of 1845. Johnson's route avoided these problems and Brereton built a line which terminated where the new docks could be best served.*

PETITIONS

Both Cornwall Railway Bills faced stiff opposition. There were substantial interests ranged against them as the examination of Pendarves by Rowe shows[12]

Q In your judgement what would be result to the County of Cornwall if that line was suffered to pass?

A I think it would be prejudicial to the county at large and I think it prevents our having for many years a direct line to Exeter.

Q Do you know that that feeling is largely participated in the west?

A It is certainly

Q Have you yourself, in your capacity of member for the Western Division presented in the House a petition signed by 37,000 people against the South line and in favour of a Central communication?

A I do not think it was that number. I think 35,000 was stated. It was a large petition and it was very strongly in favour of the direct line first to Exeter and then on to London.

The most articulate opposition to the 1845 Bill concerned Moorsom's proposals for the crossing of Penryn Creek. There was a provision to enable any parties to submit a memorial complaining of non-compliance with Standing Orders[13]. The Cornwall Railway Bill fell foul of a 'memorial' from the Penryn Town Council. The failure of the promoters to heed this memorial was one of the reasons why the 1845 Bill did not succeed. The following exchange reveals a certain detachment on Moorsom's part under cross examination by Rowe[14]

Q Have you the consent of the Admiralty in writing for the passage of Penryn Creek?

A I had a conditional assent from the Admiralty some time ago but I believe the parties have entered into a new negotiation upon that particular point.

Q Has there been a memorial presented by the Town of Penryn against the passing of your Railway over Penryn Creek?

A Merely against the particular viaduct as I understand: I have not seen the memorial.

Q Have you not seen it?

A No, I have not indeed.

Q Are you aware a memorial has been deposited with the Board of Trade?

A No, I don't know it.

By the Committee:

Q Do you know it of your own knowledge? Have you ever seen it?

A No, I have not seen the memorial.

Q By Mr Rowe. You are every day in communication with the promoters of this Bill I presume?

A Quite so.

Q Do you know from the promoters of this Bill themselves that in point of fact a memorial was prepared by the Town of Penryn against your passing a Railway over that arm of the sea?

A Certain traders who had some interests there did present some memorial.

Captain Plumridge, MP for Falmouth and superintendent of her Majesty's Packets then gave evidence:[15]

Q In your judgement as a nautical man, should you say the trade of that harbour and Penryn would be considerably impeded by the passage of a railway across the creek as the coast railway proposes to cross?

A What is it to cross on?

Q On an embankment with a drawbridge opening to allow ships to go out at stated times of the tide, with a viaduct and a drawbridge.

A Yes I think it would impede the trade considerably.

Q Do vessels at present beat up the channel?

A Yes, a large part of them do.

Q Would that be utterly out of the question after such a staging was put up?

A They could not pass through while the railway carriages were passing. They might be passing just at the top of the water where it might be necessary for them to [get] out...

Q The evidence is this. They proposed to carry a viaduct there of I think timber arches and that these will be at high spring tides only the distance of $4^1/_2$ feet clear between the surface of the water and the centre of the creek. Do you know if that will be a serious obstacle to the trade of Penryn?

A Of course it must – they must strike their masts to get under it. It depends upon the span of the arch whether the boat can get through.

It is amazing that Captain Moorsom appeared to know so little about the objections to this part of his plans bearing in mind just how controversial they were. The Committee then asked:

Q Have you looked at the allegation in the Petition and referred to the Plan in consequence?

A I have, but I do not remember them.

Q You have no note of them?

A No.

In order to overcome the uncertainty the Committee brought forward a clause:

> providing that the viaduct or bridge proposed to be constructed across Penryn Creek should not be made without the consent of the Lords Commissioners of the Admiralty.

However, as the bill failed, the clause was never put into effect.

The 1846 Bill generated some 20 petitions against it. Apart from some essentially local objectors there were two groups of petitioners, those who favoured the central line and those concerned with the crossing of the Hamoaze. Foremost among the petitioners were 'the Promoters and Members of the Committee of Management of a proposed Railway from Exeter to Falmouth and Penzance, to be called The Cornwall and Devon Central Railway', praying that the Committee might entertain their project. They alleged:

> The promotion, Advantages, and Position of this Scheme, the disadvantages of the Cornwall Line, that the Scheme of the Petitioners should be entertained by the Committee, and praying that it might be an Instruction to the Committee to entertain their project: Counsel applied to be heard in support of this Petition; but the Committee received no Instructions from the House in Compliance with the prayer thereof.[16]

Further support for the petition came from 'The Mayor, Aldermen, and Burgesses of Bodmin, in Town Council assembled':

> Alleging that the Construction of the Railway would injure their Lands, and with the streets or highways under their control; that it was not adapted to the wants of Cornwall, if made would prevent the Construction of a better line, and that it would not be the best line between Plymouth and Falmouth; that the estimated Expense was inadequate, the Traffic insufficient, the Tolls excessive, and the engineering features of the Line objectionable.

There was also a group concerned with interests in land. They alleged:

> That the railway was not adapted to the wants of Cornwall; that it was projected as an Extension of the South Devon Railway, which the Petitioners were advised was in an embarrassed State in its Finances, was unable to raise Funds for its completion; that it was not the best Line between Plymouth and Falmouth; with Allegation as to estimated Expense, Traffic, Tolls, Curves, and Gradients as before mentioned.

The second group of petitioners related to the River Tamar and were concerned about the height of the proposed Saltash Bridge. They included mining interests, fishermen, watermen, and others residing on the banks of the Tamar, owners of quays and others interested in the navigation of the River Tamar, ship owners, masters of vessels, and inhabitants of Saltash and Tavistock. Essentially they all raised the same point. The following extract from the Lords Journal gives a flavour of their submissions:

> ... who receive their Coal, Timber, Iron, and other Materials, and ship their Minerals by Vessels, navigating the Tamar, alleging that the Height of the proposed bridge across the Tamar was insufficient, whereas for the Bridge at Runcorn and other Places the Admiralty had insisted on arches 100 Feet clear

in Height; that the Bridge would obstruct the Navigation, and prove a serious Injury to the Owners of Wheal Maria and other Mines receiving their Supplies and shipping their Produce: counsel were heard in support of this Petition.
... of crossing the Tamar at Saltash was ill adapted for the Purpose, the Height of the Bridge insufficient, and its numerous arches would prevent the ferry crossing, and that it was not intended for general Traffic, but merely for the Purposes of the Railway.
Petitioners, as owners of Property in Saltash, had a Right by prescription, for themselves, their Horses and Carts to pass over the ferry which would be destroyed, that they were informed the Promoters intended to vary the Line from that specified in the Plans and Sections, and otherwise than provided for in the Notices served on them, and injurious to their Property.

THE COMMITTEE ON THE BILL, THE KEY ROLE OF THE ADVOCATES

The passage of a bill through the Parliamentary Committee depended on the skills of barristers drawn from the Parliamentary Bar[17]. This was the Victorian equivalent of today's Planning Bar. They represented promoters and objectors to private bills for developing infrastructure. The 'railway mania' of 1845-47 ensured that there were plenty of bills for aspiring advocates and opportunities for the Parliamentary Bar to make considerable fortunes. The skills of the barrister were fundamental to the success of turning bills into acts. Both the Cornwall Railway Company and the objectors were represented by two highly respected and, self - evidently, extremely able exponents of the art of examining and cross examining technical witnesses, both with strong west country roots, John Alexander Kinglake and William Carpenter Rowe.

It was their role in the proceedings which determined the outcome of the Cornwall Railway Bills. As Counsel for the Bills, Kinglake was supported by Messrs Montague Smith, Austin, Merevale and Burke: As Counsel for the Petition against the Bill Rowe was supported by Messrs Cockburn, Talbot and James. These two leading counsel and their teams clashed twice over the Cornwall Railway Bills in 1845 and 1846.

From the records of the proceedings JOHN ALEXANDER KINGLAKE (1803-1870) Sergeant at Law and WILLIAM CARPENTER ROWE (1801-1859) both emerge as highly tenacious and persistent. Kinglake had enjoyed an education at Eton and Cambridge and was called to the Bar at Lincoln's Inn at the age of 27. He had become Sergeant at Law in 1844. Sergeants were the highest order of Counsel. (This title has been defunct since the end of the 19th century.) His obituary records that he 'enjoyed a considerable practice at the Parliamentary Bar'. He was to become recorder of Exeter and Bristol and elected as Liberal MP for

5.2 *John Alexander Kinglake 1805?-1870*
NATIONAL PORTRAIT GALLERY

Rochester from 1857 until his death. He was born in Taunton and had west country connections.

Rowe was born in Launceston and was educated at Winchester and Oxford. He was admitted as a member of Lincoln's Inn and called to the Bar at the Inner Temple at the age of 29. His obituary, too, records that he practised with considerable success at the Parliamentary Bar. At the time of the hearings into the Cornwall Railway Bill he was recorder of Plymouth and also a key member of the provisional committee of the Cornwall and Devon Central Railway. In the context of the 1846 Cornwall Railway Bill he appeared on the petition of 'the inhabitants of Saltash, fishermen, watermen and others residing on the banks of the Tamar and interested in the navigation of the waters thereof ... and a petition of land owners, lessees and occupiers of land in the counties of Cornwall and Devon and shipowners and masters of vessels frequenting the Tamar at Saltash'. He was knighted in 1856 and spent the last years of his life as Chief Justice of Ceylon.[18]

At the first of these Parliamentary hearings in 1845 Kinglake called Moorsom and Brunel as his technical witnesses. Moorsom was subjected to a long and searching cross examination by Mr Rowe. This exposed all the weaknesses of his interpretation of the southern route and this was to prove fatal to the Bill.

Brunel made light of the technical shortcomings of Moorsom's proposed alignment mainly, I suggest, in order to secure funding from the Associated Companies and approval, in principle, for the southern route, whatever its deficiencies, against the rival central route. Examined by Merevale[19] Brunel explains that his prime aim had been to secure the funding of the Associated Companies, to meet the requirements of standing orders, to secure parliamentary approval and to worry about the details later:

Q You are the Engineer of the Great Western?

A Yes.

Q Has the line consented to advance £250,000 towards the construction of this railway provided you approve the plan?

A Yes, the Great Western, the Bristol and Exeter, the Bristol and Gloucester, four companies.

Q Was the argument that the works should be subject to your supervision and approval?

A That was so

Q Did you, in consequence of that agreement, examine the plans and sections of the line with Captain Moorsom?

A I did. He and I went over the ground.

Q We have heard that these companies consented to advance that capital in consequence of your approval?

A Yes, I made my report to them. At least I recommended them after the inspection of the ground and my examination of the plans to pay their quota of the subscriptions to become joint proprietors of it.

Not even his support was enough to secure approval for Moorsom's plans whose manifest deficiencies came near to dooming the whole project.

For the petitioners against the bill Rowe called a) Robert Stephenson who testified that Moorsom's proposal was intrinsically dangerous, b) James Rendel who maintained that the Torpoint Ferry was not a practical method of transporting trains across the Hamoaze. His testimony was all the more powerful as he was the designer of the ferry which had proved to be a great success for the ordinary carts and carriages of the day: And c) George Bidder who gave critical testimony on the curves and gradients that Moorsom had proposed. Each advocate could claim some success from the 1845 session. Although he failed in persuading members to accept the actual proposal, Kinglake succeeded in convincing the Committee on the need for the Railway. He had managed to have the preamble proven and established the principle of the southern route. Rowe had ensured that the proposal would not go ahead, at any rate in Moorsom's form.

In 1846 Kinglake was taking no chances. William Johnson and Brunel were the chief technical witnesses. It soon became clear that Johnson's alignment was the optimal achievable line and they both had a relatively easy cross examination from Rowe. Kinglake also called Vignoles and Hawkshaw who provided independent corroboration of this. Rowe responded by calling the formidable trio of Locke, Bidder and Rendel who, whilst sound witnesses, were only able to testify that the

5.3 *Proposals were entertained for crossing the Hamoaze either by the floating bridge between Torpoint and New Passage or by a fixed bridge at Saltash. In 1846 Parliament insisted on the latter.*

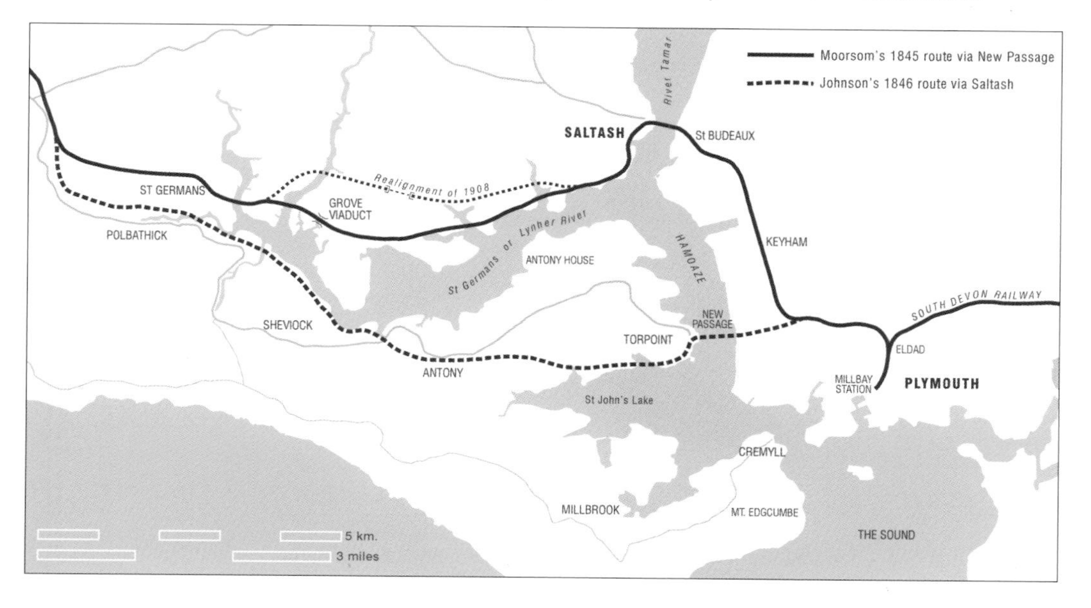

central route would be superior. But, as the central route was not being examined, this evidence did not have much force. The main weakness that they showed up was whether the Saltash bridge was technically feasible. However this was not enough to prevent the bill completing its Parliamentary process. Kinglake's success relied also on the testimonies of the Earl of Falmouth and Sir Charles Lemon who opined that the southern route, whatever its inferiority to the central route, was the only practical one. The formidable array of MPs, Trelawney, Pendarves and Tremayne that Rowe called in favour of the central route could do little more than suggest to the committee that delay would be preferable to the passing of the bill. In view of the fact that, thirteen years had now passed since the idea of the Cornwall Railway had been first formulated this argument was hardly likely to succeed.

At the end of the proceedings the Committee had to decide whether the preamble was proven. A preamble must explain, however shortly, the reasons why legislation is expedient on each of the more important subjects dealt with, and must also show, in certain classes of measures, that promoters have complied with Standing Orders or with general legislation.

The Lords rarely rejected a project that had been accepted by the Commons. The 1845 Cornwall Railway Bill was the exception. It passed the Commons and although its preamble was proven the Lords rejected the Bill. Even though the bill was lost, the proving of the preamble was a vital tool in the battle over the two prospective routes. The Parliamentary Committee reported:

> That the making of a Railway to connect the Towns of Plymouth and Falmouth with a branch to the Town of Bodmin would be of great public Advantage, by opening an additional, certain, and expeditious means of Communication between the said Places and also by facilitating Communication between more distant Towns and Places; but the Committee are also of the Opinion that it would not be advisable to adopt definitively the Plan of Railway Communications which is intended to be carried out by the Bill, without a further and most accurate Survey of the whole Line of Country to be traversed between Plymouth and Falmouth, with a view of obtaining Gradients and Curves more favourable, and of avoiding the Passage of the Hamoaze and of the Penryn River below Penryn if these last Objects can be effected without any great cost and Disadvantages: The Committee are therefore of the opinion that the Bill should not now be further proceeded with.
>
> Which Report being read by the Clerk it was ordered that the Report do lie on the Table.[20]

Act of Parliament

But the following year the successor bill succeeded: In the phrase in

Norman French beloved of Victorian Parliamentarians, 'La Reyne le veult'. The bill became the Act of Parliament on 27 July 1846 and received the Royal Assent on 3 August 1846 almost exactly a year after the failure of the 1845 Bill. It was known as an Engrossed Bill which consists of the full text of the bill written large on vellum membranes. The engrossed roll is endorsed with the long title and a note of the stages in its further progress. The membranes are stitched together in order to form a roll In the case of the Cornwall Railway Act the roll consists of some 60 membranes each 18 inches long. Eighteen of the clauses referred to the capital of the company, the names and places of residence of Directors and the amount of each shareholding. The authorised capital was £1,600,000 with power to borrow £533,333. It authorised the Associated Companies to subscribe to the undertaking. The Associated Companies are mentioned as contributing £337,500. It specifies the length of the main line from Falmouth to Eldad as 63 miles 4 furlongs and 5 chains. It says that the Railway shall be constructed to the same gauge as the GWR. There were no peculiar engineering difficulties(!): the steepest gradient on the main line was 1 in 60 and the smallest Radius of a Curve was 11 Chains (presumably not on the main line). It sets out details of tunnels, curves and gradients and most importantly that the line shall cross the Hamoaze by a bridge. Compulsory purchase must be carried out within four years of the Passing of the Act (i.e. by 1850) and the Railway completed within seven years (i.e. by 1853). It sets out terms for the carrying of passengers, goods and animals and provision for fixing of tolls. There were to be branches to Padstow, to the Liskeard and Caradon Railway, to the quays at Truro and Penryn. The company could purchase the Bodmin and Wadebridge and the Liskeard and Caradon Railways and the Liskeard and Looe Canal. The Bodmin and Wadebridge had been built many years before in 1834 for the purpose of transporting sea sand inland for use as fertiliser. One of the complications for the Cornwall Railway was whether to take it over and provide a link to Bodmin and Padstow from their main line at what is now Bodmin Parkway.

The resulting Act required the railway company to carry out the construction to the letter of the law within the specified time frame[21]. Any departures from these terms meant returning to Parliament. In the case of the Cornwall Railway the Company had to return to Parliament several more times, no doubt at considerable additional cost, to secure approval for reducing the specification, abandoning unnecessary parts of the project and for securing alternative measures for financing the project. These acts were:

1848 Act to enable GWR, B&ER and SDR to increase subscriptions to the Cornwall Railway.

1852 Act for alteration of capital enabling the company to make modifications to share capital.

1853 Act for extending capital and for extending the time for the completion of the railway.

1857 Act to enable the GW, B&E and South Devon Railway Companies 'to afford further assistance towards the completion of the Railway between Plymouth and Truro and for extending the time for the completion thereof ...' The Bill extends the time for the completion of the railway to 23 June 1860. The Bill also allowed the Company to issue 15,000 new preference shares. It also included provision for the Cornwall Company to lease the line to the Associated Companies.[22]

1858 Act to extend Capital and to extending the time for the completion of the Cornwall Railway and for making further provision as to its share capital.

1861 Act to extend the time for completion of so much of the Cornwall Railway line as lies between Truro and Falmouth.[23].

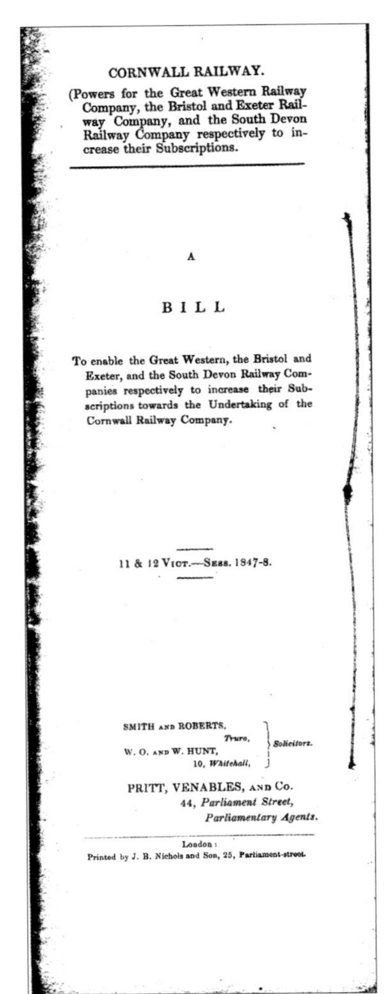

CORNWALL RAILWAY.

(Powers for the Great Western Railway Company, the Bristol and Exeter Railway Company, and the South Devon Railway Company respectively to increase their Subscriptions.

A

BILL

To enable the Great Western, the Bristol and Exeter, and the South Devon Railway Companies respectively to increase their Subscriptions towards the Undertaking of the Cornwall Railway Company.

11 & 12 VICT.—SESS. 1847-8.

SMITH AND ROBERTS, *Truro*, W. O. AND W. HUNT, 10, *Whitehall*, *Solicitors.*

PRITT, VENABLES, AND Co. 44, *Parliament Street*, *Parliamentary Agents.*

London: Printed by J. B. Nichols and Son, 25, Parliament-street.

5.4 The 1848 Bill to enable the GWR, B&ER and SDR to increase subscriptions to the Cornwall Railway. FROM AN ORIGINAL HELD IN THE GREAT WESTERN TRUST COLLECTION AT THE DIDCOT RAILWAY CENTRE.

Looking at this list of further bills, whose purpose was to amend the terms under which the 1846 Cornwall Railway Act had been passed, reflects the inability of the company to meet the deadlines and comply with the original specification. It also highlights the problems of raising funds by the traditional route of the money markets. Although railways were also able to raise money by borrowing, legislative restrictions meant that share capital was their primary means of finance, and indeed a new company was obliged to have the bulk of its shares subscribed before it could obtain parliamentary authorisation. The company had to rely increasingly on the Associated Companies to fund the project.

ABANDONMENT

One of the measures taken by the Government to overcome the financial crisis which developed after 1845 was the Railway Abandonment Act 1850[24]. This enabled companies not to carry out all or part of projects for which they had previously obtained Parliamentary approval. Lewin explains:

> The position of a company which had gone to parliament for powers to make a railway, but which had subsequently found it inexpedient to exercise those powers was therefore one of no little difficulty. In such cases the simplest course was just to let the powers expire by lapse of time, but then the company laid itself open to the receipt of a summons to show why a 'mandamus' should not be issued against it to compel it to make the line in question.

> During this period, 1848-50 ... the lot of the railway shareholder was indeed, an unhappy one, especially for those who had subscribed for railway shares in the Mania years, and had embarked their money in companies which had failed to obtain their Act. Such people were naturally anxious to get their concerns wound up and to recover what they might of their deposits.
> The Railway Abandonment Act, as it was called, authorised the Railway Commissioners on the requisition of not less than two thirds of the shareholders, to issue a warrant to allow a railway company to abandon part or all of the works, to construct which it had obtained Parliamentary powers, if, after an inspection of the company's books by the Railway Commissioners, this course met with their approval. After the issue of such warrant the company were to be relieved from their liability to make the railway or portion thereof specified ...

This was one of a number of measures to overcome 'severe pressure on the money markets', to reduce the potential calls on capital and restore some degree of liquidity into railway construction which had been in a state of paralysis. This Act came as a saviour to the Cornwall Railway Company and the Board seized the opportunity to apply to the Railway Commissioners to abandon non-essential parts of the project. On 7 August 1851 the Board of Directors resolved to call an extraordinary general meeting to determine whether to make an application to the Commissioners for Railways[25]

> ... that the several parts of the Cornwall Railway hereinafter specified may be abandoned, that is to say, the branches or proposed connecting lines to connect the Cornwall Railway with the quays or wharfs at Truro and Penryn and the Liskeard and Caradon Railway and with Bodmin and Padstow beyond the South East side of Bodmin ...

The shareholders duly agreed and on 13 April 1852 the chairman (Williams) was able to report that:

> ... the Directors have received from the Railway Commissioners their Warrant authorising the abandonment of the before mentioned portions of the line and reducing the capital of the Company to the sum of £1,125,060 divided into 56,253 shares of £20 each, every shareholder holding any share in the Company of the nominal value of £50 being henceforth entitled to two shares of the nominal value of £20 each and every shareholder holding any of these shares in the Company of the nominal value of £20 and the amounts paid in respect of the respective shares of £50.

The warrant was issued on 27 May 1852 and allowed the company to reduce its requirement for capital from £1,600,000 to £1,125,060.

Of all these hurdles, convincing the specialised committees of Parliament was the most formidable. In the case of the Cornwall Railway

Bill 1845 it passed the Commons only to be thrown out by the Lords. Dealing with the shortcomings of the Bill was a relatively straightforward exercise which satisfied many of the petitioners. The 1846 Bill raised opposition primarily from those favouring the central route. In the absence of a successful proposal for such a route their evidence did not carry much weight.

The Parliamentary procedures are complex and were a series of hoops through which the railway companies had to jump. Failure at any one of these stages spelt the failure of the whole bill. We now turn to the cut and thrust being fought out in the Parliamentary Committee room itself.

5.5 *Seal of the Cornwall Railway Company.*

CHAPTER SIX

'MEN ARE SOMETIMES MASTERS OF THEIR FATES'

WILLIAM SHAKESPEARE: *JULIUS CAESAR*

I think it is the most impracticable line for locomotive power I ever met with… I formed my opinion… that the line is entirely unsuitable to be worked with locomotive engines, that it would be both dangerous and most expensive, that it is impossible to work with locomotive engines with any regularity.[1]

… it is unquestionably the most dangerous line I ever saw.[2]

It was words like those of Robert Stephenson and Joseph Locke that meant the failure of the Company's Bill in 1845 and ended Moorsom's career as Chief Engineer of the Cornwall Railway. They were responding to Rowe who had drawn their attention to the paragraph on page 3 of the Board of Trade report which states: 'The principle objections to the line arise from the nature of its curves and gradients.'

6.1
Robert Stephenson
1803-1859
STEPHEN K JONES COLLECTION

CAPTAIN WILLIAM SCARTH MOORSOM 1804-1863

The line for which Moorsom is best known is The Birmingham and Gloucester Railway It suffered two major drawbacks. The first was the Lickey incline and the second was that it would have been more profitable if it served towns just off the route such as Stourbridge, Dudley, Worcester and Droitwich. The issues he faced were whether or not to plan a route from A to B and ignore the potential intermediate traffic and whether or not to invest in civil engineering works to avoid the Lickey incline.

Moorsom had followed the family tradition into the army and had developed an expertise in military surveying culminating in a survey of the harbour of Halifax, Nova Scotia. He left the army in 1832 at the age of twenty eight when he bought his release and became a railway engineer at the height of the railway boom. Before that he had been responsible for military surveying in the Staff Corps on the Quartermaster's general staff. He had impressed Robert Stephenson with his survey of the Ouse Valley at Wolverton which resulted in improvements to the alignment of the London and Birmingham Railway. On the strength of this he was asked to survey the route for the Birmingham and Gloucester Railway. The promoters were West Midland industrialists who were looking for accessible port facilities for the export of manufactures. So trade between the end points was their main concern. However, although the Birmingham and Gloucester gained Parliamentary approval at the first attempt on 22 April 1836, it proved difficult to raise the capital and progress on construction was slow. It was built between 1836 and 1841. Criticisms of Moorsom do seem to have some weight[3]: These include lack of experience of being a Chief Engineer. Steeped in the military tradition of obeying orders without questioning them, Moorsom appointed staff of similar leanings. He obeyed the resolutions of the directors to the letter. The Director's instruction to produce the shortest route led to the Lickey incline. Moorsom seems to have accepted this without pointing out the consequences. Nor does he seem to have had any thoroughly worked out plan for getting trains up the incline and whether to use fixed haulage or not. This notorious incline was to prove to be an expensive economy.

The incline became the benchmark case in the debate about the acceptability of steeper gradients as the performance of locomotives improved. It features strongly in the 1845 Parliamentary debates on the Cornwall Railway about what gradient was practicable.

On a positive note Moorsom did draw up a code of regulations for operating a railway. The military made up the staff of inspectors of the Railway Dept of the Board of Trade and the framework of railway discipline was largely derived from its traditions. His code brought order to the haphazard practices of the early railway operators.

Moorsom was also an extensive contributor to the proceedings of the Institution of Civil Engineers with papers entitled 'Description of the American Engine 'Philadelphia' made by Mr Norris of Philadelphia, North America ...' (no 551). For his second paper (no 611) 'Descriptions and drawings of the Avon Bridge at Tewkesbury' he won a Telford Medal. These were awarded annually for meritorious papers presented to the Institution. The paper described how:

> 'it was desirable to provide for the considerable floods, by aiding the egress of water and also to avoid any interference with the navigation of the river; a greater width of water-way was therefore given than at first view may appear necessary'.

Floods in recent years at Tewkesbury have demonstrated the wisdom of the design. The paper continued:

> 'The principal novelty in the work is the method of constructing the two piers. They are formed externally of cast iron plates filled to the first 12 feet from the bottom with solid masonry and concrete'.

This technique foreshadowed Brunel's solution to the centre pier at Saltash. The viaduct lasted for 90 years until the superstructure was replaced by the LMS Railway in 1931. Moorsom's piers survive.

Commentators such as Simmons and Conder have pointed out that his methods were slovenly and the inaccuracies of the submitted plans

6.2 *One of Moorsom's more successful achievements: Defford Bridge across the Rive Avon. Although the superstructure has been replaced Moorsom's piers remain. The historic Eckington Bridge is in the background.* KIDDERMINSTER RAILWAY MUSEUM

for both the Cornwall and West Cornwall Railways indeed show a catalogue of errors. His proposals had not been adequately evaluated before its submission to Parliament. It was never clear, for instance, whether the line was designed for atmospheric traction or not: nor was it resolved how the trains were to negotiate the Torpoint Ferry or how long this process was to take.

There were other sources of discontent with him. Ostler provides a good contemporary summary of Moorsom's shortcomings:

> Capt Moorsom had undertaken so many other engagements, that it was scarcely possible for him to give proper attention to all. As the manifold claims upon him prevented him from giving that personal attention to the perfecting of the Cornwall Line which was really necessary, the Committee became much dissatisfied ... It was urged also as an objection to his Line that he carried across three navigable estuaries. It was however so contrary to general experience to embark a Railway train, that the public, not unreasonably, regarded the project with distrust. The advocates of a Central Line were too happy to take advantage of the feeling. Another objection was the carrying of the line by a high viaduct across the Truro river, immediately below the town. No real objection lay against this, for it would not interfere with the navigation, and was really a measure of economy, for instead of one viaduct, which would suffice in crossing the river below the town, two were rendered necessary by crossing the vallies above it.
>
> A more serious fault, and one that was quite indefensible, was the proposal to carry a low viaduct across Penryn Creek, a step which would necessarily interrupt the navigation of one of the most considerable trading ports in the

6.3 A view over Penryn with Collegewood viaduct in the foreground on Brereton's route to Falmouth. Both Moorsom and Johnson's routes would have terminated in the centre of the picture, on the west bank of Penryn Creek, Moorsom having crossed the creek by a viaduct.
MICHAEL MESSENGER COLLECTION

> county. The committee felt the danger to which all these objections exposed the Line, and anxiously desired to confer with their Engineer on the means of avoiding them; but his manifold and pressing engagements elsewhere prevented him from often meeting them, and sometimes even from keeping his appointments.

We cannot know what Moorsom's attitude could have been to the task of surveying the southern route. He had already reported on the topographical and engineering disadvantages of this route. He had put his energies into the design of the central route and perhaps was less than wholehearted about the prospect of surveying what he must have perceived to be a less than satisfactory alternative with the formidable problem of constructing a line through the Fowey valley. When the House of Lords required '... a further and most accurate survey of the whole line ...' they were referring to both the inaccuracies in Moorsom's survey and proposed gradients and curves on the line.

The submitted plans show a line starting at Greenbank Quay in Falmouth, crossing the Penryn Creek on a low timber viaduct, 500 feet long with a drawbridge. It then climbs at a gradient of up to 1 in 40 to Ponsanooth and crosses the Truro River on a lengthy viaduct 600 feet long to the south of the city. It then follows the Tresillian River until it joins the line we know today near Probus. Skirting the china clay district and passes to the north of St Austell and then descends to Par passing through a 580 yard tunnel before reaching Lostwithiel and starting a long ascent through the Fowey valley passing Respryn, Glynn Bridge and Liskeard. It leaves the current line at St Germans falling steadily crossing Polbathick Creek by another timber drawbridge, proceeding across the St Anthony promontory to the Torpoint Ferry.

On the Plymouth side the proposed line climbed steeply beside the '*Glacis*' of the Devonport Dock Lines and Morice Town, with gradients of 1 in 30, to the proposed terminus of the South Devon Railway at Eldad. '*Glacis*' is a term used to describe the sloping, open 'firing ground' abutting a defensive fortification; land deliberately kept free of buildings and trees and offering no cover for an attacking force. The defences in question were the Devonport 'Dock Lines' - stone faced walls and bastions, surrounded by a deep ditch. The 'Lines' had been constructed in the mid 18th century to guard the landward approach to Plymouth Dock and the Naval Dockyard. The town of Dock was renamed 'Devonport' in 1824. West of Eldad, the proposed line of the railway would have run via Stoke village to New Passage. This was north of the 'Lines', but alongside the associated Government land or *glacis*. New Passage Hill had been cut through the 'Lines' by 1791 to give access to the Torpoint ferry crossing and new housing at Morice Town. By 1857-8, the Lines had a reduced military importance and the *glacis* to the north and north east of the Town became Devonport Park.

There was considerable doubt whether such a route would be permitted:

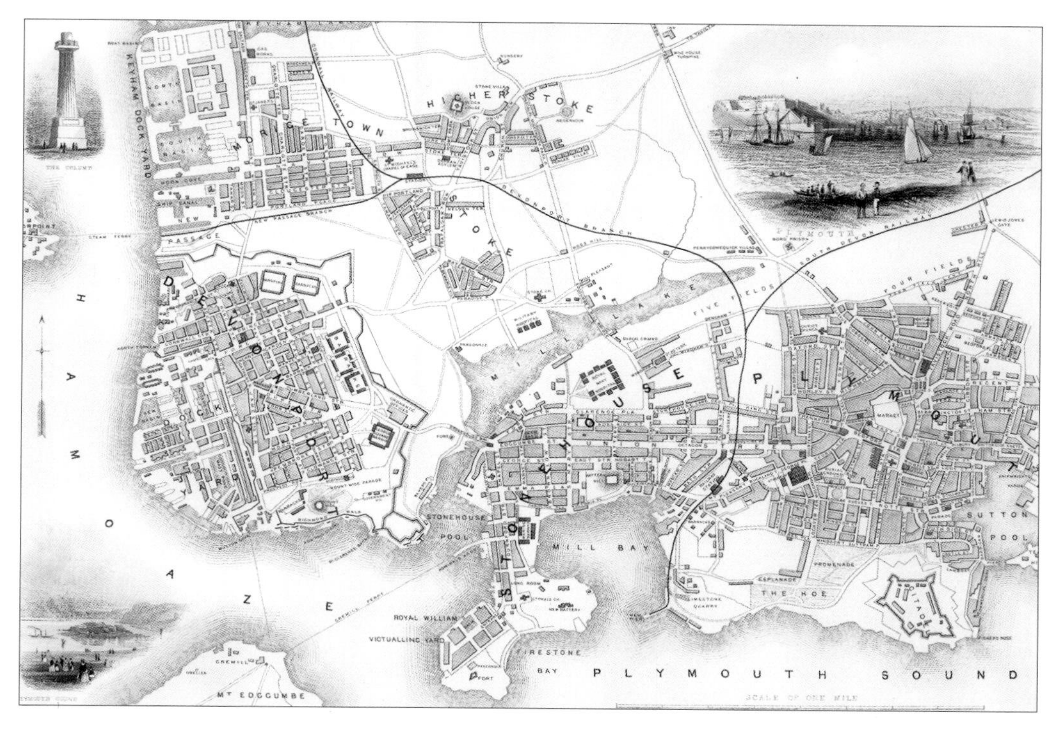

6.4 *Published at a time when both ferry and bridge were being considered as alternatives for crossing the Hamoaze, Rapkins map of Plymouth, Stonehouse and Devonport shows both routes.* PLYMOUTH CITY MUSEUM AND ART GALLERY

Q Have you heard from the promoters of the bill since yesterday that Her Majesty's Ordnance have refused their consent to you passing directly or indirectly the glacis of Devonport?

A The subject has not come before me at all since.[4]

In comparison with Johnson's survey of the following year, Moorsom's is a succession of steep gradients and sharp curves. Ostler comments:

> There was also a feeling, which none entertained more strongly than the friends of the Line, that his gradients and other works were more unfavourable than the difficulties of the County required.

INACCURACIES IN THE SURVEY

The Select Committee on Railway Bills spent much time on the crossings of the Hamoaze and of Penryn Creek. But the other main issue raised in the Petition against the Bill was the amazing number of inaccuracies in Moorsom's submitted plans. The petition then identifies three instances, where the gradient is inaccurately marked, which have occurred in copying. Then there are nine instances of inaccuracies which appear to have arisen in the calculation. The House of Commons appears to have stretched a point in giving leave for the Bill to proceed.

The Committee subjected Moorsom to what was clearly an embarrassing and painful exposure of the inaccuracies in his submitted plans. The line of questioning undermined the credibility of the whole submission. One of his problems was the contemporary methods of lithography which could distort the image. He explained:

> The lithographed paper is first prepared by damping and then engraved afterwards. I believe in this case they were dried by artificial heat. The distortion is considerable.

More embarrassing admissions and feeble excuses of which the following exchange with a member of the Sub Committee on Petitions[5] is but one ...

Q Will you look between the first mile and fourth furlong and the second mile and seventh furlong? What is stated there?

A The inclination is stated quite incorrectly I believe, 1in 60. That incorrectness arises in the figures only. The gradient is correctly stated. If you look at this line of inclination and look at this you will see that it is marked 1in 60 and it is 1in 60.

Q You suppose that this error pervades the whole of the plan?

A Yes. The actual inclination is quite correct but the statement in the figures is wrong ...

And again ...

Q Now will you take the eleventh mile and first furlong and the eleventh mile and second furlong? What is the inclination there?

A The inclination written is 1 in 130.

Q What ought it to be?

A In this case it measured out to 1 in 90 ...

Q You have seen the petition?

A Yes, but the allegations are rather too numerous to bear in mind. I calculated them all out and it appeared to me that in some few cases there were differences and that in others they were very small.

Q In this case the difference is 90 and 130?

A These had been done while I was away from my office and I think they may have been incorrectly calculated instead of doing it with accuracy. The calculation is made incorrectly.

Q You do not mean to state that they are inaccurately copied from some other document which was right but the calculation there had an error?

A In the first instance it was an inaccurate copy because I happened to calculate that myself and it was inaccurately copied from my correct calculation which still exists upon the paper. But in reference to the others as to which I have been asked I can only conjecture that it has been incorrectly calculated. It has been correctly drawn but the figures are incorrectly calculated ...

Q In all these cases that you have pointed out how the error upon the face of the plan; is an error in the figures and not in the line of the inclination?

A It is only an error in the figures – the inclination is correct.

Q The inclination is invariably correct but in some instances the figures are wrongfully marked horizontally and some upon the vertical line?

A Yes.

Q You have stated before that the inclination of the vertical lines is correct but you have stated that there are instances in which the section is incorrect in consequence of the figure being marked wrong?

A There are some instances in which there are omissions of figures of the vertical heights – I said that the only way in which I could possibly reconcile the discrepancy between the two parties measuring was by supposing that the vertical height figured here was taken by the parties and that the vertical height was incorrectly marked.

These examples give a flavour of the incidence and nature of the inaccuracies.

GRADIENTS AND CURVES

The attitude of engineers to steeper gradients was changing quite rapidly at the time that both bills were before Parliament. More powerful engines had made them practicable.

> Behind this level-road policy of his (Robert Stephenson's) was his father's axiom that it was best to eliminate gradients even at a greatly increased first

cost in tunnelling or earthworks, so that all the power of the locomotives could be economically applied to draw a maximum load instead of to surmounting inclines. Locke became the great exponent of the opposite school of thought, which favoured going up and over natural obstacles which the Stephensons would either go round or tunnel through.[6]

The Board of Trade report (Appendix one) points to the number of gradients and tight curves included in Moorsom's plans for the southern route. However it does not consider them to be 'absolutely impracticable' or a reason for rejecting the proposal outright but clearly has considerable reservations about them.

6.5
George Parker Bidder 1806-1878
INSTITUTION OF CIVIL ENGINEERS

GEORGE PARKER BIDDER 1806-1878

Over-shadowed by the big three, Bidder was a very able and successful engineer with many railway and docks works to his credit. Bidder is perhaps best known for his work on hydraulics in connection with London's drainage and land enclosure from the sea in the Netherlands and was also an enthusiastic exponent of the potential of the electric telegraph. He had achieved distinction in his work for Robert Stephenson on the London and Birmingham Railway and in particular the incline out of Euston Station and had also been engineer on several railways in the eastern counties.

Bidder had an extraordinary mathematical ability which made him a powerful witness before parliamentary committees. When he appeared before the Parliamentary Committee of the Cornwall Railway Bill he already had a formidable reputation as a debater. He was President of Institution of Civil Engineers in 1860/1.

Despite the prevalence of gradients throughout, it is those at either end of the line that provoked the most attention; the immediate climb out of Falmouth and the short section from New Passage to Eldad as demonstrated by Rowe's examination of Bidder:[7]

Q Now then looking through the section on that line and looking on the curves on the plan will you apply your mind to the paragraphs of the Report of the Board of Trade to which I called Mr Stephenson's attention? (concerning curves and gradients.)

A Yes.

Q In the first place the Board of Trade assumes a more favourable inclination than actually exists, is it not so? They say nothing of 1 in 40?

A No they do not.

Q Nothing also of 1 in 30?

A It is not mentioned here.

Q Regard being had to all that traffic on the line including the Devonshire end will you state what is your opinion as to that line, first as to

6.6 *Cover of plans accompanying 1845 submission showing Moorsom's name.*

punctuality and the possibility of its working with punctuality at the speed of 20 or 30 miles an hour?

A It cannot work with punctuality at 20 miles an hour. I do not think it could even with an engine without a load work with punctuality at 20 miles an hour: the gravity of an engine upon those gradients would be equal to about 40 or 45 tons on a level with 30 miles an hour the gravity alone would be equal to a train of 30 tons ...

Q Now with respect to the safety of working such inclines and accompanied with such curves as this, will you take the Penryn case - 1 in 40, an incline with three curves of 15 chains to say nothing of all the other curves?

A That would require an incessant vigilance and attention to preserve the safety of the public. Should any accident happen, should an occasion occur by which any part of the engine gets deranged, such as the breaking of an axle, the consequences would be most serious indeed. On gradients of this character it is also to be remembered that engines are exposed to very great force and to very unequal power... .

Q What is the ascent from the water up to Eldad?

A At Torpoint it is 1 in 30. I think that will have to be worked by an assistant engine and a rope, there is no doubt of that.

Q Captain Moorsom proposes to use no assistant power on that main line in the passage from Eldad to New Passage and Penryn up an incline of 1 in 40 and those intermediate inclines of 1 in 30 but he considers that he shall go at 25 miles an hour without assistant power. Do you think that can be done?

A I do not think it can be worked at that speed at all.

The doubts about the gradients and curves were sufficient for the House of Lords to reject the details of the Bill. It passed the Commons but

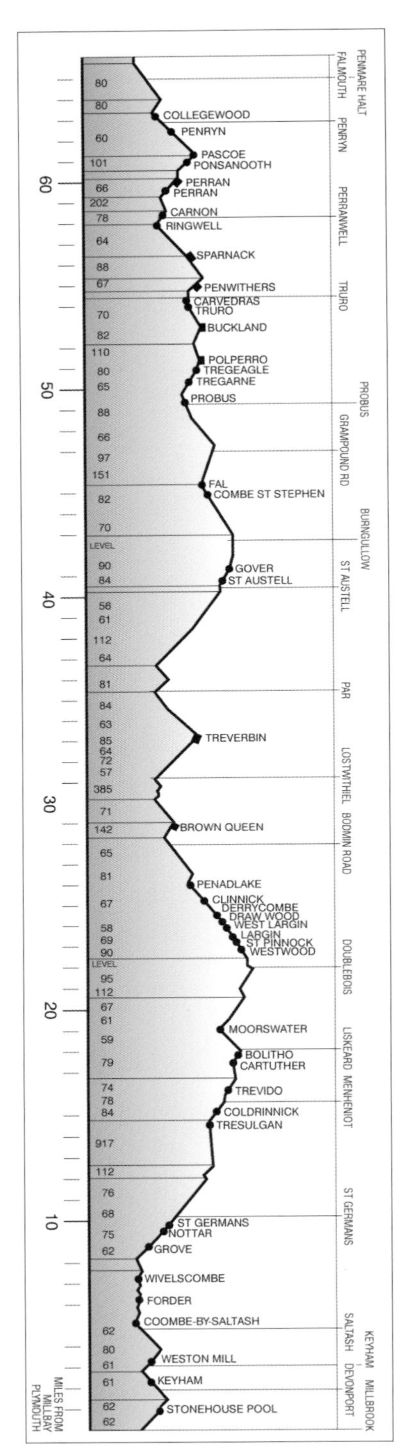

6.7 '... the route presents one continued series of engineering difficulties.' The gradient profile of the Cornwall Railway illustrates the scale of the problem faced by the promoters of the railway. With hardly any level track the terrain results in a series of switchbacks from virtually sea level at Falmouth and Par to an elevation of 385 feet at Doublebois. The frequent tunnels and viaducts demonstrate the heavy, and expensive, engineering works that were necessary to overcome a difficult terrain.

the Lords took the view that the shortcomings were so serious that a fresh survey was required. The Report from the Select Committee recommended 'that the Bill should not now be proceeded with'. It is little wonder that the House of Lords recommended 'a new and more accurate survey' for the Cornwall line[8]. The decision on the 1845 Cornwall Railway Bill did help to resolve the technical issues concerning the railway. However the 'Civil War' was far from over. The issue of the route refused to die down.

Meanwhile in contrast to the triumphalism of the meeting on the central route supporters of the southern route took a more sober line. Following the rejection of the Cornwall Railway Bill by the House of Lords in 1845, the Provisional Committee of the Cornwall Railway took stock. The Committee of Management reported to a meeting of shareholders and set out a course of action to secure Parliamentary approval in the following session. A meeting of the Associated Companies and members of the Provisional Committee of the Cornwall Railway met at the offices of the GWR on 25 July to consider the resolution of the House of Lords. It was resolved: 'That it is important for the interests of the Cornwall Railway Company, that immediate steps should be taken to give full effect to the said resolution'. The meeting on 26 August of shareholders received a report on the course which the Directors 'recommend for adoption under the circumstances in which the Company is placed' to bring another Bill before Parliament. In order to prove the financial strength in the interest of clearing Standing Orders the Directors report that the Great Western and Associated Companies will become shareholders to the extent of £250,000 and 'by the support of an unusually large and influential local interest amounting to nearly £300,000'.

The promoters saw that they had an approval in principal. It was a question of redesigning the line to meet the Lords technical requirements. They recognised that the Preamble had been proven and that they now needed to put right the estuary crossings at Penryn and the Hamoaze and rectify the engineering shortcomings of Moorsom's survey before resubmitting in the following session. The Provisional Committee expressed thanks to The Right Honourable the Earl of Falmouth and to Sir Charles Lemon Baronet for their invaluable support in carrying the Bill through Parliament 'to the advanced stage which it attained'. Thanks were also recorded to the Company Secretary, Protheroe Smith (Solicitor), 'in the arduous and responsible duties imposed on him by having to contend with an opposition as unexampled in its character as it has been determined in its conduct'.

Dismissal of Moorsom

Under the circumstances that Parliament had approved the preamble, i.e. the need for the line, but had rejected the detail, the Directors took the view that Moorsom could not be relied on to produce a line that would receive Parliamentary approval. The Provisional Committee and the Great Western promptly dismissed Moorsom and appointed Brunel:

> ... for the purpose of recommending such improvements or alterations in the Line of Railway as may seem to him expedient.

The committee resolved:

> That in consequence of the resolution of the Committee of the House of Lords it appears to this Committee very desirable that a change should take place in the Engineering and Captain Moorsom having expressed his willingness that such change should take place.
>
> It was resolved that Captn Moorsom be thanked for his handsome letter to Mr Smith and that Mr Brunel be requested to accept the office of Engineer to this Company and to carry out the recommendation of the Lords Committee[9].

The 'handsome letter' does not appear to have survived; nor do we know what the 'change' was to which Captain Moorsom expresses his willingness and still less about any correspondence between him and the company. It is clear that some misunderstanding may have taken place concerning any future role that Moorsom might have played which comes to light when he submits accounts for further work. The Board queried these expenses. There is no record of how the matter was resolved but it marked the end of Moorsom's involvement with the Company[10]:

> Capt Moorsom's account amounting to £369 7/- having been submitted to this Board Moved by Mr Gill Seconded by Mr Tivery
>
> Resolved that the Secretary be instructed to ask Capt Moorsom by whose authority and at what dates he undertook the journeys and rendered the services referred to in his account.

We do know that Brunel was in Italy for most of September and early

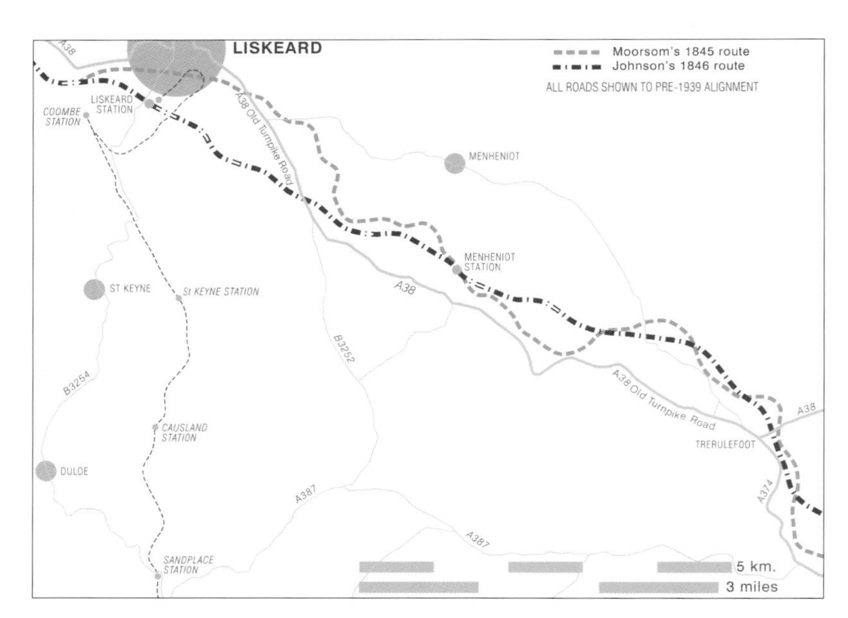

6.8 A sample comparison of Moorsom's and Johnson's surveys for the 1845 and 1846 Cornwall Railway Bills respectively, clearly demonstrates that Johnson achieved a much superior alignment.

October 1845 and Moorsom may have assumed that Johnson may have needed supervising during that period. Brunel trusted Johnson implicitly as a safe pair of hands and Johnson was quite clear that he was taking orders from no one except Brunel. The only clues to the misunderstanding are the somewhat intemperate letters to Moorsom in Brunel's own letterbooks, for example[11]:

> I do not think it worth altering the accounts. It won't alter the fact that you consider that you have been engaged or at any events have occupied yourself in arranging for the survey – 'revising sections' and 'overlooking the surveyor'. I merely say that you were not authorised nor asked to do so and that neither my surveyor nor myself were aware of it - and that at all events for the future I must beg of you not to do anything for me. By whatever strange means such a mistake can have arisen I wish to say no more about it but will endeavour to have the Cornwall account settled merely suggesting the question.

Despite his support for Moorsom's survey Brunel appears to have been well aware of the shortcomings:

> As I am upon the question of sections however I must tell you that whilst I have not opened my mouth about it to any body else and I have no intention of doing – those who made your Parliamentary sections for you have most grossly 'fudged' them. I can use no other term of the incorrectness of the whole plans and sections was beyond anything I have had experience of.

The Cornwall Railway Company lost no time after the rejection of their 1845 bill. Brunel had indicated that a fresh survey could be completed within three months. He commissioned William Johnson to carry out the survey required by Parliament. Within three months Johnson had completed his survey and the new bill was lodged on 30 November 1845 for consideration in the 1846 Parliamentary session. It went before the Committee of Standing Orders on 27 February and was considered by the Select Committee from 21 May until 15 June.

Brunel made it quite clear that the survey was, indeed, a fresh one and not simply a tidying up of Moorsom's line:

> I took the whole subject of communication between Plymouth and Falmouth into consideration entirely anew, without reference to the old plans than, of course, in reference that those plans furnished; and obtained all the information I possibly could as to what was desirable in the way of communicating with the principal towns of Cornwall, and also to any objections which had been lodged against previous plans. I had the country generally between Plymouth and Falmouth re-examined and any line, that appeared likely to offer any advantage, tested by surveys and levels.[12]

The Committee had little to say on the technicalities of the revised survey which speaks loudly for Johnson's work. Essentially his task was to improve on Moorsom's alignment and to survey an alternative to the Torpoint ferry of a bridge at Saltash. The main issue was the balancing of capital costs of civil engineering works against economy of operation. Again Johnson was adjudged to have achieved an optimal balance. The only other issue concerned the admissibility of the central route. Despite the best of endeavours of Kinglake to have the question ruled *ultra vires* its proponents were allowed their day in court. However the logic of the views of Lemon and Lord Falmouth who, as we have seen, were converts to the southern route, won the day.

WILLIAM JOHNSON

The plans and sections for the 1846 Cornwall Railway Bill were drawn up in the autumn of 1845 by William Johnson (born 1801) and Henry Hornor Johnson (born 1816) whilst Brunel was in Italy. They are described on the plans as 'engineering surveyors'. They were respectively the eldest and youngest children of William Johnson to whom Brunel had been a client over several years. William senior had been born in 1771 into a Quaker family and had worked on several projects for Brunel. Most of his work was in Cheshire, Lancashire and Manchester. He was based in Manchester and is described on his marriage certificate as 'Land Surveyor'. Latterly he is known as an 'engineering surveyor'. At the time of the survey of the Cornwall Railway the brothers were 45 and 29 years old respectively.

In a letter Brunel stresses that he wants 'great accuracy and great detail' and this is exactly what he receives from the Johnsons who commanded great respect in railway engineering circles. William was described by Hawkshaw as 'the best man in England for the purpose Mr Brunel has put him'. And Ostler says of him:

> It would be unjust to close the history of this protracted contest without briefly noticing the merits of those who contributed to its success. Mr Johnson, who laid out the line, had previously enjoyed the very highest reputation as a Surveyor, and was therefore selected by Mr Brunel to fulfil the requirements of the House of Lords. His merit was severely and triumphantly tested by the hostile scrutiny his work encountered, and which failed to detect one error.

The *Royal Cornwall Gazette* confirmed what a good job Johnson had done:

> ... so judiciously has the Line been laid down, that from Truro to the Tamar there are only three tunnels, neither [*sic*] of them long, one indeed does not lose the light; while of the gradients it may suffice to say, that the train on Tuesday, which could not have contained less than 800 passengers, or weighted with its two engines much less than 200 tons, ran the 54 miles including the stoppages in two hours and a half.

The relationship between Brunel and Johnson is significant. Clearly Brunel trusted Johnson for his accuracy and reliability. But it was equally clear that Johnson was answerable to Brunel and no one else. This is shown by the cross examination of Johnson by Rowe who was clearly trying to find out whether Johnson had been influenced by Treffry[13]:

Q You say got your instructions as to the laying out of this line?

A Yes.

Q Did you get your instructions from Mr Brunel alone or did you see Mr Treffry the Chairman of the line?

A I got them from Mr Brunel alone.

Q Did you communicate with Mr Treffry about it when you came to Cornwall?

A I did not.

Q Not at all?

A Not at all.

Q Not up to this time?

A I did not see Mr Treffry until after the plans were deposited nor any agent of his.

Q And your instructions were to observe the course that you have spoken of – that you were to touch Liskeard, Lostwithiel and Saint Austell?

A Yes.

Equally he had no contact with the displaced and, no doubt, disgruntled Moorsom:

Q Mr Brunel I presume laid down the general course of the line?

A He gave me general instructions before I went into Cornwall.

Q You were not then tied to Captain Moorsom's line but what were your general instructions from him?

A They were that it had been settled that the line should pass near St Austell, Lostwithiel and Liskeard.

Q Did you also survey the Country between Saltash and the alternative line between Saltash and the Junction?

A Yes.

Q That was the line I believe that you discovered by yourself did you not?

A Yes, myself and my assistants.

Q Did you select that as the best line which in the observation of the district you could find?

A Yes.

Q I need hardly say that you have very much improved the curves and gradients on the line?

A Yes I have.

(See Appendix eight)

CHARLES BLACKER VIGNOLES 1793 – 1875

Considerably older than the other witnesses, Vignoles had had a military career at the tail end of the Napoleonic Wars. After this he had been involved in surveying in South Carolina and Florida. His engineering career had started with work on Thames bridges and the second survey of the Liverpool and Manchester Railway. He sponsored the *Novelty* at the Rainhill Trials, arguably the second most successful entrant. At this time he developed the flat bottomed rail for which he is, perhaps, best known. He was engineer of several railways in his native Ireland before embarking on the Midland Counties Railway. In 1835 he was appointed engineer to the Sheffield and Manchester Railway whose main civil engineering work was the three mile Woodhead Tunnel. This brought him financial ruin and replacement by Locke. (The irony is that Locke hated tunnels and avoided constructing them whenever possible.) He then carried out the only successful atmospheric line at Dalkey before bringing his expertise to bear at the Parliamentary Committee into the Cornwall Railway. His most celebrated achievement was the multi span suspension bridge over the Dneiper at Kiev.

6.9
Charles Vignoles
1793-1875
STEPHEN K JONES COLLESCTION

6.10
John Hawkshaw
1811- 1891
Institution of Civil Engineers

John Hawkshaw 1811-1891

It was the fate of Hawkshaw and other engineers who were born only five years after Brunel, Robert Stephenson and Locke, never to achieve the popular recognition of their illustrious predecessors despite glittering careers in their own right. Hawkshaw was to have a distinguished, longer and arguably more productive career than the eminent pioneers not only in railways but also in docks and harbours, drainage works, flood defence and sewerage schemes. In London he was engineer for the East London Line and was responsible for two railway bridges over the Thames, Charing Cross and Cannon Street. Abroad he engineered railways in Russia and the ship canal from Amsterdam to the North Sea and the Leipzig and Dresden Railway 1835.

His appearance on the Cornwall Railway Bill came at a relatively early stage in his career. When he gave evidence to the Parliamentary Committee this was all in the future. He was however able to bring to bear extensive experience of building railways in the Pennines with heavy engineering works and steep gradients. He was 35 years old and younger than most other witnesses.

' So young and successful an engineer was naturally associated with many important undertakings'. Two years before he appeared before the committee on the Cornwall Railway he had been appointed engineer to the Manchester and Bolton Railway. This was followed by a similar post to the Lancashire and Yorkshire Railway. It was the engineering of these lines through hilly country that gave authority to his pronouncements of what gradients were realistic and which were not. Hawkshaw had engineered gradients of 1 in 50 at both Bradford and Leeds. He expressed authorative views on railway incline planes and in particular those at Lickey and Dainton:

> The change of views of Engineers, on this subject had been very great. He remembered the time when a gradient of 1 in 100 was thought to be the utmost that ought to be ventured upon; and that with 1 in 50, locomotives must be put aside, and ropes must be employed. The incline on the North-Western Railway, from Camden Town to Euston Station, was for a long period worked by a rope, which was considered the only practicable mode, although the rise did not average more than 1 in 66.

The Severn Tunnel will rank as his greatest achievement in view both of the commercial importance and the physical obstacles which were overcome. Notably he gave advice on the feasibility of the Suez Canal and the Channel Tunnel. He had been a key figure in the 'battle of the gauges' and the Gauge inquiry of 1838. Now he was to be a key figure in the 'battle of the gradients'.

He was President of ICE in 1862/3 and knighted in 1873.

ARGUMENTS BETWEEN CIVIL ENGINEERING COSTS AND OPERATIONAL COSTS

One of the issues emerging from the two hearings was the problem of balancing the capital costs of earthworks against the likely returns from easier operations. Clearly there was no chance that a straight and level railway could be engineered in Cornwall. The challenge for Johnson was to achieve a balance between heavy civil engineering works and the capacity of the locomotives of the day. He had to find a line that was neither too steep nor too expensive. Brunel under examination by Merevale a year later spells out the difference between Moorsom's and Johnson's lines[14]:

Q As the noble Lord and the Honourable Members do not know Cornwall can you tell me how many curves you will have altogether upon your line – the main line?

A The line, as on all good lines through difficult countries, is on continuous curves of course and on any drawing a strait [*sic*] line through a rough ground is in 99 cases out of a hundred a piece of bad engineering... .

Q Will you tell me the smallest radius of those curves?

A 25 chains.

Vignoles, under examination by Merevale, thought that the line was easily within the capabilities of the latest locomotives[15]:

Q Do you consider that the line relating to the plans and sections can be safely speedily and efficiently worked with economy and practically?

A Oh there is no doubt about that at all; it is the mere question of the size of the Engine. The great difficulty with respect to the gradient, in the original laying out, it was supposed the engine had not sufficient adhesion on the rails – that is it had not the bite enough to propel itself forwards. All the early lines were laid out under the apprehension that the engine could not be made sufficiently powerful to overcome such gradient, the experience of the last five years has proved that we can get up the gradients now of an acclivity that were formerly thought quite impracticable and the gradients of this line 1in 60 are now comparatively from the advance of engineering what a gradient of 1 in 100 was five years ago.

Q (by the Committee). Is that from an improvement from the Engine?

A From the larger size of which the engine is made – the general arrangements and improvements and also on the principle of working, which is to send the train more frequently with lighter loads.

Q Have you made any Estimate of what the additional expences per ton on the maximum would pay for the extra expence for working gradients such as these?

A No, I have not but I do not think it can be much. If you have an Engine for instance of such cylinder and two feet stroke you will be able to do any amount of work that is likely to come over that line – an engine such as that will weigh perhaps 18 tons and the adhesion of that Engine will be perhaps 10 or 12 tons. It will weigh 10 or 12 tons and then you have got an adhesion of two thirds of that weight of the Engine upon the driving wheel and that is a measure of the load which the Engine can carry. The measure of power is the capacity of the boiler to generate steam so that with these two elements you can command gradients of a very much steeper character than 1 in 60.

He confirmed under cross examination that the line was as good as could be hoped for:

Q I believe you gave evidence last year on the Committee on the Cornwall Railway?
A Yes.
Q Since then have you examined the plans and Sections on the present line?
A I have.
Q You remember perhaps the Select Committee of the House of Lords recommended the postponement with a view to getting better gradients if possible?
A A general improvement of the line.
Q Do you consider that the recommended line has been followed in the course now taken from the plans and sections you have seen?
A I think the best line and the best gradients have been got consistent with any moderate degree of outlay.

Now in 1846 Locke confirms the point when examined by the Committee[16]:

Q If it were thought indispensable to construct a line, a coast line from Falmouth to Plymouth do you think one could be constructed with better gradients than this one?
A Yes my Lord, I think it could but I must say at the same time that I cannot say whether you ought as a commercial question or not, to spend so much money in order to obtain those better gradients.

Hawkshaw agrees:

Q Looking to the fact that Cornwall and that part over which this line passes is a rough county and intersected with the valleys does it appear to you from the sections it is judiciously laid out with reference to the gradients?
A There can be no doubt about it. The country is a very rugged country and to seek gradients flatter than those proposed would involve an enormous cost without any corresponding advantages in my opinion.[17]

At last the company had their Parliamentary approval and got to work promptly. Little were the members to know the paralysing financial difficulties that they were to face.

Ostler considers it:

... fortunate that all the earlier attempts had failed. Even in Cornwall there was much apathy, not to say opposition, on the subject of the Railway. There were many who believed that either the engineering difficulties were insurmountable, or the capital could not be raised, or the Line would not pay.

At the opening ceremony the chairman, Smith summarised the complex process they had been through:[18]

> Now I do not know whether I am not giving a piece of information to one or two persons present when I tell them that the course of this line was not at all chosen by the persons who represent this railway. You have heard – I have heard – a thousand opinions as to the propriety of the course of line of this railway. Well, I do not know but that this Board would take credit to themselves for having selected this course, but that credit they have no right to. Preliminary measures were taken long before the incorporation of this company; gentlemen of the county subscribed and carried out a partial survey, but all had for their object the communication by railway from Truro to Exeter, and it was only at the close of 1844 (a long time ago), that the incorporation of the South Devon Company, and the commencement of their works, induced a public meeting on the spot we now stand upon. The county had been canvassed in various ways with reference to this matter; a public meeting on this ground, presided over by the late Earl of Falmouth, was called expressly for the purpose of considering what course should be taken under the altered circumstances of the times - those circumstances being altered by the incorporation of the South Devon Railway Company and the prospect of a speedy railway communication as far as Plymouth – so that the County of Cornwall should secure a similar communication for its interests. I attended that meeting – the first meeting for any railway purpose, I ever had the honour to sit at. This meeting, it was prognosticated, would disclose the elements of dissimilarity of purpose and intention; but those elements by some strong overruling power brought into perfect unison. I never saw such an effect as the long and able debate produced; the discussion was full and well sustained; the result was clearly and satisfactorily brought out – the meeting was perfectly unanimous. Without offence every objection was fully and fairly met and it was voted unanimously that the increasing interests of the county required and called for the construction of a railroad from Falmouth to Plymouth. A provisional committee was appointed – not to decide on the best route that was considered settled but to carry out the fixed and predetermined position of the county. On that committee I acted from the commencement; therefore I am perfectly cognizant of all the facts, and I know how wisely, how ably, and how perseveringly that committee laboured until the company was incorporated.

Although the 1845 Cornwall Railway Bill must be regarded as a failure it did succeed in clarifying all the technical issues which would need to be addressed in the 1846 Bill with the exception of the crossing of the Hamoaze: an issue that was to tax engineering technology to its limits and the finances of the company to breaking point.

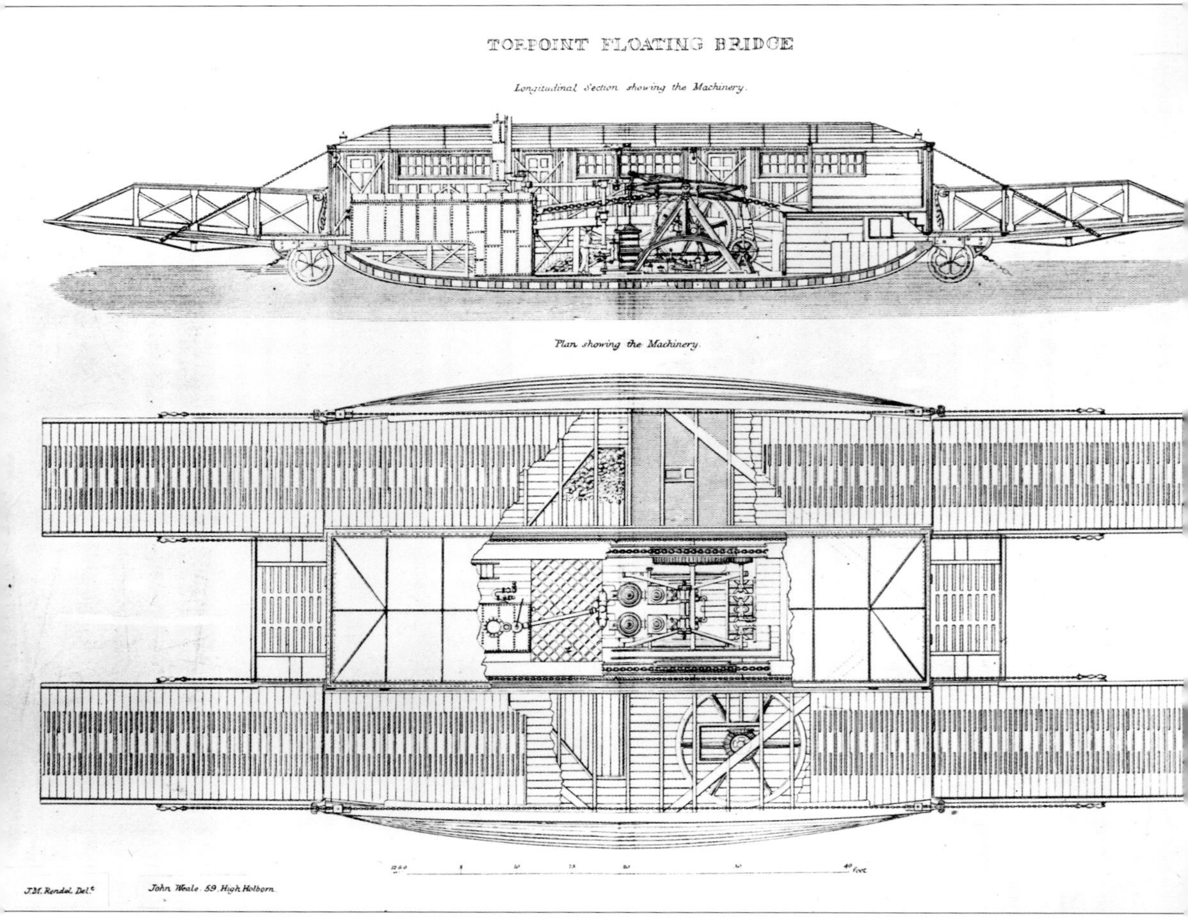

TORPOINT FLOATING BRIDGE

Longitudinal Section showing the Machinery.

Plan showing the Machinery.

J.M. Rendel. Delt.

John Weale. 59. High Holborn.

7.1 *The Torpoint Floating Bridge.*
Moorsom proposed to run three seven ton railway carriages onto each of the road vehicle decks.
KEITH PERKINS COLLECTION

Chapter seven

'The most difficult engineering work which has ever been attempted in this or any other country'

The Times 4 May 1859

As the divisions between the supporters of the central route and the southern route became deeper, the latter, belatedly, started to consider how to deal with the greatest natural obstacle on their route, the River Tamar. Meanwhile the former envisaged that the southern route might founder over this issue and were working out tactics for destroying it once and for all. Ostler summarised the situation:

> It was, however, so contrary to general experience to embark a Railway train, that the public, not unreasonably, regarded the project with distrust, and advocates of a Central line were too happy to take advantage of the feeling.

Such had been the success of Rendel's floating bridge[1] at Torpoint that Moorsom seized on the idea of using it for transporting trains across the Hamoaze. This concept was included in the 1845 Cornwall Railway Bill and was tested very rigorously by the Parliamentary Committee. During these proceedings doubts began to crystallise about it with the result that the House of Lords concluded that the whole idea was not only impractical but downright dangerous. The proposed use of the floating bridge was one of the main reasons for the failure of the bill. The evidence of its engineer, James Rendel, proved pivotal. He was the first to testify that, despite its self-evident success in terms of the road traffic of the day, it would not be suitable for transporting trains.

James Meadows Rendel 1799-1856

A Devonian by birth, Rendel's works are concentrated in the West Country, hence his opinions on West Country engineering matters were highly respected. He is best known for his 'steam floating bridges' several of which, notably the Torpoint Ferry, still exist, albeit in more modern form. It had operated since 1834 and ten years later had established a good reputation for reliability. Rendel never regarded these floating bridges as more than stop gaps until permanent bridges could be built as replacements and drew up plans for suspension bridges at Saltash and the Fowey estuary, neither of which came to pass. His design for the Clifton suspension bridge competition reached the last four but ultimately lost out to Brunel's design. Neither of them lived to see the completion of the bridge in 1864.

Rendel set up his own practice in Plymouth in 1822. The cast iron Laira Bridge, which was built between1824 and 1827, made his reputation. It lasted until the 1960s. The Institution of Civil Engineers awarded him a Telford Medal for it. He moved to London in 1838 living in a house on the site of what is now the Institution and achieved great distinction as its president in 1852/3, being also made a member of the Royal Society. His other major achievement was in harbour works which were much in demand in the 1840s, a period of unprecedented maritime development in the UK.

He gave evidence at the 1845 hearing that he had surveyed a line for the Cornwall Railway with superior gradients. The only surviving evidence of it lies in his examination by Rowe in 1845[2] :

A Will you allow me to say it is a line I recommended myself: The line, from Plymouth to Falmouth through this country now selected as the line before the Committee, is to the best of my recollection. There is no gradient on that line of more than 1 in 90, that is the impression I have. I think that the country will admit to that gradient …

Q If you were now laying down a railway would you not get gradients more severe than those you did five years ago?

A I think, like all the other good things, good gradients might be purchased at too high a price. The impression on my mind is that the country will admit of gradients that had to be taken, by the advantage of certain ridges and tunnelling through the other ridges of ground being peculiarly favourable for tunnelling.

Clearly such an alignment would have been expensive as William Johnson himself summarised the argument:

Q You spoke to this section as being the best the Country will afford – do you know that a section has been had between Falmouth and Plymouth showing for its worst gradient one in 90 by Mr Rendell [*sic*], a very eminent Engineer

A It is possible to put gradients on bad sections but I am quite sure that any line from Falmouth to Plymouth with a gradient of 1in 90 must be outrageously expensive. I have no hesitation in saying so.[3]

THE BALANCE OF OPINION SHIFTS FROM THE FERRY TO A BRIDGE

The use of the ferry, with its interruption to rail traffic, had received only qualified support from the Board of Trade:

It does not appear, however, that this passage is in itself so objectionable as to weigh materially in a consideration of the sole practicable line proposed into Cornwall.

Rowe had spent a great deal of time in cross examining Moorsom on the viability of the gradients and curves of the proposed line for the

Cornwall Railway. Now he turned his attention to the crossing of the Tamar. His cross examination revealed, all too clearly, that Moorsom had not thought through how the use of the floating bridge between Torpoint and New Passage would work out in practice, any more than he had looked into the implications of crossing Penryn Creek. Rowe also called a formidable quartet of James Rendel, George Bidder, Robert Stephenson and Joseph Locke to provide evidence on the impracticality of Moorsom's proposal.

Essentially there were three arguments against the use of the ferry:

a) That the process of getting trains on and off the ferry was ill-thought-out and inherently dangerous,
b) That the gradients between the ferry terminal at New Passage on the Plymouth side and the South Devon terminus at Eldad were so severe as to be almost unworkable,
c) That the time taken to achieve the crossing could be more than made up by many additional miles.

When you consider the rigorous requirements of the Parliamentary Standing Orders it is surprising how little thought had been given to the crossing of the Tamar. Trundling trains down ramps on a gradient of 1 in 10 onto the ferry does not seem to have rung any alarm bells with Moorsom. Each carriage of the period weighed over 7 tons. Light as this may seem by today's standards the thought of a breakaway on such a gradient does not bear thinking about. Yet Moorsom proposed that the carriages be run onto the ferry by gravity. Neither did the steep gradients up the Devon side to Eldad appear to have caused him much concern. Under cross examination by Rowe Moorsom reveals a blend of optimism and complacency beyond belief[4] :

7.2 *A broad gauge first class six wheel carriage of the Cornwall Railway typical of what might have been placed on the Torpoint Ferry.* KIDDERMINSTER RAILWAY MUSEUM

Q Now then, supposing you arrive at Tor Point will you tell the Committee how long you anticipate it will take you to get your train in the boat before the boat begins to move?

A I should think rather less than a minute.

Q Do you propose to run your train on with your engine upon the boat?

A Probably not, probably the first mode will be to work it by letting the engine stay there.

Q In so serious a matter as this have you not arrived at a conclusion whether it would or would not be possible to carry your engine across the Hamoaze?

A I never arrive at any conclusion on such an important point until the exact period at which it is necessary for me to make my final judgement.

As witnesses were called for the petition against the bill, the weakness of Moorsom's position becomes all too apparent. Rendel, examined by Rowe later the same day, proved to be a particularly devastating witness about the use of his Torpoint ferry[5] :

Q Captain Moorsom states that the bridge being double he will divide his trains and run one half down the rails on one side and the other half down the other to get them upon the bridge. Do you think it convenient and practicable, regard being had to wind and tide, and the circumstances which you have spoken of as affecting the bridge?

A I think it would be a very inexpedient plan. I think it might be accomplished infinitely better.

Q Do you think that the plan suggested might even be attended with dangerous consequences?

A The objection that I feel to it is that at all times and especially in rough weather there will be no possibility of bringing the rails which would be laid upon the deck of the bridge into such immediate contact with the rails laid down over the plains as to make it at all safe to attempt to get the trains in that manner. It would require altogether an amount of control and management and for persistence which could make it altogether an inexpedient plan.

Q I am sorry to put such a question to you Mr Rendel as it may appear to a man of science bordering on the absurd, but I am obliged to put it – in your judgement could the process which Captain Moorsom speaks, of dividing the train and running it down and putting on board in 2 portions, be done in a minute?

A I cannot conceive it possible.

Q Do you think it could be done in 1 or even 10 in the way I have described it?

A I think there are circumstances that would prevent it being done even in 10 ...

Then, cross examined by Kinglake:

Q As a practical engineer having had your attention called to the line of communication by which you propose that the Railway should be conveyed across at Torpoint, was it not your proposition that it should make a circuit round by Saltash?

A That was my advice.

Q Taking into consideration the expense and such other considerations as must come into the making of a railway, should you not be inclined, if your opinion was asked, to recommend a (floating) bridge of the sort you were describing, at Saltash for a railway?

A No, I should not.

Rowe sows further seeds of doubt in the Committee's mind as he examines Bidder[6] :

Q Do you concur in the opinion which was stated to the Committee that the loss of time in passing according to the manner proposed by Captain Moorsom, even with the bridge used by Mr Rendal [*sic*], which he says is infinitely better, would be increased by a loss of about fifteen miles run?

A Even contemplating that a complete arrangement could be made by which the carriages could come on the boats always at the same places, I think the better thing would be to take the passengers out of the train and put them in the boat. I should take them over and put them in fresh carriages that I think would be the plan that will be resorted to and I think it will be done with a saving of time when you consider the difficulty of taking carriages weighing five, six or even seven tons upon the boat, even with all the mechanical facilities which can be applied there must be a great loss of time and I am not sure in the end that the passengers will be transhipped.

Q Should you think it undesirable, if you could avoid it, to cross by boat in any case?

A I would go a great deal round to avoid such an inconvenience.

Robert Stephenson, examined by Rowe was even more forthright[7] :

... I repeat that in crossing any river of that kind that the stoppage, and the inconvenience, and the influence (of the) weather, and many other objections which may operate together, I have no hesitation in saying that those will make it equal to 15 miles going round; as you cannot put two large ponderous masses like that upon a boat and freight them over in the manner proposed without great difficulty.

The ever alert Rowe asks Brunel[8];

Q Do you think there would be any danger in running your train through the boat into the Hamoaze?

To which Brunel, no doubt thinking of the opportunity of building the bridge, replies:

A I think, and decidedly.

And finally, of the engineers, Locke hammered home the point[9]

Q ... it has been suggested by Captain Moorsom that his trains having arrived at the Cornish side he proposes to break the train in two and run three carriages on one rail and three on another, down into this double boat, in your judgement can that arrangement be carried out with convenient practice?

A A floating bridge cannot be considered a convenient thing for a railway, and therefore it cannot be carried out conveniently. It is a thing which I would go a great many miles round to avoid.

Q Now then, following that, will you allow me to ask you whether you think the process of dividing the trains and running those carriages upon such a bridge by gravity and being hard to the wind and weather and tide one that you could accomplish in a minute?

A No, certainly not.

Q May I assume 5 or 10 minutes for it?

A At least.

Q Now we have heard the distance across and the mode of transit that has been mentioned here. Taking all of these circumstances into view what do you suppose would be the loss of time by the Railway in passing the ferry?

A I should say in practice it could not be done in less than half an hour.

Rowe then leads Lemon in confirming that the crossing should be avoided altogether:[10]

Q Do you know that in addition to the 20 miles of increased distance that the passage of the Hamoaze, including the putting of the trains on the boat and taking them out was estimated by engineers of great knowledge as equal in time to 20 miles of railway run?

A There were many different estimates given; it was computed so differently by different engineers that I cannot say. Some conjected it would be only 7 miles some others I think said 3/4 of an hour.

Q However I take it for granted there must be a delay of some time?

A Yes.

Q And it is an obstacle very much to be avoided if it could be done?

A Yes, quite so.

Q I believe it is an obstacle highly objectionable to a very large portion of the County of Cornwall?

A Yes.

Q Have you any doubt of that?

A No.

Rowe then draws this admission from Moorsom:

Q Do you consider the passage of the Hamoaze to be a matter of considerable inconvenience to the Railway?

A It would be much better to go on dry land if it could.

Apart from the inconvenience of using the ferry a further deterrent of the New Passage route must have been the formidable gradients on the Plymouth side. This was summarised by Moorsom under cross examination by Rowe[11].

Q Now Captain Moorsom I am going to direct your attention first to the pink line between the New Passage and Eldad and to ask you this, whether you have an inclination of 1 in 30?

A Yes, on the Eldad extension I have an inclination of 1 in 30.

Q Is that on the 64th mile and 4 furlongs?

A Yes.

Q At the 65th mile have you an inclination of 1 in 30, 1 in 40 for 3 furlongs?

A There are 2 inclinations I think after the 65th mile but both that - 1 in 40 and 1 in 30 in the same extension line.

Locke, normally a proponent of steeper gradients, commented:

Q Will you look at the gradients going up from the water to Eldad?

A Yes.

Q They are very severe I believe?

A Yes.

Q 1 in 29?

A Yes.

Q Will you tell the Committee if in your judgement those gradients can be worked at so many miles an hour with safety?

A I have already stated that in my opinion it cannot be done on a gradient of 1 in 40, and of course on a gradient of 1 in 30 it would be still more dangerous.

There can be little doubt that the strength of objection to using the ferry, with its consequent gradients, by such a strong team of technical experts effectively doomed the bill.

It is at this point, on 2 June, that Rowe introduces the idea that a high level bridge at Saltash would be more desirable than the ferry. He presumably understood that such a concept was at the limits of technology and beyond the budget of the Company. One can conjecture that he felt that this requirement would sink the southern route and play into the hands of the supporters of the central line. However he reckoned without the combination of the muscle of the Great Western Railway and the inventive genius of Brunel to save the southern route. He examines

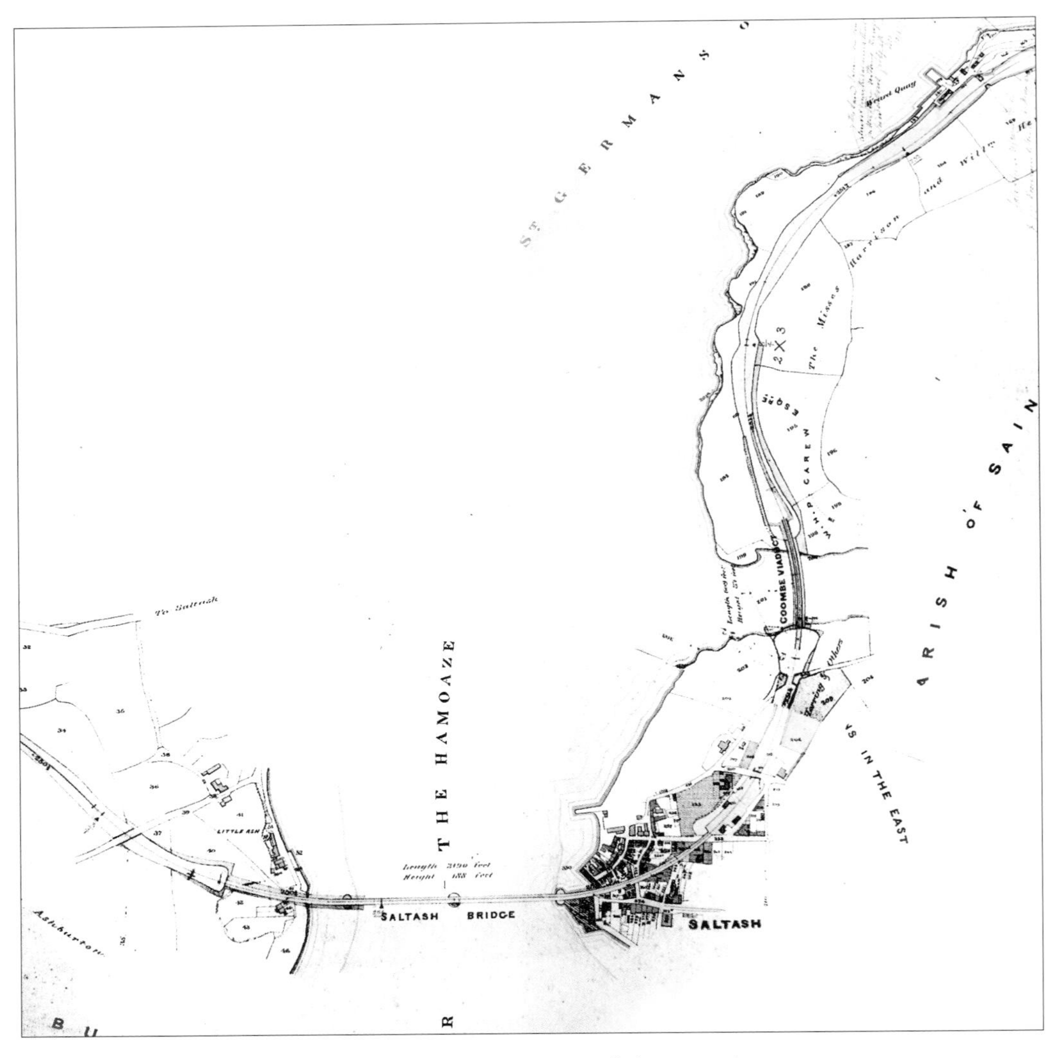

7.3
The parabolic alignment of the railway across the Tamar allows a panoramic view of the Hamoaze.

Pendarves, an ardent supporter of the central route:

Q Do you know the character of the river at Saltash?

A Yes

Q Would a high level bridge there give great facility in commanding the level westwards?

A Of course it would.

... and on re-examination Pendarves confirms,

Q Allow me to ask you upon that point with regard to this matter, if you have belief that a line other than this line to Plymouth avoiding the Hamoaze and going by Saltash might meet with favour and support in Cornwall?

A I think it would ... I believe the Hamoaze is a great objection for many purposes and is to me I know.[12]

The Provisional Committee reacted smartly to make sure that the option of a bridge was included in their Bill the following year. The Parliamentary Committee, faced with a choice, specified that the crossing should be by a bridge even though it was far from clear what sort of a structure might be possible. The prospect of a bridge at Saltash raised a range of new issues not least the question of whether such a bridge could actually be constructed. Following the success of the Bill, Brunel promptly began investigating the bed of the river. Despite the post-mania recession which halted progress on the rest of the line, work continued on the preparatory work for the bridge. The survey of the river bed was completed in March 1848 but construction only started in May 1854 with the floating out of the 'Great Cylinder'. Brunel had hoped to finish the bridge in 1857. In fact it took another two years in no small measure because of the bankruptcy of the contractor Charles John Mare. The bridge was finally opened in 1859 along with the rest of the railway from Plymouth to Truro.

Smith in his speech at the opening ceremony, summarised how the idea of a bridge gradually supplanted that of the ferry:[13]

On coming to Saltash it was proposed to cross Hamoaze by the very simple means of the steam-bridge like the one now in use only longer and more powerful to carry over a train of steam carriages. They applied to parliament for an act of incorporation for that line of railway and encountered a very formidable opposition; the most powerful arguments of their opponents were brought to bear upon them and it was represented to Parliament that it would be very much better to cross the Hamoaze by a bridge. The Cornwall Company never projected the bridge, but Parliament no doubt influenced in a great measure by the objection to crossing the Hamoaze by a steam ferry, and after a large sum of money had been expended would not sanction the plan. The directors had in another session of Parliament to reiterate their application and it then became a serious question what they were to do. Were they to risk another application to Parliament, and another large sum of money in fruitless application, or were they to adopt the suggestion that a bridge should be made – a thing without which it would be useless to go to Parliament? After the most careful consideration they adopted a course which I think was most proper. They went over the whole site of the line to half-way between Liskeard and Plymouth, had a very careful survey made, and suggested two plans to Parliament, but again recommended the ferry. I don't speak in jest. I don't utter a sneer when I say that the wisdom of Parliament overruled their recommendation; for the ferry was condemned and the bridge sanctioned. Parliament inflicted a serious cost on the company, but the result has been a beautiful and substantial structure.

THE DESIGN OF THE BRIDGE TAKES SHAPE

Just as Moorsom seemed to have had little idea about the practicalities of using the ferry so a year later Brunel appeared remarkably vague about the bridge at Saltash. It is described in the 1846 Bill as:

> Viaduct 360 yards, central arch 250 ft span and six arches of 100 ft span all 70ft high.

Such a structure would have borne little relationship to the Royal Albert Bridge as subsequently built. There seems to have been some precedent for passing bills where the single most formidable engineering work had not been fully resolved. The Chester and Holyhead Act was passed on the assumption that trains could pass over Telford's Menai suspension bridge. When it was realised that the bridge was not suitable for railway traffic Parliament was found to have passed an Act 'leaving a gap in the communication across the Menai Straits to be filled up by the construction of the necessary link.'[14] The precedent of the Britannia Bridge enabled Parliament to approve the Bill even though little detail was available. In view of this precedent the Parliamentary Committee on the Cornwall Bill of 1846 were prepared to approve the Bill even though the details of the crossing of the Hamoaze were far from complete.

However the Cornwall Railway Act of 1846 goes as far as possible to define the nature of the crossing in the absence of a detailed design from Brunel:

> Be it enacted that the said railway shall cross the river Tamar at Saltash by a bridge to consist of four spans only with strait soffits all with spans and all be of such dimensions together and construction as shall be previously approved of by the Lord High Admiral or the commissioner for executing that office of Lord High Admiral, such approval signified in writing under the hand of Secretary of the Admiralty and that said bridge shall not be constructed until working plans and specifications of that same shall have been deposited at the Admiralty and approved of in like manner.

Brunel first alluded to the possibility of a bridge when examined by Kinglake in 1846.

> Q With reference to the crossing of the Hamoaze we have heard that there is an alternative line by way of a bridge crossing the Tamar at Saltash. Is that so?
>
> A Yes, the only means of avoiding the crossing of the Hamoaze, if it were considered objectionable, appeared to me on an examination of the country to be to cross at Saltash by means of a fixed bridge.[15]

However under cross examination by the ever persistent Rowe, he seems to know remarkably little about whether it was feasible to construct a pier, or piers, in deep water in a tidal estuary. This had never been done before and there was no guarantee that it could be achieved. Nevertheless it is quite surprising that Parliament was prepared to approve the Bill without further convincing evidence that the bridge was a realistic possibility.

Q How many piers will you place in the deep water?

A I do not exactly know yet. That depends on the Admiralty. I imagine about 4

Q According to your plans and sections?

A According to the plans and sections there would be five.

Q In the first place, I take for granted you have taken the soundings?

A Yes.

Q Take if you please the centre pier. What is the depth of water there: high water?

A I am afraid I have left all the sections of Saltash at another place. There are about 40 feet from low water mark. (*This is clearly an understatement*)

Q And the others will be how many feet from low water mark?

A I cannot speak from recollection ...

Q Do you get at once to rock or many feet of mud?

A Generally speaking, at once to rocks. The bottom of the river is rough where there are light holes. There is gravel and sand upon rock.

Q These things have been done under your superintendence?

A Yes.

Q It is suggested to me that where your centre pier will be placed you have about 15 feet mud to get through before you get to rock?

A It is not so.

Q You have had borings made?

A I have had soundings made.

Q Soundings are one thing and borings are another. Have you had any borings there?

A No.

Q How can you possibly tell whether you have to deal with 15 feet of mud or not?

A The bed of the river is rock there entirely and it is merely where from the irregularity of the form of the river that in certain parts there is a deposit of sand or gravel . . .

Q That being the depth from low water at the centre pier what will be the height of that pier? What will be the height of that pier from low water up to the clear of the Arch?

A About 140 or 150 feet

Q Measuring from low water?

A No, from the bottom altogether.

Q 140 feet up to what?

A Up to the road line. (*Another under-estimate*)

Q The surface of the rail?

A Yes.

Brereton, Brunel's right hand man and ultimate successor in the practice at 18 Duke Street, explains in his paper to the Institution of Civil Engineers, how the design for the bridge evolved[16] :

> It was first proposed, that the bridge should consist of seven openings, one of 250 feet, and six of 100 feet each, of uniform height of 70 feet; but in consequence of objections raised by parties interested in the navigation, plans were submitted to the Admiralty with the increased dimensions of one span of 255 feet, and six of 105 feet, at a height of 80 feet above high water, all to be built with timber trussed arches. The Admiralty, however, required that there should be four spans only, two of 300 feet and two of 200 feet each, with straight soffits, and a clear headway above high water of 100 feet. To comply with these requirements, it became necessary to apply to Parliament, for amended powers, which were obtained in 1847 ...
>
> By this time the construction of wrought-iron railway bridges had become general; and in the cases of the Conway and Britannia Bridges, spans up to 460 feet had been obtained without difficulty. In determining the dimensions of the bridge at Saltash, it was considered whether it might not with advantage, be constructed with only one pier in the deep water, instead of three, as would have been necessary for the spans required by the Admiralty; and the experience obtained of the nature of the foundations, having shown that the rock was favourable for the construction of the piers for a span of 465 feet over the western half of the river, designs were made in 1850 for a bridge with two main spans of 465 feet each. In 1852, when it was determined to proceed with the building of the bridge, it was considered practicable to reduce the spans to 455 feet each. The drawings from which the bridge was executed were prepared accordingly, and early in 1853 the work was commenced.

Brereton's paper is primarily concerned about the centre pier of the bridge. The President, Hawkshaw, who chaired the meeting of the Institution of Civil Engineers on 11 March 1862 expressed the hope that the author would give an account of *the manner in which the superstructure of the Saltash Bridge had been erected*. Sadly, however, he never did.

BUILDING THE ROYAL ALBERT BRIDGE

Before work could start on the Royal Albert Bridge the bed of the Tamar had to be thoroughly surveyed to find firm foundations. The iconic superstructure is justifiably well known. However the real pioneering work was the building of the centre pier which is hidden under water. This work proceeded on investigating the bed of the river whilst everything else had ground to a halt following the financial crisis. The construction of the whole Cornwall Railway project was to depend on finding firm foundations for the centre pier of the bridge. The company minutes suggest some anxiety about this. At that stage the design of the

7.4 *The Devon truss being floated into position in the autumn of 1858.* STEAM MUSEUM OF THE GWR

bridge could not be completed without assurances that the outcrop of rock, identified by divers, did in fact exist. On 24 July 1848 Brunel explained:

> ... the Saltash borings and soundings which I have much at heart as most important to the future prospect of the Company[17].

The technique for carrying out the survey was to suspend a wrought iron cylinder 6 feet diameter and 85 feet long between two old Admiralty vessels. The cylinder was lowered into the mud, and water pumped out, over the area where, as Brereton explains:

> ... on a thorough examination of that part of the bed of the river where the centre pier would probably be built. He is able to report that the bed of the river for a space of 50 sq ft had been carefully examined by 175 borings.

William Glennie reported on 25 May 1848:

> Yesterday evening I had the satisfaction of standing on the mud at the bottom of the Tamar and examining it minutely.
> NB. I did not forget to smoke a cigar at the bottom of the river!

Accordingly Brunel was able to complete the design work before construction of a much reduced railway restarted in 1852. The sinking of the construction cylinder did not take place until 1854 and the completion of the work inside was achieved in October 1856.

This part of the operation took 2½ years and was the longest single stage of the construction. Binding suggests that the completion of the pier rather than the superstructure was responsible for the overrun in costs from £162,000 to £225,000.

On 7 August 1848 Brunel reported:

> With the view to our future proceedings when the time may come for carrying on the works – it will be a very great relief and add much to public confidence if we have determined every thing connected with the bridge at Saltash – ascertained the exact state of the rock at the points which appear likely to be suitable for the pier and proved the practicability of getting down to the rock through a cylinder such as we are using for the soundings and borings and of keeping the water out if need should arise by closing that cylinder and using it as a diving bell. I am strongly of the opinion that ... the works for determining the character and practicability of the Saltash bridge are the most important and will be of the greatest value to the Company when the good times come.

On 26 August the Committee resolved:

> That the sum of £350 be placed at Mr Brunel's disposal and which Mr Glennie has stated to the Board will be sufficient for the purpose of completing the examination of the bed of the river at Saltash so as to enable Mr Brunel to determine the nature of the structure and expense of its construction which will be required to carry the line across the Tamar.

Six months later Brunel was able to report to the Directors:

> We have succeeded in making a detailed examination and minute survey of the work which would form the foundation of the centre pier of the bridge; and by ascertaining the exact state and form of the surface have been enabled to determine the proper site for the pier and have satisfied ourselves of the excellent quality of the rock. This survey has been effected and most accurately at a depth of about eighty feet below high water mark and as is well known in strong current.
>
> Having determined most satisfactorily the nature of the foundation we have also tested the efficiency of the plan by which it has been proposed hereafter to construct the pier and I am happy to say that nothing could have proved more satisfactory or more completely have realised my most sanguine expectations.
>
> By sinking the cylinder through the tenacious clay which covers the bed of the river down to the rock we have on several occasions made immediately a simple and almost perfectly tight coffer dam from which we have withdrawn the water and have been able to descend and examine the bottom at leisure. On the last occasion in order to complete the experiment we cleared away the clay and excavated two or three feet into the rock which was exceedingly tough and sound and built down some masonry before removing the cylinder ... The success which has attended our trials here will I think have amply repaid the exertions and expense incurred and by removing all doubts upon this important part of the line will I trust considerably increase the probability of an early renewal of the works.

Reading between the lines, the Board shares the sense of relief, expressed by Brunel, that the bridge could now be confirmed as feasible. The Board was now faced with another two years of frustrating inaction because of the ongoing financial crisis. Not until May 1852 was the Board able to instruct Brunel to obtain tenders for the construction of the bridge. The board also authorised him to purchase the links of chain manufactured for the Clifton Suspension Bridge some 20 years earlier for the sum of £8 per ton. These chains provided fewer than half the number of links required to complete the Royal Albert Bridge. One can only speculate on Brunel's feelings about the irony of the situation. 'Clifton, my first child, my darling', as he had described it, had been on ice for twenty years. Buying the chains must have seemed like its death sentence. (It was completed but only five years after Brunel's death by Hawkshaw and then to a much simplified design and using the chains from Brunel's Hungerford footbridge.) However these self-same chains now enabled his last bridge to be completed. The final design for Saltash was completed by the end of October 1852 and the ill fated contract with Mare (1815-1899) was concluded at the start of 1853. On the face of it he was the ideal contractor. He had set up the Thames Ironworks on Bow Creek with every modern piece of equipment for metal work fabrication. On the strength of these facilities he had constructed the box section tubes for Robert Stephenson's Britannia Bridge across the Menai Strait.
On 4 February 1853 the Committee reported that:

> Mr Brunel concluded contracts with Mr Mare for the completion of the Saltash Bridge, foundations and approaches for the sum of £162,000 and that Mr Mare had agreed to take 1,000 shares at £3.15/- discount in part payment of the sum stipulated to be paid.

And on 23 February:

> Towards the iron-work of the bridge, considerable progress has been made with all the preliminary works; a lofty and substantial scaffolding is constructed for the purposes of the erection on shore of one entire span. The pontoons for sinking the cylinder and subsequently floating the Bridge, are nearly completed. The cylinder itself is nearly ready for launching and preparations are making for floating and sinking it. Like other works in iron however, very great delays are caused by the great difficulty experienced at the present time in obtaining materials.

On 24 May 1854 Brunel reported:

> The Directors will be glad to hear that our preliminary operations of floating off the cylinder and sinking it in its place have been very fortunately & successfully completed. We pitched it on Saturday morning and with the help of a remarkably quiet state of wind and tide – fixing or rather ascertaining the position of the Bottom – and fixing it when we had obtained the right

> position and by the excellent - the perfect – assistance of all engaged we succeeded in pitching the bottom at the place required with a degree of accuracy which must of course partly be the result of fortunate accident – but which was approached by the means I have referred to.

However financial storm clouds were gathering and Mare was suffering cash flow problems in the face of rapidly rising costs of both labour and materials and was pursuing Brunel for £10,000 on account.

As Brunel discretely put it on 22 February 1855:

> The rather strong measures we took and which a little alarmed me have turned out in every respect right - Mare as you have seen has 'stopt payment' or at all events come to such a pass as to justify any proceedings for securing ourselves and we can do him no harm – than he has done himself.
>
> It is a serious matter and one which I suppose will involve a meeting of the board as soon as Mare's position is clearly settled. I believe myself that he cannot fail to become bankrupt – in which case we must take possession of the works and carry them on. If he is not made bankrupt his creditors will I apprehend throw up the contract, either by arrangement with us or without it.

Brunel urged Bond to handle the matter sensitively. In September he wrote:

> I have not referred to the reports current as to Mr Mare's pecuniary difficulties. We need not increase them by talking of them if they exist and, if they do exist, we must take great care not to afford him any just grounds for saying that we have done anything to embarrass him or to afford any excuse for his relinquishing his contract. I wish particularly to impress upon you, however, that I have no knowledge of the existence of any such difficulties; or of any probability of his seeking to avoid carrying out fully his contract. But when such reports are current we must prepare for the possibility of their being true and my advice under such circumstances is to take great care not to do anything that can be interpreted into a hostile act or which could provoke a contractor to throw the work on your hands before his bankruptcy and thus compel you to take some steps for the mere protection of the works, which might destroy the contract, and put you at the mercy of the assigneer. If he is in difficulties and should unfortunately fail we can take possession of the works under the contract without any notice, and be tolerably well protected; but if, contrary to the terms of the contract, we interfered or took possession before he became bankrupt, I don t think we should have any such protection.

Mare went bankrupt in October1855. There are two possible reasons for this, one prosaic and the other colourful: The surge in inflation to 15%[18] and the overrun on the central pier explain the difference between his estimate of £162,000 and the eventual out-turn of £225,000. However the alternative reason is that, having just won a contract to supply ironwork for Westminster Bridge it is said that he put his advance on a horse at the Derby and lost![19]

Despite these problems work had been proceeding. On 2 August 1855 the Board received this generally encouraging report:

At Saltash the works of the Bridge have proceeded slowly but still successfully. Shortly after the last half yearly meeting, the excavation for the foundation of the center [*sic*] pier having been carried to what appeared after careful examination to be a sufficient depth. The masonry was commenced and although the carrying on of work under a pressure of three to four atmospheres has proved a tedious operation – a complete ring of masonry 35 ft in outside diameter and varying from 6ft to 9ft in height has been built upon the rock and forms the foundation of the pier.

The year 1856 began with the laying of the masonry in the body of the cylinder which was completed in October after which the iron columns were erected to receive the trusses.

The Times reporter[20] summed up the problems of the deep water pier:

> It is however, on the main pier, in the centre of the river, on which both the great spans rest that all the pressure and vibration comes and for this was required a tower of such proportions that nothing short of the solid rock itself would suffice for its foundation. But to reach this was a matter of no ordinary difficulty in as much as some 70 feet of sea water, with 20 feet of mud and concrete gravel lay between Mr Brunel and the stone on which he wished to build. A cofferdam for such a depth and in such a tideway was out of the question, yet by a novel application of the cofferdam principle what seemed an insuperable obstacle was overcome. An immense wrought iron cylinder of boiler plate, 100 feet high and 37 feet in diameter and weighing upwards of 300 tons, was made and sunk exactly on the spot whence the masonry was to rise. From this the water was pumped out and air forced in; the men descended, and working as in a gigantic diving bell at the very bottom of the river, cleared out the mud and gravel till the rock was reached and hewn into form to support the cylinder evenly all round. Powerful steam air-pumps were necessary to keep the labourers supplied below, and as a matter of course they worked at an atmospheric pressure of upwards of 35lb to the inch. At first this affected them severely; many were constantly seized with cramps, faintness and insensibility, but this was only at the commencement, and after a time 40 labourers could remain at once in the large diving apparatus with apparently little inconvenience. But it was always dangerous and unpleasant labour, and all were glad when the first great difficulty was over, and the noble columns of granite, built inside the cylinder, rose above the water's edge at last.

In contrast to the problems of the pioneering construction of the deep water pier the erection of the superstructure went smoothly. Using the

7.5 *The recently completed Royal Albert Bridge* THE EDWARD HAMER COLLECTION

experience of the earlier bridge at Chepstow and through meticulous planning Brunel and Brereton were able to complete the formidable tasks of raising the two trusses, 455 feet long, through100 feet to time. *The Times* was able to report:[21]

> The enormous iron tube, which with the rail attached weighed 1,100 tons, was this afternoon successfully floated by Mr Brunel from the Devon side of the Tamar. Shortly after 3 o clock one end was safely lodged on the Cornish side and the other on the pier in the centre of the river.

Nine days later the Board reported:

> That this Board desires to offer its congratulations to Mr Brunel on the successful and satisfactory result of the important operation of transferring the western section of the Royal Albert Bridge from the Company's yard to its position across the river.

On 23 February 1859 the Board reported that:

> ... the second or Eastern Span of the Saltash Bridge, which was floated into place in the middle of July (1858), has been raised to its full height and the piers built up; this was accomplished by extraordinary exertions by the middle of December last, since which the lifting machinery and engines have been removed, the flooring of the Bridge completed and the ballast laid. The

> remaining piers of the side openings on the Eastern shore which could not be proceeded with till after the Bridge had been floated away have since been finished and the superstructure raised and completed and in two or three days the Bridge will be tested by the running of heavy trains across it ... Saltash Bridge having been completed sooner than was by many expected.

However just before Christmas 1858, Brunel had been advised to go abroad for health reasons.

SUCCESS AT LAST

It was hardly surprising that the press was euphoric about this major engineering achievement and icon of the west even if it was an expense without which the company could have done. This was an occasion for considerable pride as the *Royal Cornwall Gazette* recorded that the Chairman had been unstinting in his praise for Brunel at a 'Dejeuner' held at the council chamber in Truro on the day after the official opening[22].

> We have heard a great deal of late – and the longer we live the more we do hear – as to the span which united the counties of Devon and Cornwall, the Royal Albert Bridge. I have heard very strange opinions as to the origin of this bridge; there are some very wise individuals who in places of public resort are remarkably fond of dogmatising on this subject, and who will tell you, as one told me a few hours ago, that this grand and marvellous structure is due to the ambition of Mr Brunel. In an evil moment he was tempted to raise up a monument to his engineering ability that should astound the world. He has done so. He has completed a work which will yield him world-wide fame and will be talked of in every part of the globe and in every department of language. Depend upon it people who attribute that bridge to such a cause are utterly mistaken. Some say that the bridge proves nothing but a reckless, uncalculating determination of the Board of Directors, and that having once determined on such an erection they stuck to it regardless of expense. There is no more truth in that than in the other rumour.
>
> Parliament inflicted a serious cost on the Company but the result has been a beautiful and substantial structure ...
>
> As long as ever the Bridge stands it will be testimony to people of every period and country of one of the first men of the age. We cannot look at the structure without amazement at the great mechanical ability and vast intellectual power which exists in the man who excogitated [*sic*] that grand work and carried it to a successful completion. Mr Brunel needs no eulogies from me, or you, or Cornwall; his monument is raised.

May 1859 was a good month for Victorian engineering as, in addition to the opening of the Royal Albert Bridge, Big Ben was first started on the 31st. These were, indeed, exciting times in the civil engineering world.

FROM MENAI TO THE MERSEY VIA SALTASH

At the 1846 Parliamentary hearing there had been much discussion about both the predecessor of the Royal Albert Bridge, the Britannia Bridge and its successor, the Runcorn Bridge. These three bridges are seminal in the technical thinking about railway bridges with long spans. The question is often asked: Why, when the Royal Albert Bridge is an acknowledged masterpiece, was its design not followed elsewhere?

The Times[23] reporter stressed the scale of the advance that the Royal Albert Bridge was over the Britannia:

> About eight years ago all England was talking of, and Europe wondering at, the importance and magnitude of that great engineering work, the Britannia Bridge. Since then viaducts and bridges of all kinds and sizes and each one possessing one or more features of peculiar difficulty have been erected without notice or comment. We have grown accustomed to the great strides with which our engineers have advanced, and look with comparative indifference on what in other countries would be regarded justly as national works, the standard of what their mechanical and scientific skill could ever accomplish. There needs no greater proof of this than the case of the Saltash viaduct, now nearly built, but with which we have no doubt the majority of our readers are so little acquainted as perhaps to be even unaware of the precise part of the United Kingdom in which Saltash is situate. Nevertheless, in this obscure little village near Plymouth, a bridge is being raised across the Tamar which is second to none in the world and which in size and engineering difficulties of construction far surpasses even that of Angelsey.

So the Royal Albert Bridge represents a significant step in the design of railway bridges. In the nine years since the completion of the Britannia Bridge, Brunel had achieved a significantly lighter structure. Walters explains[24] :

> While, if the Saltash Bridge be compared with the Britannia Bridge, it will be noticed that the greater economy of the form is due to the metal being concentrated along the lines of strain, which is claimed as a peculiarly American practice, but it was only introduced by Mr Brunel in 1859.

He describes the Britannia Bridge as 'structurally primitive' whereas the Royal Albert Bridge is 'considerably more advanced'. However he also points out that 'despite its virility, it sired no progeny'.

The subject of the Runcorn Bridge had come up at the hearing into the Cornwall Railway Bill in the context of the clearance required by the Admiralty. '... at the time Committees were sitting on the Runcorn Bridge they had an idea that a ship canal might be made up to Manchester'. The possibility of a canal had been around for several years and, even though the Manchester Ship Canal was not to be opened for nearly another half century, headroom had to be provided for sea-going ships.

7.6 *Standardised lattice girders which could be erected in situ proved to be the way forward. Runcorn Viaduct was the next estuary crossing after the Royal Albert Bridge and used this much simpler technique. From* THE ENGINEER *29 June 1866.* INSTITUTION OF CIVIL ENGINEERS

The Runcorn Bridge was started in 1863 and completed in 1868 by William Baker, the Chief Civil engineer of the London and North Western Railway[25]. It was a significant advance in that the close mesh lattice girders offered greater rigidity than the suspension system at the Royal Albert Bridge and had the advantage of being assembled from standardised parts. Furthermore, the complications of floating out completed trusses were avoided by erecting them in situ. Runcorn was a considerable step forward in long spans in that it demonstrates a more rigid, less complex and cheaper system than either Britannia or the Royal Albert bridges.

These three major bridges demonstrate the advances of civil engineering techniques. Whilst the Britannia and the Royal Albert Bridge were pioneering and unique structures in their own right it was the lattice girders of Runcorn that were to provide the model for many future railway bridges.

The tubes of the Britannia Bridge were destroyed by fire in 1970 but both Runcorn and the Royal Albert Bridge are still with us in their original form. The latter still carries all current types of trains and loads which include High Speed Trains and mineral trains. There is a 15 mph speed limit. Listed Building consent was granted in 2010 for a £10m major refurbishment with particular attention to the hangers and the diagonal, longitudinal and cross bracing. The most difficult part of the refurbishment concerns the point where the vertical hangers are attached to the main tubes where corrosion has occurred and has given trouble over the years. The restoration will involve remaking these joints. Apparently they can only be inspected by abseiling and even then only a finger tip investigation is possible. The full extent of corrosion is not therefore known. Thirty coats of paint on the wrought ironwork will be removed by grit blasting for the first time in the life of the bridge. It will be repainted in 'goose grey'. The guiding principle of the restoration will be to replicate the original detail as far as possible.[26]

Even after the pioneering engineering success of bridging the natural barrier between Devon and Cornwall this was far from the end of the Company's troubles. It was to face years of financial struggle.

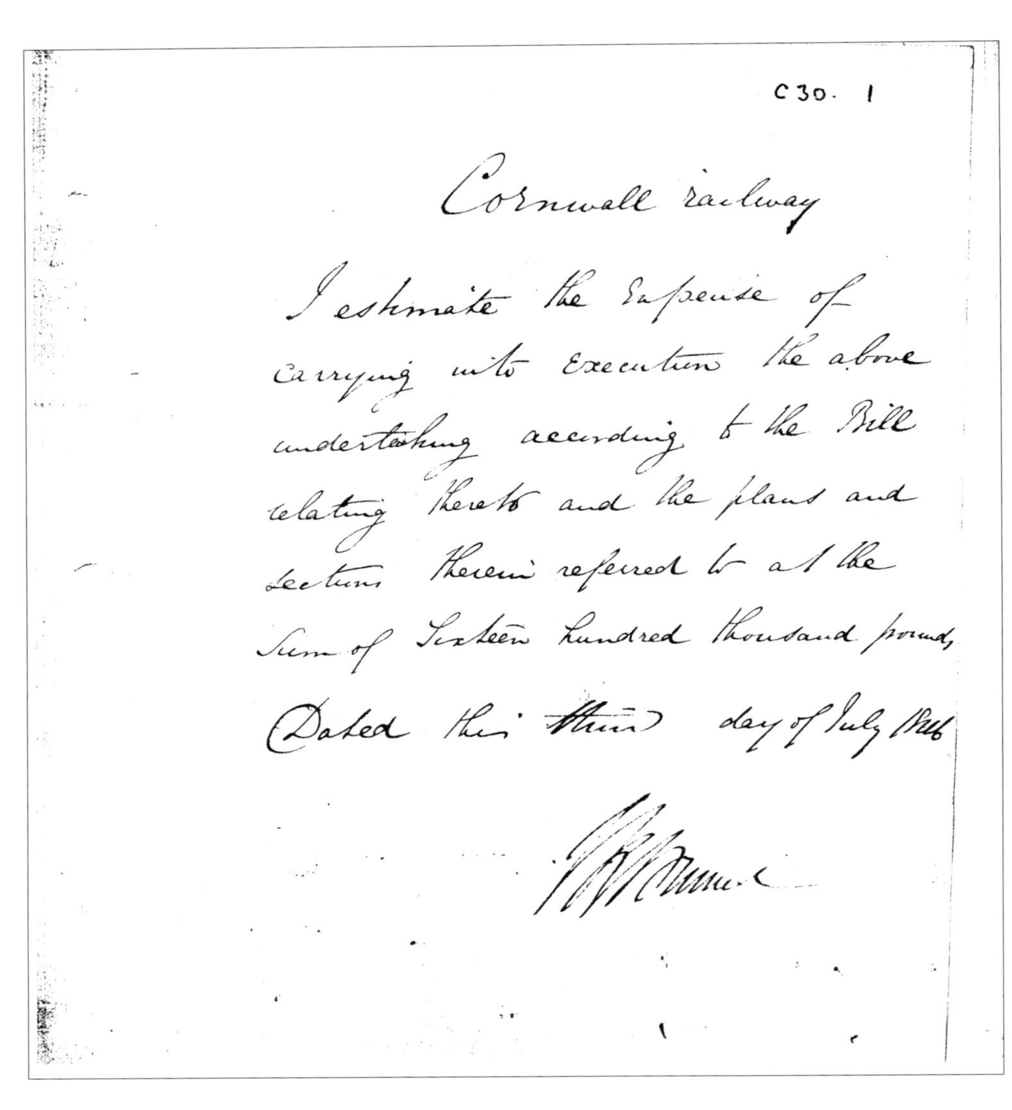

C30. 1

Cornwall railway

I estimate the Expense of carrying into Execution the above undertaking according to the Bill relating thereto and the plans and sections therein referred to at the Sum of Sixteen hundred thousand pounds

Dated this third day of July 1846

I K Brunel

8.1 *Brunel's 1846 estimate for the Cornwall Railway*

CHAPTER EIGHT

... ON BUDGET, ON TIME?

> I estimate the expense of carrying into execution the above undertaking according to the Bill relating thereto and the plans and sections therein referred to at the sum of Sixteen Hundred Thousand pounds
> Dated this third day of July 1846
> I.K. Brunel

Brunel's estimate for the Cornwall Railway was a simple document on two sides of quarto. It was deposited on 4 July 1846. His estimates provided much discussion in the select committee and were shown to be far from accurate.

One of the problems facing the cash-strapped Cornwall Railway Company was that of obtaining an accurate estimate of the cost of the project. The art of large scale contracting, as pioneered by Locke, was at that time in its infancy. The Company was faced with a range of estimates for building the railway. Moorsom's calculation of £1,000,000 was based on a scheme involving heavy gradients and sharp curves but comparatively little in the way of civil engineering works. His estimate amounted to £16,000 a mile for the 63 miles from Plymouth to Falmouth. As it was to use the existing steam ferry no allowance was made for crossing the Hamoaze.

As soon as Brunel, never one to overestimate the cost of engineering works, replaced Moorsom as engineer to the Cornwall Railway Company in 1845 he promptly indicated that Moorsom's estimate should be increased to £1,600,000 to provide for branch lines. This consisted of £839,000 for the main line and £761,000 for the branches which, ironically, were soon to be the subject of abandonment orders.

The Company was not alone in finding that the out-turn was at variance from the estimates. The cost of railway building had already shown a wide variation. The original Great Western main line had cost £56,300 per mile (Brunel's original estimate had been for less than £20,000 per mile) and the London to Birmingham £53,100 per mile as landowners understandably drove some hard bargains. Brunel's estimate for the Cornwall Railway would have worked out at just under £14,000 a mile. This is perhaps characteristically low, bearing in mind that his

8.2 *Isambard Kingdom Brunel 1806-1859*
STEPHEN K JONES COLLECTION

estimate was for a double track line which involved heavier engineering works than Moorsom's. The details of the estimate as submitted to the Parliamentary Committee in 1846 were:

Main Line Falmouth to Torpoint	
Earth work 6 chains 470,000 yards	£292,083
Bridges culverts	£101,750
Tunnels 2,358 yards run	£90,000
Ballast fencing £5,800 per mile	£55,250
Sub total	£839,083
Moorswater and Caradon Branch	£3,429
Penryn Branch	£2,056
New Passage to Eldad	£20,891
Carvedras to Newham	£6,597
Padstow Branch	£106,841
Launceston Branch	£250,910
Land	£196,274
Stations and contingencies	£173,919
Total	£1,600,000

Locke was called to give evidence about Brunel's estimate and threw doubts on it:[1]

Q ... you told us you were not satisfied with Mr Brunel's estimate, you did not tell us the amount in which you differed?.

A In round numbers for the whole of the line and upon which of the estimates I think there will be a difference of £400,000.

Q And have you the details by which you get at that?

A I have the whole details. Mr Brunel's estimate I understood was £1,600,000. I make the estimate for the same work £2,045,000.

Q Does that include the bridge at Saltash?

A No it does not.

Q That you put at something like £140,000?

A There was an alternative line. There is a considerable difference in the alternative line.

Q I am not taking the line by Hamoaze but the line by Saltash.

A I thought it was fair to state it by the Hamoaze as Mr Brunel's estimate states it by the Hamoaze after having shewn that comparison. I state if the Saltash deviation be taken it will cost £233,000 in addition.

8.3 *Joseph Locke 1805-1860*

He recalculated Brunel's figures and in a *'Comparative Estimate of the Cornwall Line'*. He opined that this total should have been £2,045,504 for the Torpoint line. Using his estimates this would suggest a figure of £18,770 per mile for the main line.

Proceeding to the estimates for the line as a whole Locke, in his characteristically painstaking way, has gone through Brunel's estimate and identifies significant underestimates:[2]

Q Have you gone over the estimates sufficiently?

A I have.

Q Have you any details there, any figures?

A In the first place I have taken the section and I have had the quantity of the earth works accurately measured and I make a considerable difference in those quantities and I differ also with Mr Brunel as to the price at which that work can be executed.

Q Now take the quantities first.

A The quantity I take to be 8,300,000 instead of 6,500,000 as stated by Mr Brunel.

Q By the committee. Of earth work?

A Yes.

Q How do you get at that?

A By accurately measuring the section of Mr Brunel as accurately as it could be done.

Q Cubic yards?

A Cubic yards.

Q That is the only way you could get at it?

A Of course it is.

Q That is the only way any engineer ascertains the work to be done that is by the measurement of the section?

A It is the price of the earthwork. I differ also with Mr Brunel that I see here. Taking the total quantity and dividing it by the money it comes to 10d 3/4d [a] cubic yard. In a country like Cornwall where there is a good deal of shale and rock I think it is more difficult to excavate than ordinary land gravel or earth such as is usually met with and I have estimated that 15d 1/2d a yard.

Q What has he his at?

A 10d 3/4.

Q Is 10d 3/4 the average price in a country where the material is much better?

A It is rather less from 11d or a shilling would be about the average in a sandy clay or moderate soft earthy country. In Cornwall where there is a good deal of rock and a good deal of shale there is no doubt the excavations will cost more money.

The greater part of Cornwall is primary and secondary formation. It is in reference to the tunnels, I find according to the length and the total quantity estimated for those tunnels, it comes to £38 a yard. My opinion is those tunnels will cost £50 and on this side of Exeter Mr Brunel himself I know has estimated £60 and £50 a yard for tunnels and therefore I cannot see why they could be made cheaper in Cornwall.

There is a report of a meeting in Cardiff in November 1844[3] at which Brunel gives some figures on the cost of tunnelling: Box Tunnel had cost £100 per yard, White Ball Tunnel £59 and Cheltenham Tunnel £34. The feature is headed *Diminished Cost of Railways – Tunnelling* and Brunel indicates that within the previous three weeks he had contracted for tunnelling at £28 per yard.

No allowance seems to have been made for purchasing the Hamoaze ferry from Plymouth Corporation, a matter that had been under discussion as is revealed by the examination of Philip Protheroe Smith, Company Solicitor to the Cornwall Railway:[4]

Q I wish to ask you whether you have contracted to purchase the ferry at Torpoint?

A Yes we have entered into a provisional contract.

Q Will you be kind enough to give me the date of the contract near about?

A Executed with an agreement last year.

Q And the same abides?

A And the same abides with some variation.

Q And the same price?

A I think I may say the same price, there is some little difference between the lessee and proprietors as one year more has elapsed in reference to the price generally. You may take it the same.

Q £66,000?

A No pardon me – not so large a sum, £52,000 subject to a question as to £5,000 – a legal question which I referred to in my examination last year.

Q £52,000 absolutely and with a contingent payment of £5,000 more?

A Yes.

From the evidence presented by Locke it would seem that Brunel's estimate for the route by the Hamoaze, of £1.6m is out by at least £440,000 in addition to which there would be the cost of purchasing the ferry of £57,000. The total cost of this line would therefore have been £2,097,000.

Brunel's estimate for the line with the 'Saltash Deviation route' was £1,836,897 which included the £40,000 for the bridge:

Alternative Line by Saltash

Earth work 1,296 chains 670yds	£59,000
Bridges and culverts	£84,379
Permanent way including Ballast and fencing at £5800 per mile	£63,800
Land	£29,718
Total	£236,897

The additional cost for the 'deviation', according to Locke would be £233,776, which gives his total cost of the railway at £2,279,280. However his estimate for the bridge of £140,000. His final figure would have been an additional £100,000 giving a figure of £2,379,280, or £37,800 a mile for the whole line.

In view of the uncertainties of the costings surrounding the projected railway it is perhaps surprising that Parliament was prepared to approve the scheme. Just as the engineering deficiencies of the 1845 Bill had been enough to destroy any prospect of Parliamentary success, so, one might have expected that the manifest shortcomings in financial planning to have sunk the 1846 Bill. However this did not happen. The railway was somewhat unusual in having low land acquisition costs and high civil engineering costs and one might have thought that under these circumstances Locke's evidence might have carried more weight than it did.

In 1851, at the height of the financial crisis, Brunel provided an estimate of £850,000 for a single track railway without branches, a figure which included the bridge. This represents a cost of £13,400 a mile. The final bill on the opening line which included an only partially completed line between Truro and Falmouth was £1,491,324 11s 11d[5]. Taking out the cost of the bridge the Cornwall Railway had eventually cost £22,580 per mile for a much reduced specification. The Royal Albert Bridge had increased the cost by £3,930 per mile to £26,500. At the time that Brunel made this estimate the costs of building railways were low because very little building was taking place. There was surplus capacity in both the markets for materials and for labour. Furthermore land owners in Cornwall were prepared to settle cheaply to the company. By the late 1850s construction was picking up and costs were rising rapidly which, to some degree, accounts for the overspend. It is little wonder that Smith and Tweedy had 'talked over the whole matter and have retired to bed as dark as midnight as to the future and not known what steps to take' and, no doubt, spent sleepless nights on the project.

ESTIMATES FOR THE SALTASH BRIDGE

Budgeting for the Saltash bridge had proved to be an even wilder exercise than for the main line. If Brunel's early designs for the bridge had been controversial his estimate caused astonishment. In all fairness only Locke comes up with a realistic figure based on his experience of estimating for the construction of the Runcorn Bridge. He produced an accurate estimate for the bridge right from the outset. If we exclude the costs of the very long approach viaducts, it is exactly the same as the final cost of the Royal Albert Bridge i.e. £225,000. Both bridges required deep foundations. However, the multiple piers at Runcorn required to take a double rail track were less deep at 40 feet and were completed by using unpressurised cofferdams. The single pier at Saltash for a single line required a much deeper pier, at 90 feet below water level for which this technique would have been inappropriate. There was no precedent for the cost of the deep water pier which was where the overspend occurred. Because of its pioneering nature it was to be the biggest single underestimate.

Brunel's estimate of £40,000 is staggeringly optimistic and was received with astonishment by Rendel, Locke and Bidder. Rendel uses the precedent of his own design for a suspension bridge at Saltash and Bidder considers his bridge over the Medway to illustrate how inaccurate Brunel's figure must be.Brunel is cross examined by Rowe on costs of the Saltash Bridge:[6]

Q This is important to enquire into now as I find upon the alternative two lines for Saltash that you return as your estimate £84,379 for bridges and culverts. Does that include the large viaduct or bridge at Saltash over the Tamar?

A Yes.

Q Will you be kind enough to tell me how much of that sum is to be attributed to that bridge over the Tamar?

A £40,000.

On the basis of the following evidence one can almost hear a collective intake of breath in the committee room. Bidder, for one, cannot resist some irony:[7]

Q You are aware that there exists a material difference of opinion between Mr Locke and Mr Rendel on the one hand, and Mr Brunel upon the other, as regards the expence of that bridge?

A Yes, very much so.

Q Do you agree with Mr Rendel and Mr Locke that the bridge could not be constructed for £40,000?

A Most decidedly. If it can be done for that, all I can say is it is a pity the discovery had not been made many years ago. We should have saved many millions of money in this country ... If there is a scheme for building that bridge at that cost, all I can say is that it is the most valuable discovery of the age!

Rendel, too, can hardly contain his disbelief.[8]

Q You being skilled in these matters do you think that such a bridge Mr Brunel proposes could be constructed for £40,000?

A For what!

Q For £40,000?

A A bridge of the description here given?

Q Yes he has said so.

A Not by any means that I am acquainted with. I think there must be some mistake ... I do not know any means by which a bridge of this description can be built for £40,000.

8.4 *The sheer complexity and expense of building the Royal Alabert Bridge can be gained from this engraving of Brunel and Brereton overseeing the floating of the first tubular truss on 1 September 1857.* BODMIN TOWN MUSEUM

Q What was your estimate?

A I think the lowest estimate for the bridge at Saltash (*referring to his own design*) was at £85,000; that also as I said before a suspension bridge spanning the entire opening calculated only for road traffic. I wish to explain the great difficulty there would be in building a bridge at Saltash in grounding the piers in such a depth of water, the low water spring tides – there is the difficulty.

Kingslake cross-examined Rendel who provided the most realistic estimate for the bridge but still underestimates the final cost. This is unsurprising bearing in mind that his proposal for a bridge at Saltash had been for a suspension bridge with a long central span which would have obviated the need for the central pier.

Q You have been asked something about the proposed bridge [at] Saltash? Is that rather a visionary scheme in your judgement?

A Why I should say it is so, as some years ago I made a design for it.

Q Would it be a very expensive affair? May I say it would cost £100,000?

A Yes, or £200,000.

Locke under examination does not disguise his disbelief in Brunel's estimate:[9]

Q Mr Brunel has given his estimate for that bridge at £40,000 do you consider that sufficient?

A No I do not.

Q Mr Brunel's bridge is proposed to be one of seven arches, or if he adopts the Government view of four arches and spans of 300 feet in the centre arches. Do you think £40,000 will be enough?

A I do not believe you could build any bridge at all for £40,000 across there.

Q What do you think it would be?

A Why, that would depend upon the height. £140,000 would be much nearer the mark I think – I have made an estimate for a similar bridge for crossing the Mersey at Runcorn this year for a Bill which has passed the Committee of the House of Commons of the height of 100 feet above high water. That was the height fixed by the Admiralty and that bridge although it is built on rock in the tideway which is dry at low water, the cost of it with its approaches was £225,000...

Q You say you think such a bridge and that which Mr Brunel has proposed himself could not be erected for less than £100,000 more than he has put to it?

A That is my very strong opinion I have not made an accurate estimate of the cost of this bridge. I believe it would turn out to be even larger than that. I have not made that estimate and therefore I feel with reference to this particular bridge I cannot speak with so much certainty as I can with reference to the other parts of the estimate.

The Britannia Bridge had cost £602,000. If the Royal Albert Bridge had been completed as a double track bridge the final cost would have been an additional £100,000, giving a total of approx £325,000. It seems clear from this that Brunel had given a lot of thought to building a cheaper and lighter bridge than the Britannia. The advance in terms of lightness and cheapness of construction is something for which Brunel is rarely given credit. Simmons is one of few authors to recognise this. He takes a favourable view of Brunel's approach to his clients' finances:

> The price of iron, when the Chepstow bridge was built, was exceptionally low. The first three of these bridges (Conway, Chepstow and Britannia) all carried a double track. The cost of the Saltash Bridge was reduced by £100,000 through restricting it to one track only, in order to meet the Cornwall Railway's financial difficulties. On the other hand that bridge including its approach on the west side was substantially longer than the Britannia. It seems fair to say that in each case, with the smaller and the larger works, Brunel's cost about half as much as Stephenson's. Berridge attributes the difference to the much tighter control that Brunel kept over his work. But it must also be remembered that Stephenson's work preceded Brunel's and that Brunel therefore had the great benefit of his friend's experience.[10]

On the debit side his initial estimate for the Royal Albert Bridge of £40,000 appeared absurd to other engineers at the time. Also his estimate of £850,000 for the construction of the single line railway, including the Saltash Bridge, proved woefully inadequate.

The problems of a single major engineering work absorbing a high proportion of the total budget for a line is illustrated by the comment of one potential contractor:

> The proposed bridge at the Tamar at Saltash must be abandoned or it will swamp the undertaking as a paying line – as the Britannia tubular bridge over the Menai Straits has the Chester and Holyhead Railway.[11]

The Birth of Project Management

Joseph Devey's book, *The Life of Joseph Locke*, was published in 1862 just after the deaths of Brunel and Locke. It therefore enjoys an immediacy and provides a perceptive insight into the financing and engineering issues of the day. Although the author's sympathies clearly lay with Locke it nevertheless illustrates the difference of approach towards contracting between the two. Where he refers to *'the delusions practised on other lines'* he may well have been referring to lines engineered by Brunel.

Brunel (1806-1859) and Locke (1805-1860) were almost exact contemporaries. Yet their approaches to railway engineering and to budgeting were very different. There is no doubt that Brunel was an engineering genius who relished the challenges that nature had put in the way of his railways. He seems to have thrived on a degree of risk in overcoming these obstacles. Devey describes him as the 'Michaelangelo of Modern Engineering'.[12] Locke, on the other hand, avoided major civil engineering works if he possibly could[13]. His avoidance of tunnelling wherever possible, for example, reduced construction costs at the price of steeper gradients than had hitherto been attempted. On his line from London to Southampton there are several long deep cuttings which reflect his dislike of tunnels. As Devey puts it:

> Upwards of 16,000,000 cubic yards of earth had to be removed; for Mr Locke disliked tunnels, and had recourse to them only when no other means could attain his object; for steam, operating upon an imprisoned atmosphere, generated much carbonic acid gas, which was not particularly calculated to improve the health of the passengers.

He might also have added that long tunnels had acquired a reputation for overrunning their estimates as Brunel's experience at Box and Robert Stephenson's at Kilsby had shown.

Locke also tried to avoid the heroic bridges and viaducts that so appealed to Brunel. He has several excellent structures to his credit, the Weaver Viaduct, the initial designs for the Runcorn Bridge and the Penkridge viaduct. He had seen how the Britannia Bridge had pushed up the cost of the Chester and Holyhead Railway from £38,000 to £45,000 per mile. Devey summarises the difference between the two engineers:

> ... but it was a principle of his (Locke's) that nothing should be called into existence which did not subserve the public interests to such a degree as to make them remunerate the projectors for the capital invested in its creation. Railways and steam-ships, with Mr Locke, were commercial speculations; hence, if they failed to pay, they ought never to have been constructed. With Mr Brunel, public roads and carriages ought not to be constructed, or arches raised, unless one can be made to look luxurious, the other lofty, and the third imposing. The profit was of minor consideration.

And Rolt, writing nearly a century later says:

> The brilliant Isambard Brunel was a perfectionist with little concern for the pockets of shareholders. Locke showed too much concern for them.

Brunel provided a tribute to Rendel[14] which said more about the author than the subject of the comment! It concluded with the following somewhat equivocal judgement . . .

> He was always considered a safe man – one who would seldom do anything that he had not, or others had not done before – and this is, strange to say, a recommendation with men of business, who do not understand engineering. But it is quite clear this quality is not the characteristic of a Smeaton, a Stephenson or a Watt, or the world would make no progress.

Locke's Grand Junction was notable, when it opened in 1837 for being the first trunk line in Europe. It had been built on time and within its financial estimates. It was in marked contrast to the lines mentioned above as it had only cost £14,000 per mile. This was partly due to the comparative lack of engineering works, partly to early agreement with land owners on acquisition costs, partly to his efficient attention to detail but most of all to his contractual arrangements. Locke's particular skill was as an organiser. He closely controlled contractors and expenditure and, unlike many contemporaries, completed his lines on time and within estimates. His experience of contracting the Penkridge viaduct had been an object lesson. One contractor had submitted an estimate for £26,000. When Locke had revised the specification the same contractor tendered for it at £6,000. The Cornwall Railway Company was still learning the same lessons some forty years later when they were tendering for the replacement of the Moorswater viaduct they received tenders for between £35,000 and £56,000. Peter Margery, the resident engineer, paid detailed attention to the specification and found that the work could be done 'in house' for £28,520.

Locke had been critical of George Stephenson's estimates for the Liverpool and Manchester Railway. This had lead to a major falling out between the two on the Grand Junction Railway. The Directors recognised Locke's superior estimating techniques and dismissed Stephenson from this project as explained by Devey:

> On account of the wasteful expenditure incurred by this hand-to-mouth system, the Manchester and Liverpool line cost upwards of a million, while it need not have cost more than half the money. Owing to these sad experiences, Mr Locke decided to let all his works to large contractors by open tender; and, influenced by his recommendations, the directors of the Grand Junction and of the Sheffield and Manchester unanimously determined that no work should be done by private contractors but that a bond should be taken from every person employed. It was a constant principle upon which Mr Locke subsequently acted, to test the accuracy of his estimates and save shareholders

from the delusions practised on other lines, by getting responsible contractors to undertake the work under the cost and the time named in the specifications, and to guarantee its execution by depositing with the directors 10 per cent. of the capital at stake, which they agreed to forfeit in case of violating their engagement.

Locke's contribution to civil engineering was in sound contractual arrangements which meant that his projects were delivered on budget and on time. Rolt[15] goes as far as to say ... he probably exercised a greater influence on railway engineering... than either Stephenson or Brunel . He entered discussions at an early stage into estimates with a limited number of well tried large scale contractors. Thomas Brassey is the best known of these.

Devey leaves us in no doubt about how the process of contracting changed over the years. His book shows that Locke provided a blueprint, the main element of which was a detailed specification, which was to serve the civil engineering profession well.

Most biographers of Brunel in recent years have been critical of his approach to what today we would call project management. He would not have scored highly in delivering projects 'on time and on budget'. Vaughan, for example, describes his estimates and contracting practices.

The contractor arrived at his price for a job by simple arithmetic – he estimated the cubic yards of earth to be moved or piled, the number of bricks required, and the number of horses. There seems to have been no allowance, or inadequate allowance, made for additional costs owing to bad weather or unforeseen difficulties, and as a result a contractor frequently got into financial trouble ... Isambard employed far too many low calibre contractors and as a result spent far too much time supervising their efforts to the detriment of his proper work and indeed his health.[16]

Contractual problems are cited by Dr Smith as the main cause of delay:

Other mishaps have followed, but except for the failure of the contractor for the works between Truro and Falmouth, which has had the effect of postponing that part of the Line, none of these misfortunes have interfered with the progress of the railway. The contractor for the Royal Albert Bridge, Mr Mare, failed, but the gigantic undertaking was steadily carried on.[17]

As a result of these practices Brunel's estimates were far too low and the contractors were unable to build to his indicated costs. He was not alone in dealing with such contractors; of the thirty contractors engaged on Stephenson's London to Birmingham apparently ten went bankrupt. It was estimated that, at that time, no contractor could estimate his costs closer than to within 25%.

So, how well did Brunel respond to the financial constraints on the Cornwall Railway?

He does appear to have made two decisions which were more in the Locke tradition. It was unfortunate that neither achieved its objective. The first was to open negotiations with Sir Samuel Peto (1809-1889) who was a well established railway and building contractor. The minutes of Cornwall Railway Company record that on 23 Feb 1847 …

> From the information your Directors have received from Mr Brunel they have the satisfaction to state that an offer has been made by an eminent contractor to construct the whole line including the Saltash Bridge on terms which your engineer considers it will be decidedly advantageous to accept and which will ensure the early completion of the works.[18]

And three months later:

> Received a letter from Mr Brunel dated 17th instant stating that he had arranged a preliminary contract with Mr Peto. The time for the completion of the works being entirely under the control of the company so as to adopt the progress to the means.

Peto had won the contract for the Wharncliffe viaduct at Hanwell on the Great Western Railway. There had been disputes over payments and Peto appears to have found Brunel 'overbearing and inconsiderate'. Maybe this is why these discussions seem to have faded out when the financial crisis put an end to hopes of building the line in the immediate future. This seems to support Brindle's contention that 'Brunel seems to have treated most of his contractors with an air of haughty disdain'. Peto may well have seen that the economics of building the line would be difficult, profit margins small, and feared a succession of disputes with Brunel[19]. He may also have realised that he might have to accept a substantial payment in shares which were hardly likely to yield any significant dividend.

The second of Brunel's decisions was to engage C. J. Mare to build the Saltash Bridge. Mare was another experienced engineer with a business in Greenwich. He had successfully built the Britannia Bridge and was therefore a strong candidate to build the Royal Albert Bridge. Unfortunately he underestimated the cost by £58,000 and, in consequence, went bankrupt. He had agreed to take 1,000 shares (presumably £20 shares) at a £3.15s discount in part payment for the sum stipulated.

With the failure of these two initiatives Brunel and the Cornwall Railway Company were forced into taking a far more direct involvement with the construction of the railway than should have been necessary to the worry and detriment of both. He employed a number of small contractors for the 60 miles from Plymouth to Falmouth whereas one might have expected Locke to have let a contract to one large contractor. They were Messrs W. and H. Drew (Plymouth – Saltash, 3 miles), Messrs Ritson (Saltash to east of Liskeard, 10 miles), Messrs Sharp and Sons (east of Liskeard – Truro, 39 miles). This contract was by far the biggest involving 21 viaducts and five tunnels (Bosvigo, Buckshead, Polperrow, Treverrin and Brown Queen). There were also G. H. Findlater for the 3/4 mile east of Truro including the Carvedras viaduct and Sam Garratt (Truro- Falmouth, 10 miles). The bankruptcy of the latter resulted in a four year delay and the permanent demotion of this section of what was to have been a main line to that of a relatively minor branch. In addition Longmans and Mead were contracted to construct the higher viaducts in the Liskeard area. During his last months Brunel was also far too greatly involved in the day to day tasks of completing the famous Great Eastern steamship. This, too, had given rise to ever deteriorating relationships between engineer and contractor. It also shows up yet another case of gross underestimation. Brunel had estimated the cost of his leviathan at £500,000. The out-turn cost was £920,000.

Nevertheless, given that he had been obliged to employ several small contractors Brunel does appear to have done everything possible in terms of nursing contractors in order to bring the Cornwall Railway project to a successful conclusion. The company minutes reveal the details of the struggle to complete the line. The Directors were all too aware of the potential pitfalls. On 27 October 1852 the minutes record their concern:

> That, as it is most important that the Directors and the public should have the most ample guarantee for the proper completion of this important work the board requests Mr Brunel to consider the propriety of letting the work in such a manner as to preclude any question of divided responsibility; which this Board fears might arise if the work be let in two contracts, without each contractor being answerable for the completion of the whole work.

In a letter to the company secretary dated 15 June 1853 Brunel showed that he was all too aware of the rapid inflation in the costs of both labour and materials.[20] He was finding it inadvisable to let adjacent contracts.

> If one let large contracts adjoining to and beyond this at higher prices and to be completed at the same time as there is already work going on this side of the line the consequences be inevitably a rise in wages. Amongst his men and increased difficulty in obtaining men – we should run the risk not only of injuring Mr Sharpe (the contractor for Truro to St Austell) very seriously to the extent probably of compelling him to stop but in all probability of breaking up the entire length of our line the cheap system on which we are now proceeding.
>
> What I propose to meet these difficulties - is that Mr Garratt should not commence work till after the harvest and that he should then proceed only with the works of tunnelling and a certain limited but gradual increasing quantity of earthworks and masonry during the next twelve months – very little ultimate delay will be caused by this arrangement and I should hope that serious consequence of a sudden demand for labour in a rather remote district may be avoided.

Unfortunately this policy of delaying the less urgent works backfired on the company. Whatever the benefits to the cash flow were offset by inflation which meant that the final costs were higher than they would have been if the works had been completed when materials and labour costs were lower.

Only a month later on 22 July 1853 the Board received a further letter from Brunel concerning the impact of inflation on the works and whether to agree to contractors exceeding their contracted prices:

> I have to lay before the Directors a subject of considerable importance for their consideration, a circumstance having occurred which might have exercised a very serious and injurious effect upon our proceedings but which I trust may be almost entirely prevented if the arrangements I am about to recommend are approved of.
>
> I have for some time past been expecting and fearing that our Contractors would find it impossible to execute at the prices of the contract owing to the great and rapid rise in wages and the prices of most materials and although temporary variations of this sort must of course be at risk of the Contractor yet it would be useless to hope that large contracts extending over two or three years would be carried on at a constant loss and indeed our contractors would not of course be able to do it even if they were willing.
>
> Mr Sharpe after one or two appeals has written and come to me himself in Town to represent that he was working at loss and that his means would be shortly exhausted, when of course he must stop and whilst he would be ruined by such a course he should gain nothing. I am as well aware as he is that such is the simple fact. The question therefore to be considered is also a very simple one. It is cheaper for the Company to make such an increase in price as will just enable a willing and active man to proceed with the works or to force this man to become a bankrupt and have the works stopped and thrown into confusion and to be obliged to relet the works as well as any extension of them after having let the world know both Contractors and workmen that prices have risen very much, I have no doubt, and I believe nobody can doubt, that it would be most important to prevent these difficulties.

Sharpe had contracted to build the line from the junction with the West Cornwall Railway to St Austell for £90,200, or £4,500 per mile. Under this arrangement a contractor would take shares as part payment of the contract. He would then raise a loan on these shares. This was a fairly common arrangement but one which exposed contractors to difficulties in raising loans should the share price fall. Brunel says:

> I shall assume that we wish them to take 10 or 15% of the total amount in share.

This is presumably what Sharpe had agreed to. Under these far from satisfactory circumstances the Board had little option but to agree to fund the shortfall as the lesser of the two evils presented by Brunel. However the Board requested that:

> he will as far as possible obtain such security as may prevent any further difficulty with the Contracts and ensure the rapid prosecution of the works.

Their request was in vain because only fifteen months later the problem had not been solved. On 27 October 1854 the minutes record:

> That the attention of the Engineer be drawn to the fact that the payments on account of the Truro and St Austell contracts already exceed the contract price by the sum of £5,108 exclusive of the falls on the shares held by the contractors and the reserve amounts, and that the Engineer be requested to afford to the Board some explanation on the subject and to inform them whether the expenditure on other contracts is likely to be similarly in excess as the Board regard with great alarm the probability of the cost of the works exceeding the contract prices.

The consequence of these failures by contractors was to throw additional management burdens on Brunel's office at 18 Duke Street. On 25 July 1856 the Board made another attempt to secure a grip on costs which had been out of control for some years:

> Mr Brunel be requested to prepare a careful estimate of the probable sum which will be required to complete and open the line from Plymouth to Truro as early as practicable

Project management skills were in their infancy in those days. Unfortunately subsequent history of major public infrastructure projects is an all too well-known succession of underestimating and cost overruns. The lesson was learned the hard way and it was the misfortune of the Cornwall Railway Company that its project had not been tackled with the degree of rigour on which Locke would have insisted. It suffered from having several relatively small contractors struggling in a period of high inflation with inadequate contingencies. It leaves the intriguing question: How would Locke's techniques have coped with the peculiarly difficult circumstances of building a railway through Cornwall in the 1850s? The promoters of the 'central line' must have looked ruefully at the financial problems that dogged the Cornwall Railway Company during the prolonged construction period and early years of working and perhaps wondered how much they would have benefited from Locke's approach to management. One unintended consequence was that the unrealistically low estimates for the southern route must have appeared more attractive than the more reliable but higher estimates for the central route. This does begin to show why the Cornwall Railway Company ran into such financial problems. Clearly the company was the victim of inflation, unreliable estimates and unsatisfactory contracting techniques.

9.1 *Carvedras viaduct, Truro, seen from Victoria Gardens.*
MICHAEL MESSENGER COLLECTION

Chapter nine

'... STRUGGLING FROM ITS VERY INFANCY ...'

George Smith, Chairman of the Board

At last the way was open to begin building the Cornwall Railway. The Directors lost no time in convening their first meeting on 18 August 1846. They felt:

> ... it is of the greatest importance to the interests of shareholders and the public that the line should be constructed with as little delay as possible.

By the following January they had received a letter from Brunel that he was ready to proceed. Although the Board had started work with such alacrity in 1846, by 1847 the national financial crisis meant they had to bring the work to a halt not to be resumed again until 1852.

However, only two years after obtaining the Act the tone of Treffry's report to the Board reflected an increasingly grim situation:

> Your Directors regret that the change in the monetary affairs of the Kingdom which they anticipated when they last met you has not yet produced such an effect as to justify their prosecuting the works on a more intended scale
> The discredit which has been unjustly thrown on all Railway undertakings however sound has necessarily pressed with greater weight on such companies as have made comparatively but little progress in their works: and, as there appeared no prospect in any improvement at any early period sufficient to justify your Directors in calling on you for any amount of capital that would enable them to prosecute the works with vigour and economy, they have deemed it right to give directions for the suspension of all further operations for the present.[1]

It was to take thirteen years to complete the project: a completion which involved much compromise to the extent that the completed railway was far from what its promoters had hoped for and envisaged. It would take many more years before it was brought up to anything like a proper standard.

What a contrast with the early railways which were built under much more favourable circumstances! The Liverpool and Manchester, the London and Birmingham, the Grand Junction and the Great Western had all been built at a time when capital was plentiful and when it would yield a good rate of return which the railway companies were able to offer. At that time overspending on budgets was not a prime concern. It was, indeed, a time when architectural extravagancies could be indulged in, like the western portal of the Box Tunnel on the GWR and the Euston Arch on the London and Birmingham. In contrast, construction of the Cornwall Railway was dogged by sheer lack of funds. Economies had to be sought which included abandoning branches and installing only a single track. When construction resumed in 1851 it was in the middle of a financial crisis linked to inflation, spiralling wages and costs of material.

Share capital was the normal means of financing railway projects but in the case of the Cornwall Railway nearly a quarter of the capital was provided by the Associated Companies. The railway was only completed with a great deal of help from them and by delaying parts of the project as late as possible in order to improve the cash flow.

As the *Royal Cornwall Gazette* reported[2] :

> For a very few weeks after the passing of the Act, there was every prospect of the undertaking being carried out rapidly to completion. A general Railway panic then set in, which brought down the shares of the best Lines to one half, or less, swept away all doubtful or bubble-schemes and compelled the suspension of almost all new undertakings, however solid and approved. In the latter class was the Cornwall Railway, whose shares became unsaleable, and which was obliged to wait for many years, watching in hope for better times.

Even in February 1848 Brunel had reported to the Directors in a thoroughly positive manner without any forewarning of the impending crisis. Work on the tunnels between Truro and St Austell was under way, stone was being assembled at the sites for the viaducts and preliminaries for surveying the bed of the Tamar were in hand. In sharp contrast to this upbeat assessment the first intimations of the financial crisis start to become increasingly evident during 1848.

The gathering crisis

The late 1840s were hardly the best times to start the construction of a railway. The 'Railway Mania' had reached its peak in 1845, inflated by the public knowledge of the large profits earned by railways already working. The bubble had burst. A financial crisis exposed several weaknesses in the system by which railway construction was managed and financed.

So, with the exception of the work at Saltash all work on the line came to a halt for four years. The Company concentrated on 'preserving the works in such a state as may admit of their being resumed whenever circumstances may be favourable'.[3]

It was unfortunate that the Cornwall Railway Company only finally received Parliamentary approval at this time. It had taken ten years to get this far; ten years of argument over the route, the method of traversing a countryside which was unfavourable to building railways, involving the crossing of tidal inlets over which different opinions prevailed. And ten years during which the main purpose of the line, to return lost packet traffic to Falmouth, had become increasingly unattainable. Work had

The Cornwall Railway.
CERTIFICATE OF £50. SHARE.
This is to Certify that Francis Joyce
of 20 Park Road North Brixton London
is the Proprietor of the Share Number 6638 in
the Cornwall Railway Company, subject to the Rules,
Orders and Regulations of the said Company.
Given under the Common Seal of the said
Company the sixteenth day of
December One thousand Eight
hundred and forty six
Registered
No 324
Secretary.

9.2 *A £50 Cornwall Railway share certificate of December 1846.* FROM AN ORIGINAL HELD IN THE GREAT WESTERN TRUST COLLECTION AT DIDCOT RAILWAY CENTRE.

begun promptly but had to be stopped. Shares were forfeited when shareholders were unable to respond to calls and money for the new railway came in very slowly. As Lewin expresses it ...

> the progress of railway promotion and construction was checked, and brought for the time being nearly to a standstill... The abundance of money awaiting investment prior to 1846 gave place to a shortage in 1847... .Under these circumstances railway construction was stopped automatically through the inability of shareholders to meet their calls.

From 1848 onwards the minutes of the Cornwall Railway Company were primarily concerned with the financing of the project; simplifying the engineering, abandoning unnecessary parts of the railway and restructuring the finances to reflect the realities of forfeited and unissued shares, seeking funds from the Associated Companies and dealing with inflationary pressures that were undermining the already strained budgetary assumptions.

It must have been galling for Treffry to have had to write the following report to the Board. His efforts to secure Parliamentary approval had been heroic. Now, on the brink of success, through no fault of his own, he was obliged to close down the project to which he had devoted so many years. His report reflects both the generality of the situation and how the circumstances have obliged the Company to halt any further work for the foreseeable future.

> Your Directors have endeavoured to carry out this object that, while all expenditures for such further construction should at present cease they may preserve the works already completed or in progress in a state to admit of their being resumed as soon as circumstances will permit.

The next report in 1849 shows that the project had effectively been mothballed:

> During the past half year your Directors have steadily acted upon the course decided upon at the time of the last meeting and have limited the expences [*sic*] to such as are unavoidably necessary for preserving the property and conducting the business of the Company[4].
>
> The works already constructed have been preserved from injury during the winter and they are placed under such inspection as will at very trifling expense secure them from danger until it may be decided expedient to recommence operations.

It was not until 1851 that the availability of capital was beginning to improve. However it was not going to be available in the same quantities as before. Economies were going to have to be made. The Company was obliged to simplify their proposals, reduce the capital requirement and to restructure the shareholdings and to abandon inessential branches and connections. The new chairman, Williams, was able to report on more favourable times. Now the need for economy and speed of construction and the use of cheaper and quicker methods was called for.

The following was symptomatic of the state of affairs:

> The Directors, under a feeling that the affairs of the Company would not justify the payment of the remuneration appropriated for their services, have declined, since March last, to receive the amount apportioned to them[5].

Getting the shareholders to honour their obligations was proving to be unrealistic:

> That it appeared inexpedient to make a call at the present time. It is necessary to reduce the expenditure of the Company to the lowest possible amount and that the Engineer be therefore restricted to limit the amount payable in respect of the works to a sum not exceeding £7,000 before the end of August (1848)[6].

In April 1852 the company had felt sufficiently confident to issue a call of 15s on every £20 share. But 18 months later Bond was instructed to write to a significant number of defaulters informing them that proceedings would be taken against them unless they paid up. Their reluctance to do so reflected the poor prospects of uptake of ordinary shares in the Company. And again in July 1854 it was considered inexpedient to try to re-issue the forfeited shares. As late as April 1856 the non payment of calls held by contractors was becoming an issue.

At last, in May 1852, the Board felt able to instruct Brunel:

> to obtain tenders for the construction of the Saltash Bridge at the earliest possible period; that he be requested to proceed with the requisite plans for obtaining tenders for the remaining portions of the line with as little delay as

possible, especially for that portion of the line between Saltash and Plymouth[7].

From the first inklings of trouble in early1848 Brunel had told the Board that he was examining

'minutely every detail in which every indication which can in the slightest degree diminish the amount of work and consequently the cost of construction'.

Three years later he has gone further and produced plans for a railway of much reduced specification. Yet again he grossly underestimated the cost of the project by almost a half. However the directors were satisfied that the line could be constructed for the amount that he had suggested.

This discrepancy is only in part accounted for by the overspend on the deep water foundation for the centre pier of the Royal Albert Bridge and the high rate of inflation during the period of construction. He wrote to the Board on 21 July 1851

Since my interview with Mr P. P. Smith in November last I have been engaged with the assistance of Mr Glennie in most usefully revising all the details of the works determining correctly all the quantities and ascertaining what amount could with certainty obtain the execution of the whole by responsible parties. The result has fully borne out my expectations I confidently exchanged in November.

I have planned of course that no unnecessary expenditure would be incurred that in the first instance, the whole would be laid with a single line of rails but that the provision should everywhere be made for easily extending the works afterwards so as to admit of the double line being added . . . but at the present time the necessity for economy has taught Railway Companies, and the electric telegraph and other improvements now work together to make a single line with great facility and to carry on a very large traffic upon it.

Adopting these views I find that the main line from the junction with the South Devon Railway at Plymouth to Falmouth – including the bridge across the river at Saltash – and including station accommodation – can be contracted for by good and sufficient men for an amount certainly under £800,000 probably under £750,000 – and that I can find good contractors to execute it at that amount or at somewhat less – and who will be able to make arrangements as to the mode of payment which will afford great facilities to the Company. Surely such an opportunity will not be allowed to escape.[8]

The Board resolved that Brunel's report should be sent to the Chairmen of the South Devon Railway, the Bristol and Exeter Railway and the Great Western companies. In accordance with Brunel's recommendation the Directors agreed to construct a single line and also decided to purchase sufficient land to construct bridges and tunnels for a double track, a sensible decision in view of the cheapness of land in Cornwall.

Your Directors have now fully re-entered with renewed and sanguine expectations upon the progress of this great work. They have every reason to be satisfied with the policy which dictated its suspension three years since, and have the high gratification of seeking its completion under greatly improved circumstances and with the fullest expectation of securing for the shareholders a satisfactory return for the capital invested.[9]

However it was not long before further economies had to be made. On 13 April 1852 it was reported that:

The Engineer and Solicitor have offered to assist in the general effort now being made by the Directors, and with that view not to ask for payment for their professional charges, but are willing to allow the amount now owing to them as well as at the amount which may in the course of the construction of the line become due to them except for their actual disbursements, to be applied in payment of calls upon them.

On 2 June 1853 Brunel sets out the financial position to Bond:

I now send you today before the Directors meet tomorrow, the Engineering accounts for the half year ending December 1852 and also for the first quarter of 1853.

The former, as you will perceive, includes what I propose to allow Mr Glennie for the last three years during which time he has been actively engaged as it is proved by the result of our letting of contracts in working up every detail for me, so as to enable me to diminish the amount of work and consequent cost of construction to a minimum.

In the second account the salaries of Mr Glennie and his several assistants are carried out at the amount at which I propose they should be fixed since the more active progress of the work commencing the 1st January last.

I have endeavoured, and shall continue to do so, to study economy in the expenditure upon engineering superintendence. At the same time it must constantly be borne in mind that great economy in the much larger amount expended in the execution of works can only be obtained by considerable labour and skill in the original setting out of the work dependent upon the correctness of detail obtained from assistants, and by great and zealous attention on the part of those during the progress of the works to insure their execution according to the instructions and terms of the contract so that they may be sufficient and no extra quantities be required. Such services cannot be obtained except by the employment of a sufficient number of trustworthy competent assistants reasonably but sufficiently paid.

As regards my own professional charges, I have been somewhat at a loss to know how to make them. I should wish to be governed by the same spirit of economy which is essential throughout this undertaking at the same time I cannot, nor of course, could it be desired that I should deal with the Company otherwise than as a professional man – and in this case there has been a great deal of thought and time devoted to the undertaking generally, which in one single work namely the Saltash Bridge, the result of the thought and consideration of some years is concentrated – What I propose is under the circumstances and in consideration especially of the labour of responsibility attending their particular work to make a fixed charge of £5,000 which (I will take in paid up shares of the Company) and that I should receive also a salary of £1,000 a year during the construction of the railway from April 1852 since which date I have not made any charge.

On 28 October 1853 another letter was read from Brunel which reflected the rise in cost inflation, suggesting that, as timber was at that time very scarce and at a high price, the viaducts between Stoke and Saltash should be deferred. And on 25 November 1853 Charles Russell suggested:

That it seems needful to the Cornwall Railway Board to limit and reduce the Expenditure at present having due regard to their own financial condition of the state of the money market. Such limitation ought to be applied to the works beyond Lostwithiel, commencing works in the mean time with such precedent outlay between Saltash and Lostwithiel as may satisfy all parties that no preference is intended to be given in favour of completing first the Western District of the Cornwall line to the postponement of the railway through the Eastern portion of the County which must be the connecting link of that undertaking with those belonging to the Associated Companies[10].

HAND TO MOUTH ... THE STRUGGLE TO FINANCE THE RAILWAY.

In April 1856, in order to improve the cash flow it was resolved.

That Mr Brunel be further requested to consider to what extent it will be possible to delay the earth and other light works on the contracts between Liskeard and Saltash until such time as the Royal Albert Bridge is more nearly approaching completion and to report to the Board thereon, as it appears that the funds available to the company do not exceed the sum of £80 to £90,000 and more cannot be obtained until some preference shares can be issued which, it appears to the board useless to attempt to do now in the present state of the money market and of the works[11].

On 25 July Brunel provided an updated estimate for the completion of the works from Plymouth to Truro:

Works completion of contracts	£193,000
Superintendence	£25,000
Permanent Way	£120,000
Stations	£20,000
Total required exclusive of interest etc	£358,500

Total estimate required for final completion of Cornwall Railway in accordance with the above

Mr Brunel's estimate	£358,500
Further land, legal expences	£15,000
General expences of office etc	£10,000
Total	£383,500

If there had been 'doubt and uncertainty' on the engineering side this was thrown into context by the doubt and uncertainty of mobilising capital for the project for the seven years after the resumption of work. At times it must have seemed that the Company would go bankrupt and no doubt would have had it not been for the constant support of the Associated Companies. Ultimately it was the gradual deeper and deeper involvement of these companies which enabled the railway to be completed. Essentially the Cornwall Railway Company was such a liability to the Associated Companies that it could not be allowed to fail. The contractors themselves contributed a significant amount more by taking securities in the company in payment for completed contacts.

A device to ease the strain on railway companies was to arrange for a contractor to finance all or part of a line's construction, a common practice during the mid Victorian years, when new undertakings found it extremely difficult to raise capital. Instead of cash, contractors took securities in payment for work done, and either used them as collateral for their own borrowings or sold them, thus effectively acting as underwriters. They could use their shares as securities for loans. However if the value of the shares was lower than their face value, as was the case with the Cornwall Railway, then the contractor was in trouble.[12] Many contractors were at risk of coming to grief over their contracts with the railway companies who found that their projects frequently overran their initial budgets.

This may well have contributed to the downfall of C.J. Mare who had taken 1000 shares in part payment for his contract to construct the Royal Albert Bridge, albeit with a £3. 15s discount.

The Board indicated in more than one case that no further payments would be made for work completed until arrangements were made concerning arrears on called shares. Such were the downsides for contractors of accepting payment in ordinary shares. In any case this kind of threat was hardly likely to encourage contractors to complete their work to standard or to time.

It was becoming clear that neither calling on existing shareholders nor issuing new shares was going to yield enough capital. By the end of 1853 an alternative source was being sought with the increasing involvement of the Associated Companies. The Board was now considering the possibility of leasing the line to one or more of these companies in order to enable the Company to exercise its borrowing powers and to raise the funds necessary to complete the line

Early in 1856 another deputation took place to discuss 'the mode of assistance from the Associated Companies'. On 4 May 1855 an agreement was reached concerning the operation of Cornwall Railway. It was for a seven year lease of the Cornwall Railway to the Associated Companies. Management of line was to be undertaken by a joint committee consisting of four Cornwall Directors and two directors from each of the Associated Companies. In return the Associated Companies jointly agreed to guarantee interest at the rate of 5% on £300,000 of preference stock to be issued by the Cornwall Company with power on the Associated Companies to create such further number of shares not exceeding £100,000 as might be needed for completing the line.

The outcome was a memorandum drafted by Captain Woolcombe (Chairman of the South Devon Railway)[13] :

> It is suggested that for the security of the Associated Companies, the Cornwall Co shall consent that the line shall vest absolutely in the Associated Companies on 3rd August 1858 when the powers will expire if not then finished so as to open for traffic.
>
> That provision be made to enable the Cornwall Co to redeem the property at any time within [blank] years on payment to the Associated Companies of advances.
>
> That the principle of the lease shall be extended so as to make the Associated Companies guarantee the interest on £300,000 preference shares as they have guaranteed the interest on the Debenture Debt, a portion of such shares or of Debentures being impounded to provide for interest till the line produced the amount to cover the Debenture and Preference share interest.
>
> That if necessary in November 1857 application is made to Parliament for extension of time and that in this Act provision be made to enable the Cornwall shareholders to redeem within [blank] years after the Companies take possession. That the above arrangement shall be submitted to the shareholders of the several companies for confirmation at, or as soon after as maybe, the half yearly meetings in February 1857. That in order to provide funds for the vigorous prosecution of the works without interruption or delay the Cornwall directors shall engage to provide as and when required funds to the extent of £50,000 by hypothecation of the amount receivable on the arrears of calls and by application of the cash balances.
>
> That, if the £50,000 be exhausted previous to the time when the general arrangement can be completed as to the issue of the £300,000 preference shares, the Associated Companies shall engage to find a further sum of £50,000 for the prosecution of the works by hypothecation of an equal amount of preference shares.
>
> That as soon as these arrangements can be put into a legal shape for ratification in due course, meetings of several Boards shall take place for the purpose of considering these details.

Meanwhile the Board of the Great Western Railway had sought further to secure the reimbursement of these loans with interest out of preferential shares to be guaranteed by the three companies as soon as the 1857 Cornwall Railway Bill was passed.

In March 1857 the Board received a report on advances from bankers:

> Upon a representation that the Cornwall Company now require advances from their Bankers for prosecution of their works and that such advances may be obtained temporarily as they are required to the extent of £30,000 upon an undertaking that the Associated Companies will secure the reimbursement of those loans with interest out of the proceeds of the preference shares to be guaranteed by the three Companies as soon as the Cornwall Railway Bill shall have passed and the said shares be issued.

It was resolved

> That this Board will join in such undertaking with the other Associated Companies the Cornwall Railway Company agreeing so to reimburse the loan with interest and consenting to place preferential shares to an adequate amount at the disposal of the three Companies in order to redeem such loans until it shall be duly accomplished.
>
> The secretary is instructed to take the steps for giving effect to such resolution.[14]

The outcome was a further Bill submitted to Parliament which duly became *The Cornwall Railway Act 1857*. Its provisions formalised the arrangements with the Associated Companies. It enabled them 'to afford further assistance towards the completion'. It extended the period for completion of the railway. It also enabled the Cornwall Railway company to create £300,000 of Preference stock on guarantee of the Associated Companies. It could now issues new shares in lieu of cancelled or forfeited shares to the amount of £100,000 on requisition of the Associated Companies. However, in the meanwhile the Company's funds were exhausted and bankers were being pressed to release the £30,000.

The darkest hour came six months later. The minutes of the Board meeting of 20 November make grim reading

> '... the funds at the command of this Board are exhausted ... it appears impossible to issue the Preference Stock in such amounts as will meet the requirements of the Company ... that the bankers have declined to make further advances ... the Board will not have sufficient to meet the ordinary demands from this day fortnight.'

On 2 August 1858 at a special half yearly meeting of Proprietors with Tweedy in the chair it was reported that:

> 5000 shares had been created of a nominal value of £20 each and of an aggregate nominal amount of £100,000. These shares as, and when the same

shall be issued, shall bear and have attached to them a right to a fixed preferential interest at such rate or rates not exceeding the rate of £5 per centum per annum payable half yearly as the Associated Companies by whom the payment of such fixed preferential interest is under the provisions of the last mentioned Act to be guaranteed shall require, and that such shares shall be designated as 'Guaranteed Preference Shares' and shall be redeemable at par at the option of the Company at any time on or after expiration of seven years,

It is easy to see that there would be no demand for shares in a company that was essentially bankrupt. A year later the situation was so desperate that the Company sought Counsel's opinion on its financial position. The document reveals the extent of the forfeiture of shares and the sheer scale of the problems faced by the Company. His advice is that there was no scope for applying to Parliament for powers to raise further funds and that the only realistic solution was for the Associated Companies to act as guarantors for the issue of preference shares which is what the Associated Companies agreed to do[15].

I understand the estimated deficiency to be somewhere about £180,000: against this the assets are a sum of about £54,000 of which a portion is the amount retained by the Associated Companies as a guarantee unappropriated of the £150,000 (nominal value of the forfeited shares) ...
There remain therefore the other sums mentioned as alone immediately available and probably the Associated Companies might be prevailed upon to release those sums for the present exigencies of the Cornwall Company if they could be reasonably secured against further calls upon them and feel an assurance that the unappropriated Capital would be applied to making good any further requirements for the Truro portion ...
I think that such an assurance might and ought to be given to the Associated Companies and that the Board should pledge itself to the fulfilment of it ...
I cannot help thinking that a proposal made in the spirit above indicated to the Associated Companies would meet with proper consideration because it is manifestly the common interest of all concerned that the Railway should be opened as speedily as possible and that the monies remaining to be expended should be raised on the most favourable terms
Signed J H Lloyd
1 Kings Bench Walk 5th Nov 1858

The Associated Companies effectively saw the construction phase of the project through to its conclusion with the formal opening of the line on 2 May 1859 and the opening to general traffic the following day. On the face of it this would seem to be the end of the financial nightmare but even after the railway was open the Bristol and Exeter Railway Company indicated that even the preference shares were not being taken up and the Cornwall Railway Company was still seeking advances from the

Associated Companies. Only three months later, in August the Bristol and Exeter Board reported to their shareholders:

> The Cornwall Railway was opened for Passenger traffic on the 3rd May last. The necessary accommodation for Goods Traffic will soon be completed when the revenue will be increased by receipts from that source. The present weekly receipts fully equal the expectations which your Directors had formed and looking at the population and vast mineral wealth of Cornwall it is confidently anticipated that the revenue when further developed from all sources will prove at no distant period adequate to relieve the Associated Companies from the liabilities into which they have entered and will have a margin for the payment both of interest on the additional capital required to complete the line to Truro and of a Dividend to the original proprietors.
>
> The unassisted resources of that Company are however at present insufficient to meet the liabilities on construction account and the per cent Preference Shares to the amount of £15,000 which the Company has created under its Parliamentary powers cannot be issued except at a heavy discount.
>
> Under these circumstances an application has been made by the Cornwall Railway Company to the Associated Companies for a temporary advance of the required sum on the collateral security of the 6 per cent Preference Shares. From a statement of the liabilities of the Cornwall Company it is in the opinion of your Directors a necessary measure of protection to the important interests which you hold in that Company. Your Directors therefore confidently recommend you to sanction this arrangement which they have provisionally approved and which they doubt not you will readily sanction and confirm[16].

At long last the line was open from Plymouth to Truro but only after years of desperate measures to raise the finance to allow the project to be completed. However the company's troubles were far from over. They faced years of balancing a weak revenue stream against the cost of maintaining the infrastructure and paying back these loans and the interest on the preference shares. The Company did not achieve a surplus until 1882 But over and above these daily operational difficulties they had the heavy capital costs of both replacing Brunel's legacy of the timber viaducts, of doubling the track and the prospect, at some time in the future, of replacing the broad gauge. During the lifetime of the company it made substantial progress on replacing the viaducts but the prospect of further capital expenditure on relaying the whole track to standard gauge was to prove to be too much and obliged the company to sell out to the Great Western Railway.

The *Royal Cornwall Gazette* celebrated the opening of the railway with a romanticised description of the route, but starting with a sideswipe at the central route intended to discomfort its rival, the *West Briton*. It is this combination of achievements in adversity and bitter divisions that characterised the story of the Cornwall Railway

Cornwall has suffered material injury and discredit from the mistaken idea of its barrenness, naturally formed from the pictures of desolation along the old road. From Okehampton it skirted Dartmoor and went through a tract of very poor land to the Tamar. Entering Cornwall after a fertile tract immediately west of Launceston it traversed fifteen miles of high and desolate moor land, the Dartmoor of Cornwall and after the end of fertility from Bodmin to Lanivet, crossed nine miles more of desert, the Gorse Moor and then through waste and marshes to within a few miles of Truro. The course of the road as little represents the character of the County, as Dartmoor does of Devon, but the wearied and disgusted traveller did not know this; and it was by this road that all the passengers by the packets travelled to and from Falmouth. No wonder that Cornwall was stigmatised as a West Barbary when such a 'Sahara' was the specimen presented. The present line of Railway will lead to a very different estimate. All scenery, the richest in fertility, the fairest in woodland, the most interesting for unceasing variety and romantic character, the most animated as a picture of science and industry and last not least, for the moral charm is after all the greatest of the landscape, the appearance of order and intelligence in the numerous population and of comfort in their dwellings, will interest and delight the traveller all along the line.
'Ever charming, ever new, when will the landscape tire the view!'
From the station at Plymouth, it runs through gardens and suburban villas to the shore. Here is the marvel of science and skill, the Royal Albert Bridge, with the ancient and romantic looking little town of Saltash in front, and the noble estuary of the Hamoaze, covered with ships of war from the first-rate to the gunboat on one side, and Mount Edgecumbe shutting in the landscape. From Saltash the course runs along the side of the Hamoaze down to the entrance of the St Germains river, and then for five miles skirts and crosses the main stream or the various creeks or inlet, with the hills on either side rich with cultivation and bright with woodland. At one spot a good view is obtained of the ancient and noble ruin of Trematon Castle, certainly older than Domesday Book and possibly as old as the Romans. At St Germains the traveller looks down on the ancient Episcopal See of Cornwall, where Athelstan in 925 planted the Anglo-Cornish Bishopric, and over the rich Park of Port Eliot. From St Germains to Liskeard, the line crosses the succession of deep vallies which extend from the mountainous granite boss of Roughtor down to the sea, each lovely for its beauty of mingled wood and meadow, and seen to the greatest advantage from the bird's-eye view afforded by the flight over the viaducts that span them. Liskeard with the undulating and fertile country around it, is seen to great advantage, showing by its appearance the prosperity it derives from neighbouring mines. From the Moorswater viaduct immediately west of it, the traveller looks down a depth of 148 feet on a busy scene where the canal and railroad connect the mines and quarries to the North with their port at Looe. And now we enter the valley of the Fowey, and what language can adequately describe it, especially as seen from the Line to

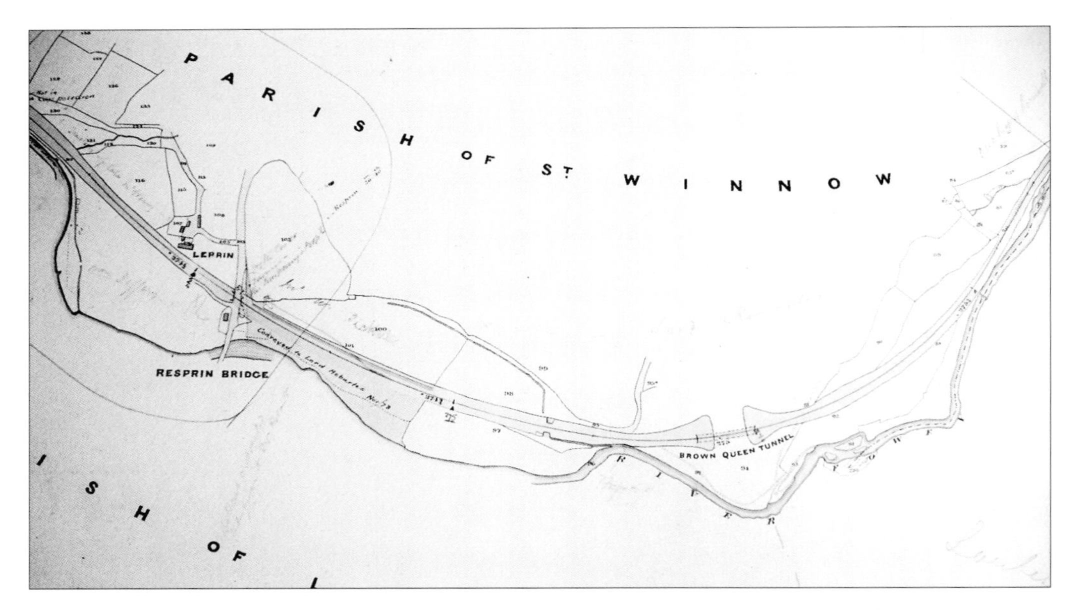

9.3 *The site of the temporary station on Lanhydrock land at Respryn before the completion of Bodmin Road Station.*

> advantage unattainable elsewhere. From high up the side of the hill along the South we look down over the extent of the romantic valley, the river winding far below us, the opposite hills clothed with wood, or bright with blossomed furze, while from time to time the vallies of St Neot, Warleggan, and Cardynham bring their tributary streams down to the Fowey, and open as we pass them extensive views shut in by the hills to the North. From time to time, a hollow indented in the hill whose side we skirt is spanned by a viaduct, and we look down at the tops of the trees below. Passing Glynn, with beautiful woods, but a house utterly unworthy of such a situation, and which the owner has considerately provided for hiding from view, by stipulating that the directors of the Company shall plant it out from sight.

There had been a long running dispute with Lord Vivian of Glynn about the construction of this station. In March 1859 the Company was able to announce that ... 'his Lordship desired to remove the restriction which prevented the Company from making a station for the public at Glynn Bridge'. However this was too late for the station to be constructed before the opening.
The *West Briton* tactfully glossed over the dispute:

> No station has yet been erected for Bodmin, owing to the site not having been immediately determined upon. It will be either near to Glynn Bridge or Respryn Bridge, and until it is completed, the Bodmin traffic will be accommodated at a temporary wooden shed erected near the latter place.

Lord Vivian had consistently campaigned for the central route and 'referred to himself power to express his disapprobation of the bill both in and out of Parliament'. He had consistently petitioned against the railway, had insisted on screening the railway from the view from Glynn. He had originally pressed for the railway to be concealed in a tunnel a luxury that the company would not be able to afford.[17]

It was at this temporary wooden shed that the ill-fated train taking dignitaries to the opening ceremony stopped 'at 9.36 to take up Mr Robartes M.P.' of nearby Lanhydrock. The *Royal Cornwall Gazette* continues:

> We pass the Bodmin road station at Respryn, Lanhydrock on the one side Boconnoc on the other. And now we have reached a low level, and pass along the very bank of the river. From Respryn to Lostwithiel is the most lovely spot on the whole Line, and the beautiful ruin of Restormal Castle, of historical and national interest is seen to great advantage. And now we cross the Fowey at the ancient town of Lostwithiel, fallen in modern times to neglect and decay, but restored to permanent prosperity, by being made the central station of the Railway, and the seat of its works. For a minute we are lost in darkness of a tunnel and, when we emerge, it is on a new scene. Mines of the first importance are now passed in succession: Fowey Consols, the great mines, the various works, the important harbour at Par, great Crinnis, the first copper mine opened East of Truro, in its day, the richest mine in the west and whose workings are now resumed; then a number of mines standing literally among the woods of Tregrehan and offering in mingled contrast the scenery of rural retirement and beauty with which an English country gentleman surrounds his residence, and the circumstances of commercial enterprise, steam engines and their attendant machinery. And now we pass on to St Austell with the Bay on one side, the hills of Carclaze on the other, and the cottages of an industrious and intelligent population thickly set on either hand. St Austell itself yields in beauty to few spots we have passed, and scarce anything can exceed the valley we cross on leaving it, its bold hills, the woodland and orchard which fill the valley above and below, with the numerous and busy population. And now for a few miles the country is bare and coarse, as we pass through the parish of St Stephens whose wealth is not on the surface but below the soil; till crossing the Fal where it flows down from the Moors towards Grampound, we again come upon fertile fields, and wooded vallies, and private residencies, and so on to Truro.

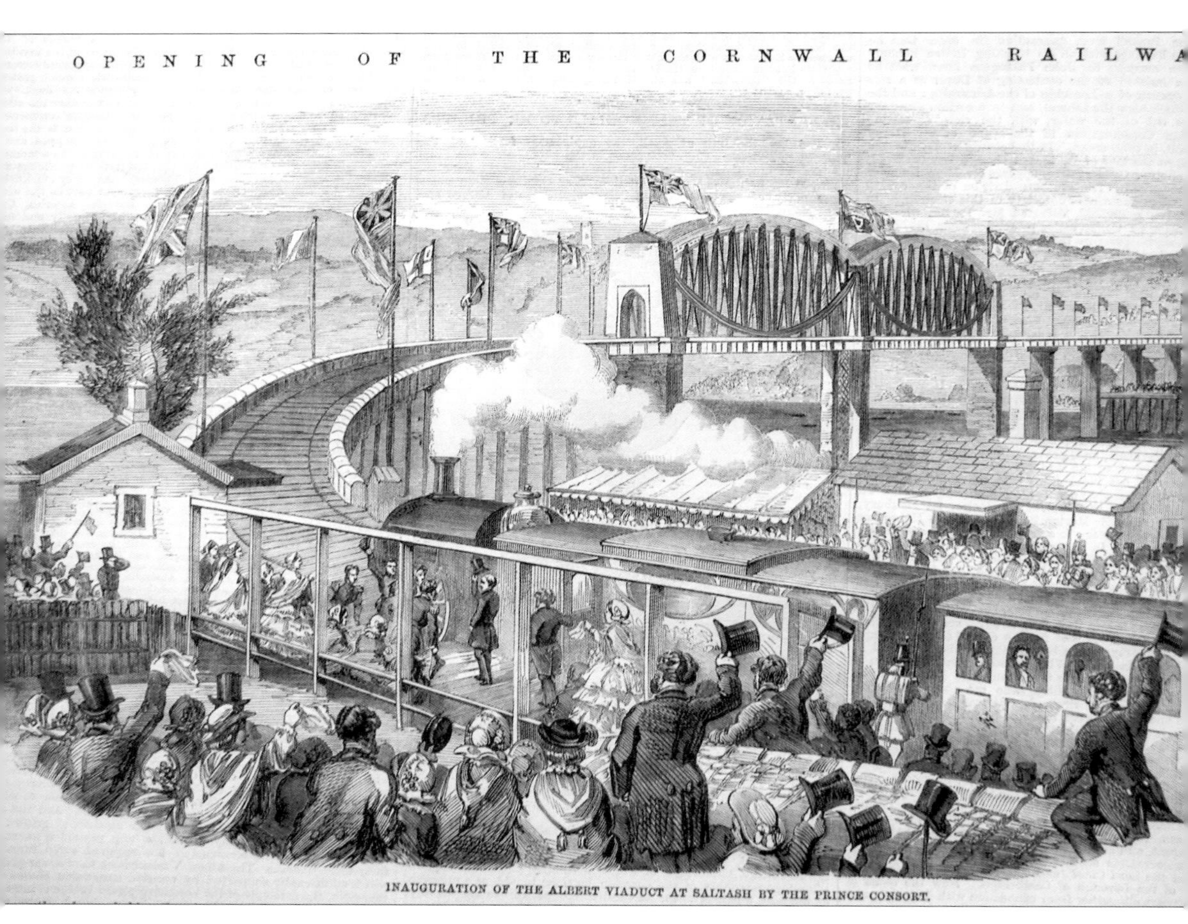

10.1 *Prince Albert,at the opening of the Royal Albert Bridge, seen alighting from the Royal train at Saltash Stat*
ILLUSTRATED LONDON NEWS

Chapter ten
The art of survival

> The Inspector of the Board of Trade having certified that the line was complete, and the directors having announced that it would be opened for public traffic on Wednesday, the first of the ceremonies with which it had been arranged to inaugurate this long-looked for event – the formal opening of the Royal Albert Bridge – took place on Monday last. To invest the occasion with greater importance and interest, his Royal Highness, the Prince Consort, after whom the stupendous undertaking has been named, was invited to perform the ceremony, and he at once signified his willing compliance with the wishes of the directors.[1]

And so, at long last, the Railway was completed, twenty years after the first serious attempts to create it. As long ago as 1852 Prince Albert had expressed an interest in the proposed bridge across the Tamar and a few months later he had agreed to the naming of the bridge. The Chairman informed the Board that he had received letters stating that Prince Albert had authorised the Directors to name the bridge 'The Royal Albert Bridge'. The Prince readily agreed to perform the opening ceremony despite the distance from Windsor.

In April 1859 Charles Gainsford, resident engineer at Saltash, reported to the Board on the state of progress of the bridge:

> The Government Inspector examined the Saltash Bridge Works and appeared greatly pleased with the results of the experiments for testing the strength of the Bridge. The principal test being a load of 386 tons including two engines and 20 wagons which in passing rapidly over the Bridge only caused a deflection in the Centre of the Roadway to the East tube of $1^1/_8$ inch and $1^1/_4$ on the West Tube.[2]

The Company could with justification enjoy the opening ceremony which took place on 2 May 1859. Such was the importance of the event that both national and local press covered the event comprehensively. The *West Briton*[3], in its editorial, stressed the advantages that the railway will bring:

> That the opening of the railway will usher in a new era in the commercial and social progress of the county, there can be no doubt, and though at present it would not be easy to estimate the full extent of the influence which it will exercise on trade, yet a slight consideration must satisfy every one that there is scarcely a person in the county to whom it will not prove a convenience and a benefit.

The Prince had already worked with Brunel on the Committee for constructing the Crystal Palace and must have missed him on this great occasion as he had not returned from convalescence on the continent. In their address to the Prince the directors alluded to his absence:

> The directors have only to regret the absence through ill health, of Mr Brunel, by whom the stupendous structure which bears your royal name was designed and completed, and to whose great talents the county is indebted for the construction of a railway through a district presenting the greatest engineering difficulties.
>
> The directors are assured that it would have been Mr Brunel's most anxious wish, and greatest pride personally to explain to your Royal Highness all the details which you will desire to know, and are so fully able to appreciate.

The only thing to spoil the occasion was the breakdown of the train carrying dignitaries and guests from Truro and stations east. However at Saltash everything ran like clockwork. Prince Albert travelled by the Royal train, which had left Windsor at 6.00 and arrived at the eastern end of the bridge at 12.10.

A technophile of progressive and liberal ideas, he was a believer in applying science to solve engineering problems. He responded to the loyal address from the Mayor of Saltash in the following terms[4] :

> It has given me much pleasure to attend here this day at the opening of the bridge which is to connect the important county of Cornwall with the rest of the kingdom; and most heartily do I thank you for your kind address, and for the cordial welcome which has marked my coming amongst you. I have to acknowledge on the part of the Queen, and of my son, the Duke of Cornwall, the gratifying assurances of your loyal and affectionate attachment; and I am sure that they will join cordially with me in the hope and trust that this noble work, which does so much credit to the enterprising men by whom it has been planned and executed, may be productive of increased prosperity to your town and county.

10.2 *The timetable for Prince Albert's visit.*
FROM AN ORIGINAL HELD IN THE GREAT WESTERN TRUST COLLECTION AT DIDCOT RAILWAY CENTRE

TIME BILL

FOR

ROYAL TRAIN,

2nd MAY, 1859.

DOWN.

Railway	Miles.		
Great Western Railway.		To leave WINDSOR STATION ... ... (Pass through Western Fork, at Slough.)	6. 0 a.m.
	21	To pass READING	6.32 „
	17	„ DIDCOT	6.56 „
	24	Arrive at SWINDON ... ... (Stop there 5 minutes.)	7.33 „
		To leave SWINDON	7.38 „
	17	Pass CHIPPENHAM	8. 2 „
	12	„ BATH	8.18 „
	12	Arrive at BRISTOL STATION ... ... (Stop there 10 minutes and change Engines.)	8.35 „
	103		
Bristol & Exeter Railway.		To leave BRISTOL	8.45 „
	46	Arrive at TAUNTON ... ... (Stop there 3 minutes.)	9.35 „
		Leave TAUNTON	9.38 „
	30	Arrive at EXETER STATION ... ... (Stop there 10 Minutes and change Engines.)	10.25 „
South Devon Railway.		To leave EXETER	10.35 „
	20	Arrive at NEWTON ... ... (Stop there 5 minutes.)	11. 5 „
		Leave NEWTON	11.10 „
	33	Arrive at the CORNWALL JUNCTION, in Plymouth (Stop there 5 minutes and change Engines.)	12. 0 „
Cornwall Rly.		To leave CORNWALL JUNCTION	12. 5 p.m.
	3	Arrive at SALTASH	12.15 „
	235 Miles.		

LONDON:—M'CORQUODALE & CO., PRINTERS

The *West Briton* reported the event:

> Precisely at the time appointed, the royal train, consisting of a state and other carriages, driven by Mr Gooch, the locomotive superintendent of the Great Western Railway, arrived at the east end of the bridge, where it stopped amid cheers of the assembled thousands ... The royal train then proceeded forward, and on passing the eastern pier the blue ensign was hoisted; on reaching the centre pier a royal salute was fired, and the royal standard was displayed, and on passing the western pier the St George's ensign was unfurled.

There were more cheers as Prince Albert alighted at Saltash station;

> and inspected plans of the bridge, the viaducts and other works of the line; and having concluded his examination, he proceeded onwards to the Coombe viaduct, 150 yards down the line, and after passing over this he returned to the west end of the bridge, where he left the state carriage and walked across to the opposite end, examining the bridge in its various parts . . . On reaching the east end, his Royal Highness declared the bridge to be opened, an announcement that was hailed with loud cheers from the bridge and the shore.

The Prince spent the whole day at Saltash with a trip on board the *Vivid*, an Admiralty yacht which had arrived the previous evening from Southampton and enabled him to see the bridge from below. There was a celebratory dinner and speeches customary on such occasions. The royal train left Plymouth at 7.00 in the evening. Daniel Gooch 'again took his station on the engine ... and the signal having been given, the train passed out of the station and was rapidly on its way'. Now the Prince had demonstrated that it was possible to fulfil this engagement far from Windsor in a single day. It had meant travelling nearly 500 miles and 19 hour day for him; no mean achievement in 1859.

On Tuesday 3 May 1859 at a reception held in Truro to celebrate the opening of the railway Dr Barham, Mayor of Truro,[5] proposed a toast:

> Gentlemen, I now proceed to give you the toast of the day, The Chairman and Directors of the Cornwall Railway . It is quite impossible for me to express that satisfaction which I feel in giving this toast, on the successful completion of your undertaking, which has occupied 13 years of struggle against difficulties altogether unexampled in any work of the kind.

He then acknowledged the role that the Associated Companies had played:

> We are largely indebted not only to the persevering energy of successive chairmen and directors of the Cornwall Railway for this happy result, but we are very largely indebted also to the aid we have derived from the companies with which we have been in connexion.

Barham then ruefully reflected on a lost generation and paid tribute to these three chairmen of the company, Treffry, Williams and Tweedy, who are the forgotten heroes of the Cornwall Railway.

> It is, Sir (addressing Dr Smith, Chairman of the Board of the Cornwall Railway), with pain that I address you as chairman of this company ... Most of you know it (the task) was commenced in 1845 or 1846 under the auspices of a man of very remarkable character and skill, and is more remarkable for his absence of selfishness. Mr Treffry was a man ... of so much disinterestedness and so much public virtue, that as he said himself, his only object on earth was the public service, and if he left enough to bury him he would be satisfied ... He was the first who may be said to have lost his life in this cause. He was succeeded by one who, perhaps, most of you knew, whether from the east or the west, as an exemplification of the particular success and particular power connected with our Cornish mining industry – the late Mr Michael Williams, who represented this county. There is no doubt that his adhesion to the line, and what I may call his disinterested exertions for it at a period of great monetary difficulty, was the cause of inspiring the public mind with that confidence in the undertaking which it would have been impossible to have infused from any other source. He was also taken from the Cornwall line after a comparatively short term of service. He was succeeded by a man (Tweedy) whom I can hardly fairly bring myself to allude to, for though unassociated with his labour for the Cornwall Railway myself, I was associated with him in almost every department of disinterested labouring in the public service. That man was so identified with, so essential to the interests of, every beneficial undertaking, and every undertaking which was calculated to advance the intellectual and moral progress of his county, that it would be, I believe, impossible to name one undertaking which was of general and unpartisan utility in which he did not bear really the labouring oar. In regard to the Cornwall Railway he was associated with it in its infancy; with the earliest struggles it had to undergo.

Dr George Smith, the newly elected Chairman of the Board of Directors, reflected on the scale of the difficulties and the cost of the achievement that lay behind the triumphant opening ceremony:

> I remember that 20 years ago, the want of railway communication was deeply felt; I remember when all the interests of the county seemed burthened with this great necessity. The mining interest wanted more ready communication with the eastern part of the kingdom; the mercantile interest cried out for a railway; the shipping interest demanded railway communication; the want of a railway was written on the heart of the county. Thank God, and I say that sincerely, we have secured this today. On opening of the railway from Plymouth to Truro, matters are brought before our minds which may appear far fetched to refer to, and which at the same time have almost died away from the public recollection. It is rather a singular fact that in the construction of

> these fifty miles of railway, we should have outlived almost a generation; and that a large mass of the population should have grown up in the midst of a line struggling from its very infancy, who are ignorant of the principles which led to the work ...

Within only a few years several others closely associated with the line would be gone ... Glennie (already in1856), Brunel (1859), Rowe (1859), Moorsom (1863), and Prince Albert himself was not to survive much longer. Two and a half years later on 14 December 1861 he died of typhoid fever.

On the engineering side Glennie was a veteran of the Box Tunnel:

> A gentleman of considerable skill as an engineer, and who was for many years engaged in the superintendence of the works upon the South Devon and Cornwall lines of railway, of which Mr I. K. Brunel was the engineer in chief[6].
>
> That the Board lamenting the severe loss which the Cornwall Railway Company has sustained by the decease of Mr William Glennie the resident Engineer, take this opportunity of recording their sense of his devotion to the interests of the Company and of his untiring assiduity, undeviating integrity and professional ability which have deserved their unqualified commendations and they desire to express their deep sympathy with his widow and family in the irreplaceable loss which they have sustained[7].

By 1858 Brunel was ailing with what was generally recognised to be Bright's disease. His son confirms that he had had consultations with Dr Bright. He took a long break from May to September and under Doctor's orders spent from December 1858 to May 1859 in Egypt and Italy. He returned too late for the opening of the Cornwall Railway and the Royal Albert Bridge. He wrote his last report to the Directors of the Cornwall Railway Company on 20 August covering the period up to the opening and beyond[8]. He reported on a range of routine matters with no indication that these were to be his last words on one of his most challenging undertakings; that goods traffic was about to begin, that sidings to connect with the quay at Par were to be constructed, that surplus materials and machinery were to be sold off and that the station for Bodmin Road had been erected at Glynn Bridge.

Brunel spent his few remaining months on the fitting out of the Great Eastern steamship at Millwall. On the very day that the ship cast her moorings, 5 September, he suffered a stroke on deck and died on 15 September.

A letter was read to the board from Brereton:[9]

> In announcing to you the painful intelligence of Mr Brunel's death I beg to say that having been for 23 years in Mr Brunel's service and for some time past chief of his Engineering staff it has been determined that I should, if it meet

> with the views of your Company, carry out the works, so far as possible with the engineering staff already engaged ...

The board responded:

> That the Board is deeply sensible of the great loss which this Company and the nation at large has sustained in the death of their eminent engineer and the Directors cannot assemble for the first time after this mournful event without placing on record their sense of the great services he has rendered to this Company their high estimation of his professional character – at the same time they feel they owe a debt of gratitude to his memory for the excellence of his designs and the able manner in which the Works on the line have been constructed – and more especially as that which is universally acknowledged to be one of the noblest structures in the World, the Royal Albert Bridge.

After the triumphant opening the Company operated the line for 29 years. Its problems were far from over. Clearly the twenty years that it had taken to build the railway were extremely difficult. Yet the Company had hardly achieved the standard of railway that it had planned. It did not have the double line railway specified in the 1846 Act, nor did it reach Falmouth. The packet traffic was never restored to Falmouth and there was therefore a black hole in the predicted revenue stream on which the whole project was founded. *The Times*[10] refers to 'the imperfect completion of the line' and that

> One of the more serious obstacles to the proper development of the traffic from the west of Cornwall ... has resulted from the continuance of the narrow gauge on the West Cornwall line.

The Company's finances were strained to the limit and further capital expenditure was going to be very difficult. There were accumulated debts of £164,000. Even basic maintenance seems to have been a problem. Thomas relates that:

> ... the track maintenance was appalling, trains rolling violently even at moderate speeds:, higher speeds were seldom obtained. This, the tenuous appearance of the viaducts and the number of mishaps, discouraged local patronage.[11]

And according to Brindle the passengers were:

> often terrified of crossing the viaducts; the trains had to slow down and the creaking and flexing of the slender structures must have been audible and alarming.[12]

It would be a new generation that had to battle on to complete the project in the face of uncertain cash flows. The engineering future of the Cornwall Railway fell into the hands of two of Brunel's very capable assistants, Brereton and Margery, who were to complete the outstanding work in Cornwall. They were both highly competent engineers and both left valuable testimony to their work in the form of papers to the Institution of Civil Engineers. The former was instrumental in completing the line to Falmouth and the latter in replacing the timber viaducts with more permanent structures.

In the meanwhile the Company was instrumental in establishing 'railway time' throughout the county. The problem of dealing with local time was more extreme than on other lines. Truro is five degrees west of Greenwich and its local time was 25 minutes behind:

> That it being highly expedient, in order to ensure due regularity of working the trains and the conscience of the public, that Greenwich time should be adopted at all towns having a station on the line, the secretary be instructed to communicate with the authorities in each town suggesting that Greenwich time should be adopted from and after the 1st June next.[13]

This was one of the less significant issues for the Company compared with completing the line to Falmouth and replacing Brunel's timber viaducts.

Completion of line to Falmouth

The long delayed opening of the railway from Plymouth to Truro must have come as an enormous relief to the Directors of the Cornwall Railway Company. However it was of little comfort to the Falmouth Docks Company or the people of Falmouth. Even the light hearted poem, composed for the opening, and quoted by Rolt, conspired to rub in the point:

> From Saltash to St Germans, Liskeard and St Austell,
> The County of Cornwall was all in a bustle,
> Prince Albert is coming the people did say
> To open the bridge on the Cornish Railway.
> From Redruth and Camborne, St Just in the west
> The people did flock all dressed in their best.
> From all parts of England you'll now have a chance
> To travel by steam right down to Penzance.

... But not to Falmouth. It was to be another four years before the twelve miles from Truro to Falmouth was completed and ready for use. As early as 1836, Penzance had been mooted as an alternative terminus to Falmouth. And now the West Cornwall Railway had already been opened for seven years. It must have been galling for the people of Falmouth to see Redruth, Camborne, Hayle and Penzance already enjoying a rail service, whilst Falmouth, whose connection with London was the main reason for building the Cornwall Railway in the first place, remained just as remote as ever. The West Cornwall Railway had become the main line and the link to Falmouth was demoted for ever to a single track branch line. Now 23 years later it must have appeared that Penzance might remain the only terminus: a prospect which would not have gone down well in Falmouth.

How very different it had appeared only a few years earlier. The directors had reported in 1852[14] :

> Your Directors cannot conclude without congratulating you upon the prospect now opened of carrying out at a small cost a line of such vast importance in a commercial, national and local point of view and which besides the large amount of traffic which it cannot fail to develop and the advantage of its connection with the port of Falmouth and Penzance will, with the West Cornwall Railway, add to the existing lines of railway from London to Falmouth and Penzance.

As early as Feb 1853 Glennie had reported that 'the line from Penwethers' (The junction of the Falmouth Branch with the main line just west of Truro) 'to Falmouth is nearly ready for letting'. And by 1853 Brunel reports to the Directors 'I am disposed to recommend that the tender of Mr Garratt should be accepted'.

Sam Garratt's tender for the Truro Falmouth section was, indeed, accepted. He was instructed only to proceed with the more time-consuming parts of his contract, namely the construction of the two tunnels. By February 1854 Brunel was able to report that:

> Between Truro and Falmouth the contract which was then reported to have been let, has been commenced, and the Contractor is proceeding with the shafts and headings of the two Tunnels, the execution of which will govern the period of completion of the whole.

The tunnels in question, together with the overbridges, were completed for double broad gauge tracks but have never accommodated more than a single line. They are the sole testimony to the long lost aspiration that this was to have been part of the main line rather than the mere branch which it has always been. Within months Garratt had gone bankrupt. Work on the Falmouth line ceased for six years whilst the Company wrestled with the completion of the Plymouth to Truro section in the face of increasing financial difficulties.

It was also becoming clear that Brunel was more concerned about completing the line to Truro than worrying about what is increasingly referred to as 'the extension to Falmouth'. On 1 April 1853 he had written:

> ... In a financial point of view there is no doubt in my mind that the completion of the link between Liskeard and Saltash is far more pressingly important than the extension to Falmouth ...

Morale in Falmouth must have hit a new low in July 1856 when the Board resolved that:

> Mr Brunel be requested to prepare a careful estimate of the probable sum which will be required to complete and open the line from Plymouth to Truro as early as practicable.

There is no mention of completing it to Falmouth. Clearly the Directors must have been keen to capture the traffic generated by the West Cornwall Railway as a first priority to support their weak cash flow. However at the opening in 1859 Dr Barham sought to reassure Falmouth that it had not been forgotten[15] :

> He said he regarded the railway communication to the West of England, taking especially into account the extension to Falmouth, as an event of incalculable importance, not only to this county, but to the nation at large, for the purposes both of peace and war; and he considered the Cornwall Railway taken as a whole from the noble Arsenal of Plymouth and the wonderful Bridge, opened yesterday by the Prince Consort, down to the harbour at Falmouth, as the most important engineering work of the century in its ultimate consequences, for, placed at the portals of the Atlantic, Falmouth must eventually become the main point for the departure and arrival of shipping.

ROBERT PEARSON BRERETON 1818-1894 was a pupil of Brunel's who rose to the rank of Chief Assistant Engineer to the GWR. He was closely involved in many of Brunel's civil engineering projects and gradually took over much of his work on the Royal Albert Bridge as Brunel, battling against ill health, became increasingly preoccupied with the completion and launch of the Great Eastern steamship. On Brunel's death Brereton succeeded him in all but name and effectively took over the practice at 18 Duke Street.

The Directors recognised Brereton's role in their address to Prince Albert left no doubt about the responsibility that had fallen increasingly on his shoulders:

> But in Mr Brunel's unavoidable absence the directors have the satisfaction to know that your Royal Highness will find he has an able representative in Mr Brereton, who has watched and superintended the whole work from its commencement to the present time.
>
> But there is a man who does deserve a word, and it is his efficient representative, Mr Brereton. From him we have had all the help we could need, and in Mr Brunel's weakness when he was unable from physical prostration to render us the assistance the pressing necessities of our line required, we had in Mr Brereton all that was wanted: he was always ready, always able, always full of energy, and took us through our work to the happy completion it is to-day.[16]

10.3
Robert Brereton
1818-1894
STEPHEN K JONES/BRUNEL SOCIETY

With the main line opened to Truro the Board was obliged to address the question of completing the line to Falmouth. Nine months after the opening of the 'main line' in February 1860 the Board requested Brereton to examine the abandoned works between Penwethers and Falmouth and report on his estimate of the cost of completing the line.

The Board of the Falmouth Docks Company was quite prepared to take matters into their own hands in order to connect their port to the *main line* and to try to raise the capital themselves. A letter from the Secretary of the Falmouth Docks Company to the Secretary of the Cornwall Railway Company dated 21 April 1860 reads:

> The great object of my Board in seeking the conference which took place on 15th February last, was to get the line between Truro and Falmouth finished on this summer and that in the event of the Associated Companies being unprepared to do this, they should afford the Docks Company or an independent, an opportunity to endeavour to carry out so desirable an object: but it was never for a moment suggested ... that the capital required to carry it out was then ready as it was stated ... that, in the event of our suggestion being acceded to, the Docks Company would make every effort to raise it.
>
> Your requirement that the Associated Companies must be satisfied of the financial and legal ability of this Company to proceed forthwith before they will take the matter into consideration virtually puts an end to negotiation, as it is evident that no Company could be formed for the purpose without the terms having been previously arranged.
>
> A further object, which my Board had in seeking the interview and urging on your Company the commencement of the line this summer, was to endeavour to remove the feeling of the Inhabitants of this Town and neighbourhood, that it was not intended to complete the Railway to Falmouth and that they were intentionally sacrificed to Plymouth and then prevent any opposition in Parliament to such extension of time as your Company may require, which opposition, if successful, my Directors felt would necessarily occasion a further delay of working the line. Could you have entertained the suggestion made by Mr Bond on 15th February, it would at all events have satisfied the public of your anxiety that the line to this place shall be constructed and that, although not prepared to make it yourselves, and you will perceive that if another Company had failed in the attempt it would necessarily strengthen any application you might make to Parliament in the ensuing session.[17]

But the Board's hands were effectively tied by the willingness or otherwise of the Associated Companies to provide further funds over and above what they had had to contribute towards opening the line as far as Truro. Although the tunnels had been built there remained eight viaducts to be constructed. A report to the Board confirmed that:

> It is no use to go again to the Associated Companies and ask for money. We must come to Cornwall, to the men who have the most interest in what has

> to be done, and I trust we shall receive sympathy and help to complete the remainder of the undertaking. I have heard some people say that, after all, the advantage of these efforts is very problematical. I have heard some people here in Truro who doubt whether they will benefit by them ... The question appears to me this - Are you as Cornishmen, with all your capital and interest, afraid to enter into competition with the wide world? A railway has been given you; will you face the world of intellect, of energy, of capital, and of labour?[18]

The South Devon Company set out the economic dilemma. If the operating return on the line would result in an annual deficit then the viability of the line would be in doubt. If however the additional traffic on the main line would help to reduce its deficit then it merited further consideration. If the Cornwall Railway Company had been starting from scratch (or *'res integra'* as Rowe would no doubt have put it) then it would seem unlikely that the Truro/Falmouth line would have been built. Members of the various boards were all too aware of the problems of raising capital from potential shareholders who had had their fingers burnt during the mania period. However a considerable sum had been spent before Garratt's bankruptcy particularly on land acquisition and construction of the two tunnels. This seems to have tipped the balance on the merits of completing the line[19].

A further issue was the location of the Falmouth terminus. The board was aware that the original proposed site for a terminus at Green Bank Quay had been based on the assumption that this was the place where the packet traffic docked. It was also well related to the business centre of the town. The new docks were a mile to the south, nearer to the sea to allow for the berthing of much larger steamships. Accordingly Brereton was instructed to 'ascertain the most desirable position for the Terminus of the Cornwall Railway'. Although Bennett, secretary to the Falmouth Dock Company had referred to 'The completion of the Cornwall Railway to Falmouth', Brereton heads his report 'Cornwall Railway Falmouth Branch'. The choice of words clearly reflects the subtly different position of the two parties.

The present docks, which were started in 1861 and completed by the time of the opening of the line, at the eastern end of the town in the shelter of Pendennis Head, required a relocation of the proposed terminus from the original proposed site at Green Bank Quay to its present location at Western Wharf. Brereton sets out the issue in his letter to Bond[20] :

> It appears that the distance along the shore in front of the town of Falmouth between the new docks and the hitherto suggested terminus of the Cornwall Railway at Green Bank Pier is about is about a mile ...
>
> Assuming that for these reasons the station were placed at Green Bank it would be next to impracticable in order to communicate with the new Docks

> to extend the Railway along the water frontage without enormous cost. If therefore it is desirable that such communication should be effected, some other direction must be resorted to.
>
> A communication from the new Docks may without difficulty be made by a Railway passing south and west of the town along the low ground or isthmus between the ornamental properties of Grove Hill and Gwyllyndune [*sic*] but without interfering with either and passing westward by the new cemetery ... and proceed to join the line of the Cornwall Railway as at present laid out near Penryn.
>
> The line above mentioned will not be difficult of construction and would enable a better gradient to be obtained than the Railway taken to Green Bank, the latter having an inclination of 1 in 60 out of Falmouth for about three miles whereas 1 in 80 might be obtained with the former for a considerable distance. This is a consideration that cannot fail to weigh largely in favour of the Dock line in the carrying out of any considerable traffic in goods.

This change extended the length of the line from Truro Station to the Docks to 12¼ miles at a cost of £18,340 per mile.

On 29 June 1860:

> Mr Brereton laid before the Board a report of the survey of the altered terminus of the line in the neighbourhood of Falmouth from College Wood to the Falmouth Docks, accompanied by an estimate of the amount which will

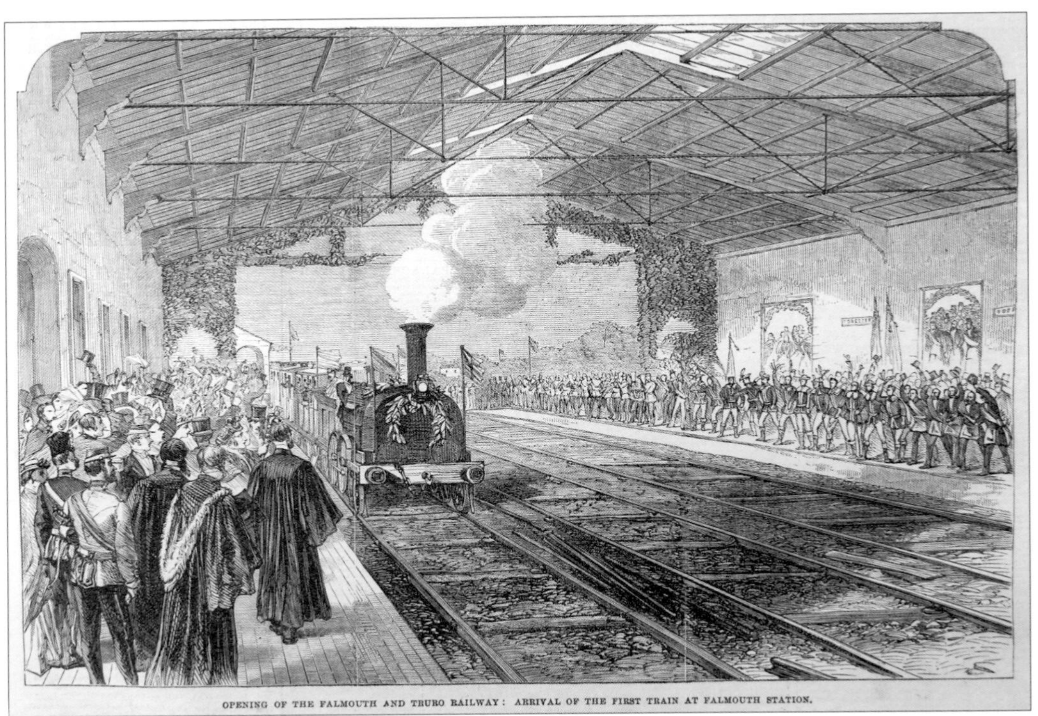

OPENING OF THE FALMOUTH AND TRURO RAILWAY: ARRIVAL OF THE FIRST TRAIN AT FALMOUTH STATION.

10.4 *The opening of Falmouth Station*
THE ILLUSTRATED LONDON NEWS

> be required for the completion being £211,000 and recommending its construction in preference to the terminus formerly proposed.[21]

The railway from Truro to Falmouth was finally opened on 21 August 1863. Dr Smith attended the opening, an event celebrated in great style. He expressed his happiness at visiting Falmouth that day on the auspicious occasion that had brought them together, and on behalf of the directors pledged himself to a hearty co-operation with the inhabitants for the welfare of Falmouth and the wealth of the county. Sure enough the line enabled the tourist industry to develop and provided a new lease of life for the hotels and lodging houses that had depended on the packet trade. The belated advent of both the railway and the new docks at last provided the new economic stimulus for the town even though its original basis, the packet services, would never return. The subsequent success of Falmouth was to be based on repairs to vessels, dry docking facilities and fisheries which enjoyed the new accessibility to London markets. It also encouraged a similar trade in early vegetables. The town, with its mild climate, also became an excellent centre for the fledgling holiday trade.

REPLACING THE VIADUCTS

Faced with the dire financial position of the company Brunel devised what was essentially a temporary standardised design of viaduct which was cheap to erect but expensive to maintain and with an essentially short life. Had cost benefit techniques been available at the time these structures would hardly have provided an economic rate of return. Indeed Brunel's son comments in the biography of his father[22] :

> ... while allowing for the cost of repairs, the total expenditure did not differ much from what it would have been had the superstructure of the viaducts been of more durable materials ...

So desperate was the company that it was prepared to go ahead with 34 of these viaducts, between Plymouth and Truro in the hope that revenues would meet the maintenance costs and provide some surplus for their eventual replacement. The biography confirms the desperation of the situation:

> ... it became necessary to reduce the capital expenditure, even at the cost of increasing the charges for maintenance. With this object the line was re-examined and modifications introduced, principally by an increase in the extent of viaducts.

They required a standing labour force of 54 men and one inspector to replace the timbers as rot began to set in. The costs soon began to amount to £10,000 a year. So by 1875, only sixteen years after the opening of the line, work started on replacing them.

PETER JOHN MARGARY 1820-1896 was, like Brereton, one of the key engineers who gradually took over responsibility from Brunel during the last years of his life. He had supported Brunel on the construction of the South Devon Railway including the traumas of trying to make the atmospheric system function economically and reliably. He also strengthened the five timber viaducts on that line when it became apparent that they would have to carry heavier trains than atmospheric ones. On Brunel's death he was appointed Chief Engineer of the South Devon. He was then, in 1868 appointed Chief Engineer to the Cornwall Railway Company. Fortunately he completed a paper in 1882 which provides a valuable insight on the replacement of Cornwall's timber viaducts.[23] He retired in 1891 having completed the replacement or rebuilding of 14 of the 34 viaducts on the main line including all the highest ones.

The question of the safety of the viaducts seems to have troubled the Directors from the beginning and *West Briton* made a point of trying to reassure the public at the opening ceremony:

> We have spoken of the safety of the Line as the most important point of all. This applies chiefly to the viaducts, which are unavoidably numerous and lofty. They add greatly to the effect of the scenery presented to the traveller as he flies like a bird through the air, and commands from above all the beauties of the rich succession of pictures spread out below him. But unless he can rest entirely at ease on the question of safety, there could be no enjoyment. We believe that the entire assurance can be given to this. There are two sources of danger – sufficient strength of the viaduct; and the train running off the rails. The first has been provided against by the skill of Mr Brunel, who has framed them as strong as wood and iron could make them, and the proof that he has fully succeeded, is the perfect absence of vibrations under the heaviest train. We travelled down in the heavy train from Plymouth, and in the last carriage, where the motion is greatest. Every viaduct was steady as a rock; and the train glided over the Line with a motion easier than even on the Great Western. As to going off the rails, that is not an accident of the broad gauge; and it is to be remembered that the railways through London, on which trains run every quarter of an hour, are on viaduct throughout.

Unfortunately this confidence was misplaced. With the ink barely dry on the paper a down train was derailed on the Grove viaduct on the day of publication. The engine and two carriages plunged into the mud of the Lynher River with the loss of three lives. Although it appeared that the cause of the accident was a derailment before the train reached the viaduct, the greater concern must have been that the superstructure of the viaduct failed to contain the train. (Appendix nine)

Margery's paper concentrates on replacing the two highest and most

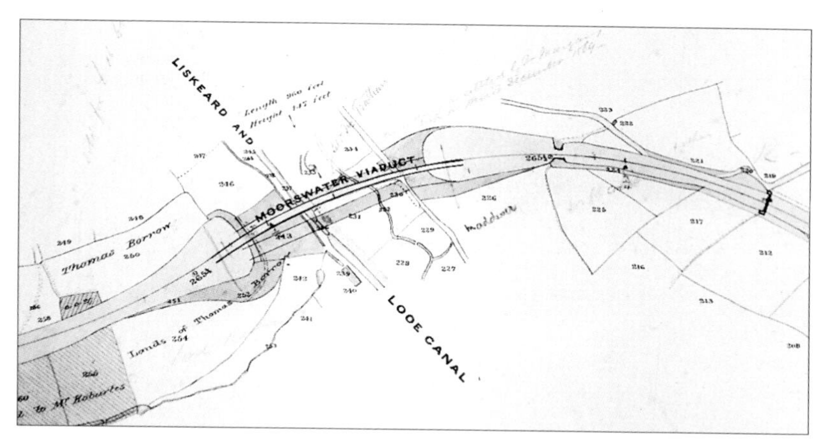

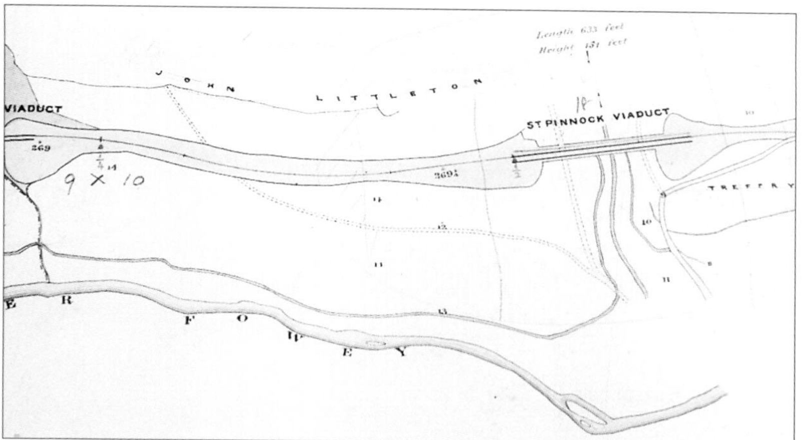

10.5 and 10.6
The replacement of Moorswater viaduct on a new alignment and reconstruction of St Pinnocks demonstrate two different approaches to dealing with Brunel's viaducts.

spectacular viaducts, Moorswater and St Pinnock with different solutions. (Appendix ten) Moorswater seems to have been particularly problematical: It was at the bottom of an incline at either end, the viaduct was built on a curve and taken in conjunction with its height, there is good reason to believe that it was the most highly stressed of the viaducts. Due to the down gradients on each side trains tended to pick up speed so that lateral forces lead to its premature weakening. This was the only one to have the extra support from a framework of twelve inch timbers.

In 1883 the chairman[24] reported:

> I believe, with regard to one viaduct, there can be no doubt upon anybody's mind as to the propriety of converting that into stone. The Moorswater viaduct, which was a very high and long viaduct, was never constructed in the way it ought to have been; and had it not been for wood structures keeping up the stone work, it would have come to grief. It was absolutely necessary for safety to convert that viaduct.

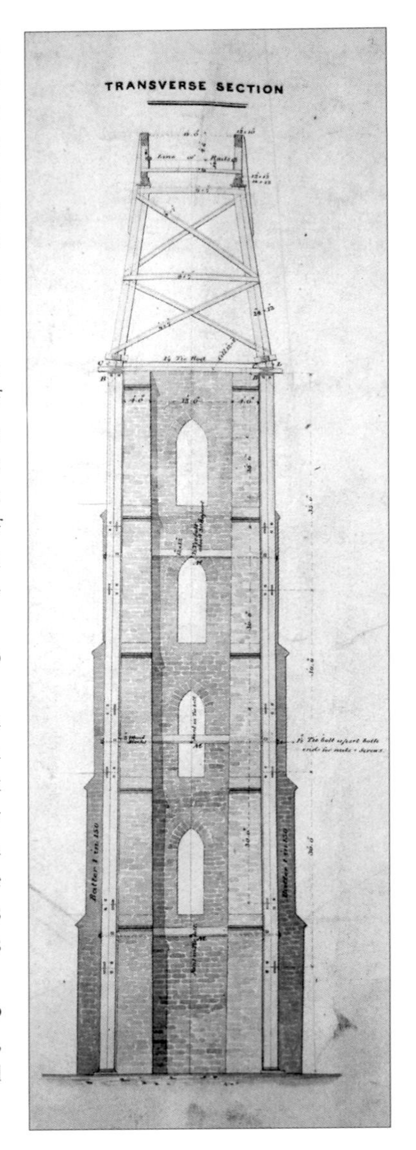

10.7 A pier of the original Moorswater viaduct showing additional timber supports.

In 1881 it was replaced by a masonry structure of eight segmental arches on an improved alignment. In contrast at St Pinnock the existing piers have been raised and an iron superstructure replaced the existing timber one. With this viaduct, which is 211 yards long and 151 feet high, this was clearly a cheaper option. Margery explains:

> The cost of the whole of the work amounted to less than one half that of constructing a new masonry viaduct alongside the existing one. This manner of reconstructing in iron is economical only in the case of viaducts 120 feet in height, and where the piers are of thoroughly good masonry and buttressed.

Clearly this did not apply to Moorswater.

The Company became involved in an arcane dispute with the GWR. In replacing the original single track broad gauge viaducts the company opted to build the replacement in masonry to a width to accommodate two standard gauge tracks. It is interesting to note from Margary's paper that:

> The viaduct is intended to carry two lines of railway, of 4 feet $8^{1}/_{2}$ gauge, but at present only a single broad gauge line is laid over it.

Between 1870 and 1883 the Cornwall Railway Company had reconstructed in masonry 12 of the 42 viaducts to a width to take double standard gauge at a cost of £88,000. The GWR, as preference shareholders, argued that these 'extravagances' reduced the Associated Companies preference stock and queried whether the rebuilding could simply be described as repairs. The GWR owned £202,500 of ordinary stock out of a total of £575,460.[25]

The lattice viaduct at Meldon (near Okehampton on the London and South Western Railway) built in 1874, has been preserved. Other viaducts

10.8 and 10.9 *Although it was cheaper to rebuild the original Brunel viaducts than to replace them, this could involve complex logistic procedures. In 10.8 the brickwork has been completed around the soon to be redundant timber trusses. In the background is the engine shed, which closed in 1918, at Liskeard Station. In 10.9 the new trusses are being lowered into place from a hand operated crane attached to a goods locomotive of the period, again around the timber trusses.*
LISKEARD AND DISTRICT MUSEUM

of this type suffered the Beeching axe, notably Belah in County Durham and Crumlin in South Wales. These had both been completed in 1857, much earlier than Meldon. It raises the thought that Brunel, not slow to adopt new technology, must have been aware of these viaducts which could be built cheaply and quickly. Why did he not consider them for the Cornish valleys? Did he, towards the end of his life, decide to stick with the timber trestles which he had pioneered in south Devon? Had this technology been used on the Cornwall Railway a lot of money spent on maintenance and replacement of the timber viaducts could have been saved.

Furthermore connecting to the South Devon Railway meant that services to and from Cornwall were subject to, not infrequent, disruption from both storm damage[26] and landslips to the sea wall between Dawlish and Teignmouth. In 1852 'a most terrific fall of the cliff ... between Dawlish and Teignmouth ... covering the line for some distance and rendering all traffic impossible'[27]. This stretch has also been subject to the risk of rock falls and, in the present era Network Rail has had to install protective netting. Following further storm damage to the sea wall in 2004 and 2009 Network Rail has commissioned a study of exposed coastal lines, such as at Dawlish, in the light of the changing climate, with a view to finding long term solutions to this recurring problem.

The notorious gradients, too, had begun to levy their toll on the South Devon locomotives. Barely had the line been opened than a locomotive burst its boiler as it was tackling the Hemerdon incline. Under the heading FATAL ACCIDENT ON SOUTH DEVON RAILWAY *The Times* correspondent[28] reported that a stoker had been killed and an engine driver dangerously wounded:

> A great pressure was put on and the train was enveloped in smoke and steam; suddenly a tremendous report was heard occasioned by the bursting of the boiler immediately after passing through Plympton Station ... the boiler plates were literally torn asunder and so violent had been the explosion that the engine was turned end for end.

The correspondent was sure that that the gradients rendered the line liable to such accidents:

> I have no doubt that the cause of the explosion arose from the driver of the engine husbanding his steam, in order to have extra power to enable the engine to overcome the steep gradient of the Hammerdon [*sic*] incline ...
> I fear that the driver is too apt to shut off the steam, that it may accumulate force sufficient to overcome the rising gradient of the Hammerdon incline ... By this means an undue strain is thrown on the boiler; indeed, the constant occurrence of these strains at the many steep gradients on this line causes the engines to become strained ... An accident nearly similar occurred this morning to one of the down trains on the Denton [*sic*] incline.

A letter from a shareholder in 1851 complains about the lack of return on his investment:

> I am, unhappily, one of the poor shareholders in the South Devon Railway, which line has been finished and in full working order for some years, but has never paid a shilling dividend in consequence of the lavish and ruinous involvement into which it was brought by the departure from the original plans ... it seems unfair, yea it is unjust, to the many poor shareholders, who like myself embarked their capital in expectation of a fair dividend soon after the line was opened for traffic to Plymouth, and have suffered and are suffering, in our daily common and necessary wants from its non-payments.[29]

Meanwhile the press reports the qualified optimism of the Cornwall Company after the first full year of operation:

> The directors report states that although the proceeds of the half year have not fully come up to what might have been expected, the resources of the county are being steadily developed; large quantities of potatoes and other vegetables, and fish, have passed over the line, and the advantages supplied by this improved mode of transit have been so appreciated in the London markets and have afforded such facilities to producers in the west of Cornwall that a continued and considerable increase of traffic from these sources may be reasonably expected when better appliances have been secured for the purpose.[30]

The passage of fifteen years from the opening reveals a more promising state of affairs as far as an operating profit was concerned. Total receipts had increased by 144%. And an operating profit of £1,124 was recorded[31]. This was hardly an impressive figure but was much better than the deficits of up to £17,000 which had been reported in previous years. During the Company's last few years its position was one of growing health.

Not only did the Cornwall Railway start to make profits at this time but the general economy had by then climbed out of the recession caused by the collapse of the private bank Overend and Gurney back in 1866. One of the directors, W. L. Martin, reports in 1883 [32] :

> I have taken the trouble to obtain some figures which may be of interest to shareholders. From 1869 to 1874 there was an increase in our passenger traffic amounting to 13½ per çent; from 1874 to 1882 an increase of 9½ per cent. The parcels traffic increased between 1865 and 1874 by 57 per cent and from 1874 to 1882 by 16 per cent. The goods traffic increased 110 per cent from 1865 to 1874 and 9 per cent from 1874 to 1882. There was a general increase of 42½ per cent from 1865 to 1874 and 9½ per cent from 1874 to 1882. I think, Gentlemen, we may safely assume that that increase is likely to go on, because, while we have a passenger traffic which is not yet anything like developed, we have the line to Newquay, which has opened up a very favourite resort for tourists; we have the new line likely to be made to Helston, which will open up the Lizard district to a very considerable extent; and, as the Chairman reminds me, the Bodmin line is also to be opened.
>
> The whole of our passenger traffic irrespective of tourist traffic is in a generally healthy condition. We have gone up several thousands a year since 1879-80, and the increase that has been made has been established. It was not for one year only, but has gone on. We have our fish traffic, which is also in a state of great development; and I look forward to this 'Fisheries Exhibition' as very likely to do great things for Cornwall, and to stimulate the fisheries generally. We have also a general goods traffic. There is no doubt the Helston line, alluded to just now, will, if it do nothing else, open up a large broccoli

and potato trade. I have no doubt that a great deal might be done in the neighbourhood of Falmouth and Penryn in that way, which has so far not been touched. I believe, Gentlemen, that the prospects of the Cornwall line are good prospects.

As Martin had predicted, despite never getting revenue from the packet traffic and the untimely decline in tin and copper mining, the Cornwall Railway Company was able to carve out niche businesses. The transport of fish, vegetables and flowers by overnight trains to the London markets became a mainstay. Accessibility by train to the holiday trade in the seaside towns encouraged a whole new business. The Great Western subsequently capitalised on this by establishing its own hotel, the Tregenna Castle, at St Ives.

His report shows that, as the capital expenditure of replacing the viaducts started to drop out, the company was hoping to break even. A very modest operating surplus was achieved for the first time in 1882. The Directors meanwhile resolved to open negotiations with the GWR either for an amalgamation of the company with the GWR or for an agreement for the working of the traffic of the company by the GWR[33].

However despite these hopeful signs there was a concern about a renewed threat from the London and South Western Railway Company, which had planned lines into north Cornwall in each of the preceding two decades. It had reached Plymouth via Okehampton in 1876 and the company was looking to extend into North Cornwall; its associate, the North Cornwall Railway, was authorised in 1882. Wadebridge was reached in 1895 and Padstow in 1899. Faced with a common enemy it was beginning to make sense for the Cornwall Railway Company to amalgamate with the Great Western in order to prevent the South Western's westward advance which had the potential to undermine the hard won economic gains.

The 1883 report shows that the rivalry between GWR and South Western was not dead and it had not been quite the end of the central route. Beeching's report *The Reshaping of British Railways*[34] condemned the line west of Okehampton as hopelessly uneconomic and unable even to cover its direct costs. It closed in 1967. The Atlantic Coast Express is now a distant memory, happily preserved by John Betjeman:

Can it really be that this same carriage came from Waterloo?
On Wadebridge station what a breath of sea
Scented the Camel valley! Cornish air,
Soft Cornish rains, and silence after steam ...

There are proposals for the restoration of part of the line between Tavistock and the Tamar Valley Line at Bere Alston to provide a commuter link to Plymouth.[35] This opens up the intriguing possibility

10.10 *The prospect of capital expenditure on converting the broad gauge was to prove to be too much for the Cornwall Railway Company. Here, at Millbay the conversion goes ahead after the GWR take-over.* COURTESY THE NATIONAL RAILWAY MUSEUM, NRM NO 780/51

of restoring the remaining 12 miles from Tavistock to Meldon. Could this eventually provide an alternative to the South Devon route at such times as the Dawlish sea wall is out of action because of either rock falls or the increased risk of flooding from rising sea levels? A belated victory for the 'central route' is just possible.

FINALE FOR THE CORNWALL RAILWAY COMPANY

A draft agreement had been floated in 1878 between the Cornwall and Great Western Companies:

The practical effect of the agreement will be to make the Cornwall Railway a part of the Great Western System during continuance of the arrangement. In November 1888 the GWR concluded a deal to purchase the Cornwall Railway which the company had leased and worked since 1861. The Great Western formally took over on 1 July the following year. The deal had been forced on both parties by the advances of the London and South Western into the far west. The price paid was £8 for each £20 share. This must have been galling for the shareholders but no doubt they were relieved that a very unprofitable investment with negligible returns was finally over. *The Times* confirmed the point[36] :

The absolute possession of the Cornwall line gives the Great Western an unbroken connexion between Paddington and Land's End, and has probably been an issue by the keen rivalry of the London and South Western.

The dying days of the broad gauge must have hung heavily over the company. Brunel's two legacies, the timber viaducts and the broad gauge between them, posed a heavy capital outgoing that was bound to tax the income stream to the limit. Between them they prevented the installation of the second track and imposed a limit on the expansion of the business. Furthermore the Directors were reluctant to have to shoulder another two great capital expenditures in the shape of converting to standard gauge and doubling the track.

Its first act after amalgamation was to convert to standard gauge in 1892 and, with the exception of the length of the Royal Albert Bridge, to install the second track. This was laid first between Plymouth and Devonport. The next section was over the Fowey Valley viaducts which had been rebuilt during the early 1880s. It was continued piecemeal as the different groups of viaducts were replaced. The last section was an entirely new alignment between Saltash and St Germans in 1906-08 involving new viaducts over the tidal creeks.

And so, half a century after the Parliamentary approval of the Cornwall Railway, it was finally completed to the standard that its promoters had originally envisaged.

10.11 *Tailpiece: Double disc bracket ex Lostwithiel Station for train following placed at the rear of the last carriage of preceding train or tender of light engine to warn permanent way staff of a following train not in the working timetable: an important aspect of safety in operating the single track Cornwall Railway. Here it is attached to a broad gauge carriage at the Didcot Railway Centre.*
Great Western Trust at Didcot Railway Centre

References

Abbreviations:

ICE	Institution of Civil Engineers
PA	Parliamentary Archive
TNA	The National Archive
RCG	*Royal Cornwall Gazette*
WB	*West Briton and Cornwall Advertiser*

Preface

1. Thomas, 1960
2. PA Brunel examined by Merevale 2 June 1845

Chapter 1: A sea of troubles

1. RCG 6 May1859
2. A list of members of the Provisional Committee of the Cornwall Railway is included as Appendix 3.
3. RCG 11 October 1839
4. RCG 6 May 1859
5. *The Times* 7 October1858
6. PA 26 May 1846 Brunel examined by Kinglake
7. PA 3 June 1846 Bidder examined by Rowe
8. PA Evidence of Mr Nicholas Whitley, Valuer.
9. RCG 15 Nov 1846 Notice of application for shares in Cornwall and Devon Central Railway
10. PA 29 May 1846 Rodd examined by James
11. WB 6 May 1859
12. *The Times* 6 January 1873
13. PA House of Commons 26 April 1844, South Devon Railway Bill, Brunel examined by Mereweather
14. PA 12 June 1846 Brunel cross examined by Cockburn
15. PA 12 June 1846 Stephenson examined by Rowe
16. PA 20 May 1846 Locke examined by Kinglake
17. PA 20 May 1846 Hawkshaw examined by Kinglake
18. Elvins *The Corn Laws and the Protection Issue 1842-52*
19. Inflation: the value of the pound 1750-1998, House of Commons Research Paper 99/20 23 February 1999
20. TNA RAIL 134/2 Fourth half yearly ordinary meeting of proprietors 26 August 1848 Chairman's report.
21. Parris and Maguire, 1995, p31-35
22. RCG 6 May 1859

Chapter 2: Connecting the capital

1. TNA RAIL 1014 Memorial dated 17 July 1839
2. PA 21 May 1846 Lemon examined by Merevale.
3. WB 26 December 1834
4. RCG 15 November 1844
5. PA. Bill for improving Falmouth Harbour 16 July 1841 P.A. Holland, Commander in Her Majesty's Navy examined by Gregory.
6. PA Lord Falmouth cross examined by Rowe 21 May 1846
7. TNA RAIL 134 25/26 Letter from R. P. Brereton to W. Bond dated 10 May 1860
8. TNA RAIL 1075/30
9. RCG 19/26 January and 9 February 1833
10. William Andrews was the legal representative of the London, Exeter and Falmouth Railway Company which promoted the central line.
11. WB 20/27 May 1836
12. RCG 26 August 1836
13. PA 3 June 1846 Stephenson cross examined by Kinglake
14. *Falmouth Packet and Cornish Herald* 27 September 1839
15. Devey, 1862, p117
16. TNA RAIL 1014/2/52

17. RCG 11 October 1839
18. RCG 1 November 1839
19. WB 6 May 1859
20. Keast, 1982, Ch V
21. *Falmouth Packet, Cornwall Advertiser and Visitors List*, 13 April 1934
22. WB 13 February 1858
23. WB 21 November 1856
24. WB 1 July 1853
25. TNA RAIL 134/1 Meeting of the Committee of the Devon and Cornwall Railway 20 November 1839 chaired by Earl of Falmouth
26. TNA RAIL 134/1 Meeting of Committee, 18 November 1840 chaired by Earl of Falmouth
27. WB 6 November 1840

CHAPTER 3: 'A CIVIL WAR BETWEEN GENTLEMEN'

1. PA 29 May 1846 Tremayne cross examined by Merevale
2. PA 21 May 1846 Falmouth cross examined by Rowe
3. Elvins, 2001
4. RGC 8 November 1844 Letter from Ed Turner re Moorsom's report
5. *Falmouth Packet* 17 April 1841
6. *Falmouth Packet* 8 May 1841
7. RCG 15 November 1844
8. TNA Rail 134/1 Provisional committee Meeting 5 February 1844
9. PA 29 May 1846 Tremayne examined by Rowe
10. *The Times* 12 November 1844
11. RCG 2 and 9 February 1844
12. RCG 15 November 1844
13. RCG 8 November 1844
14. WB 29 August 1845
15. PA discussions between Counsel and Chairman during evidence of Trelawney and Locke on 29 May and 12 June 1846
16. WB 5 September 1845
17. PA 29 May 1846 Rodd examined by Rowe
18. PA 29 May 1846 Pendarves examined by Rowe
19. PA 29 May 1846 Trelawney re-examined by Committee
20. PA 29 May 1846 Tremayne examined by Rowe
21. PA 21 May 1846 Falmouth examined by Kinglake
22. PA 21 May 1846 Lemon cross examined by Rowe
23. WB 5 September 1845
24. RCG 6 June 1859

CHAPTER 4: 'PERCHANCE TO DREAM'

1. ICE Proceedings No 681 May 14 1844
2. Ostler, 1846
3. PA West Cornwall Railway Bill 21 May 1845 Brunel examined by Rowe
4. Lords Journal 27 July 1846 p1107
5. PA 12 June 1846 Locke examined by Cockburn
6. Clifford, 1968, p57-63
7. *The Times* 14 November 1844
8. Hadfield, 1985
9. This biographical profile has been compiled from *Dictionary of National Biography* and the Proceedings of the Institution of Civil Engineers, Cantor and the *Jewish Encyclopedia*
10. *The Falmouth Packet and Royal Cornwall Gazette* of 8 November 1844 reports; 'This new act of Parliament came into operation on Tuesday. The most important provision is that made for the accommodation and convenience of third class passengers, who will, in future, be carried on all the railways at the rate of 1d per mile. The third class carriages are required to be peculiarly constructed, so as to afford every shelter and protection from the wind and weather; and the inspectors of the Board of Trade have been engaged during the past week in examining the new vehicles. The Act requires the third-class trains to travel at the rate of twelve miles an hour inclusive of stoppages.'
11. RCG 2 February 1844
12. TNA RAIL 134/1 Provisional Committee 9 March 1844

13. TNA RAIL 134/1 Provisional Committee 3 August 1844
14. PA 29 May 1845 Moosom cross examined by Rowe
15. PA 3 June 1845 Stephenson examined by Kinglake
16. ICE Proceedings No 714 February 25 1845
17. PA 12 June 1846 Brunel cross examined by Cockburn
18. PA 12 June 1846 Locke examined by Cockburn
19. PA 12 June 1846 Brunel cross examined by Cockburn
20. *The Times* 3 March1848
21. *The Times* 31 August 1848
22. *The Times* 21 December 1848
23. *The Times* 28.November 1848
24. *The Times* 9 January 1849

CHAPTER 5: THE PARLIAMENTARY LABYRINTH

1. Williams, 1949, p67
2. Clifford, 1968, p865
3. Simmons & Biddle, 1997, p363
4. Clifford, 1968, p88
5. OCBRH p400-401
6. PA Lemon 21 May 1846
7. TNA RAIL 1075/13
8. Clifford, 1968, p788
9. PA 5 June 1845 Thomas Cooper examined by Merevale
10. PA HL/PO/CO/1/135: Proceedings before the Standing Order Committee on certain Railway Bills & Opposed Private Bills.13 February 1846-17 August 1846
11. PA 1846 Protheroe Smith examined by Kinglake
12. PA 29 May 1846 Pendarves examined by Rowe
13. Williams, 1949, p109
14. PA 29 May 1845 Moorsom cross examined by Rowe
15. PA 21 May 1846 Plumridge examined by Merevale
16. PA Lords Journal 27 July 1846 p1105
17. Simmons & Biddle, 1997, p95
18. For the biographical detail I have consulted Selden Society Supp Series 5: The Order of Sergeants at Law, Selden Society supp series 7: Law officers and King's Counsel, Holborn: Biographical Information of Past Lawyers, Venn's Alumni Cantabrigenses and *The Law Times*.
19. PA 2 June 1845 Brunel examined by Merevale
20. PA Lords Journal Vol 77 p879 22 July 1845
21. Williams, 1949, p175
22. *The Times* 20 March 1857
23. *The Times* 10 December 1860
24. Clifford, 1968, Vol p88; Williams, 1949, p109
25. TNA RAIL 134/2

CHAPTER 6: 'MEN ARE SOMETIMES MASTERS OF THEIR FATES'

1. PA 3 June1845 Stephenson examined by Rowe
2. PA 3 June 1845 Locke examined by Rowe
3. Conder, 1868
4. PA 31 May 1845 Moorsom cross examined by Rowe
5. PA 5 May 1845 Moorsom examined by a member of the Committee
6. Rolt: 1960, p240
7. PA 3 June 1845 Bidder examined by Rowe
8. TNA RAIL 134/1 General Meeting of Shareholders 26 August 1845
9. TNA RAIL 134/1 30 April 1846
10. TNA RAIL 134/1 Board Meeting 30 April 1846
11. Brunel letterbook 4 Letter dated 27 December 1845
12. PA 1846 Johnson cross examined by Rowe
13. PA 26 May 1846 Brunel examined by Kinglake
14. PA 26 May 1846 Brunel examined by Merevale
15. PA 28 May 1846 Vignoles examined by Merevale
16. PA 10 June 1846 Locke examined by Committee

17. PA 20 May 1846 Hawkshaw examined by Kinglake
18. RCG 6 May 1859

CHAPTER 7: ' THE MOST DIFFICULT ENGINEERING WORK WHICH HAS EVER BEEN ATTEMPTED IN THIS OR ANY OTHER COUNTRY'

1. Kittridge 2008, p50
2. PA 3 June1845 Rendel examined by Rowe
3. PA 1846 Johnson cross examined by Rowe
4. PA 29 May 1845 Moorsom cross examined by Rowe
5. PA 3 June 1845 Rendel examined by Rowe
6. PA 3 June 1845 Bidder examined by Rowe
7. PA 3 June 1845 Stephenson examined by Rowe
8. PA 2 June 1845 Brunel cross examined by Rowe
9. PA 2 June 1845 Locke examined by Rowe
10. PA 21 May 1845 Lemon cross examined by Rowe
11. PA 29 May 1845 Moorsom cross examined by Rowe
12. PA 2 June 1845 Pendarves examined by Rowe
13. RCG 6 May 1859
14. Clifford *A History of Private Bill Legislation Vol 1* p85
15. PA 26 May 1846 Brunel examined by Kinglake
16. ICE Proceedings 1861/2 session, Paper 1,062
17. TNA RAIL 134/2 Meeting of the Board 9 August 1848
18. Inflation: the Value of the Pound 1750-1998 House of Commons Research Paper 99/20 23 February 1999
19. *Biographical Dictionary of Civil Engineers* p523
20. *The Times* 4 May 1859
21. *The Times* 2 September 1857
22. RGC 6 May 1859
23. *The Times* 7 October 1858
24. Walters, 1963
25. Cowan C, *Runcorn Railway Bridge , Crossing the Runcorn Gap, 3,* Halton Borough Council, 1990
26. Planning application 10/ 00473/LBC, Plymouth City Council PA HL/PO/60/1

CHAPTER 8: ON BUDGET, ON TIME?

1. PA Locke 12 June 1846 cross examined by Talbot
2. PA Locke 12 June 1846 examined by Cockburn
3. RCG 15 November 1844
4. PA 29 May 1846 Protheroe Smith cross examined by Rowe
5. WB 6 May 1859
6. PA Brunel cross examined by Rowe 29 May 1846
7. PA 15 June 1846 Bidder examined by Cockburn
8. PA 12 June 1846 Rendel examined by James
9. PA 12 June 1846 Locke examined by Cockburn
10. Simmons, 1991, p28
11. TNA RAIL 134/51 Notes on the construction of the Cornwall Railway
12. Devey, 1862, p189
13. Simmons & Biddle, 1997, p275
14. Lane, 1989
15. Rolt, 1970, p68
16 Vaughan, 1991, p68
17. RCG 6 May 1859
18. TNA RAIL 134/2 Directors report 23 February 1847
19. *Biographical Dictionary of Civil Engineers*, p614
20. TNA RAIL 134/2 letter from Brunel to Bond 15 June 1853
    Other Refs; Simmons & Biddle, 1997, p158-9 on financing, p107 on construction costs

CHAPTER 9: 'STRUGGLING FROM ITS VERY INFANCY'

1. TNA RAIL 134/2 Board meeting 26 April 1848
2. RCG 6 May 1859
3. TNA RAIL 134/2 Board meeting 22 February 1850

4. TNA RAIL 134/2 Board meeting 23 February 1849
5. TNA RAIL 134/2 Board meeting 26 August 1852
6. TNA RAIL 134/2 Board meeting 13 May 1848
7. TNA RAIL 134/2 Board meeting 24 May 1852
8. TNA RAIL 134/2 Half yearly meeting 28 February 1851
9. TNA RAIL 134/2 Board meeting 28 August 1852
10. TNA RAIL 134/2 Board meeting 25 November 1852
11. TNA RAIL 134/3 Board Meeting 26 April 1856
12. Simmons & Biddle, 1997, p160
13. TNA RAIL 134/3 Board meeting 10 October 1856
14. TNA RAIL 134/3 Board meeting 28 March 1857
15. TNA RAIL 134/3 Board meeting 11 November 1858
16. TNA RAIL 134/3 Board meeting 12 August 1859
17. WB 5 September 1845

CHAPTER 10: THE ART OF SURVIVAL

1. WB 6 May 1859
2. TNA RAIL 134/3 Report on the Saltash Bridge works 16 April -14 May 1859
3. WB 6 May 1859
4. *Plymouth, Devonport and Stonehouse Herald* 7 May 1859; WB 7 May 1859
5. RCG 6 May 1859
6. WB 27 June 1856
7. TNA RAIL 134/3 Board meeting 4 July 1856
8. TNA RAIL 13417 Letter dated 20 August 1859
9. TNA RAIL 134/3 Letter dated 28 September 1859 reported to Board Meeting October 1859
10. *The Times* 27 August 1860
11. Thomas, 1960
12. Brindle, 2005, p164.
13. TNA RAIL 134/3 Board Meeting 6 May 1859
14. TNA RAIL 134/25/26 13 April 1852
15. RCG 6 May 1859
16. RCG 6 May1859
17. TNA RAIL 134/3 Letter from Bennett to Bond dated 21 April 1860 reported to Board Meeting 4 May 1860
18. RCG 6 May 1859
19. TNA Minutes of South Devon Railway Company dated 14 August 1860
20. TNA RAIL 134 25/26 Letter from Brereton to Bond dated 10 May 1860
21. TNA RAIL 134/3 Board Meeting 29 June 1860
22. Brunel, 1870
23. ICE Proceedings No 1848, 1882
24. TNA RAIL 1034/79 Report of meeting held at Paddington, 20 April 1883
25. TNA RAIL 134/36
26. *The Times* 31 October 1846
27. *The Times* 31 December 1852
28. *The Times* 29/30 June 1849
29. *The Times* 15 September 1851
30. *The Times* 5 March1860
31. Simmons & Biddle, 1997, p113
32. TNA RAIL 1034/79 Report of meeting held at GW Hotel, Paddington, 20 April 1883
33. TNA RAIL/134/43
34. British Railways Board, 1963
35. http://www.kilbridegroup.com/tavistock
36. *The Times* 19 November 1888

Sources & Acknowledgements

FACTS ARE SACRED, COMMENT IS FREE
C. P. Scott

I have relied, wherever possible, on contemporary accounts, books of the period, newspapers and archival material for their immediacy.

Contemporary accounts appear in the *West Briton* (WB), the *Royal Cornwall Gazette* (formerly the *Cornwall Royal Gazette, Falmouth Packet* and *Plymouth Journal*) (RCG), the *Plymouth, Devonport and Stonehouse Herald* and the *Plymouth and Devonport Journal*. As will be seen in Chapter 3 these papers politicised the issue of the route of the railway and must be read in the context of their political loyalties, for which Elvins (*see below*) is an invaluable guide. They were influential. Their reports on the opening of the railway in May 1859 give comprehensive historical accounts of the problems that the promoters and the Company faced over the previous 20 years. The *West Briton* issued a special 4 page *'Illustrated Railway Supplement'* to commemorate the occasion. It covered in some detail the history of the company, the engineering works, the scenery, topography and antiquities of the country as well as the opening ceremony. It is a valuable source document on which I have drawn to a considerable extent. I have also used material from *The Times* and *Manchester Guardian* newspapers.

The search for archive material has taken me to The National Archives (TNA) at Kew, the Parliamentary Archives (PA) in Westminster, Bristol University and the Institution of Civil Engineers. The principal sources are detailed below.

The National Archives at Kew contains records of pre-nationalisation companies. The catalogue reference RAIL 134 relates to the Cornwall Railway Company. Within this file I have consulted:

RAIL 134/1	Railway Committee for promotion of railway between London and West Cornwall
RAIL 134/2	Board meetings
RAIL 134/3	Board meetings
RAIL 134/17	Letters and reports from Brunel
RAIL 134/19	Royal Albert Bridge, reports by resident engineer
RAIL 134/25/26	Falmouth extension reports mainly by Brereton
RAIL 134/36	Arbitration between CRC and GWR about reconstruction of viaducts
RAIL 134/39	Amalgamation with GWR
RAIL 134/43	Agreement of lease and conditional purchase of CRC, 1855
RAIL 134/47	Plan and elevation of Moorswater viaduct 1860
RAIL 134/48/49	Falmouth to Torpoint submitted plans
RAIL 134/51	Notebook of estimates for construction of Cornwall Railway
RAIL 134/79	Report of Meeting of CRC held at GW Hotel, Paddington on 20 April 1883
RAIL 134/113	Warrant of abandonment of branches and reduction of capital
RAIL 1014/2/18	Meeting of Directors 1845
RAIL 1075/13	Direct London and Exeter Railway. Prospectus and application for shares.

At the Parliamentary Archives:

The House of Lords and House of Commons Journals which provide a record of decisions reached in Parliament.

The transcripts of the Parliamentary Select Committee on Railways for the Cornwall Railway Bills of 1845 and 1846. The Committee was set up to provide expert advice to members of the House of Commons and the House of Lords, few of whom understood railway affairs. These are substantial volumes hand written by the clerks of Parliament. Their value is that they provide the actual words used by the witnesses under examination or cross examination. In a few cases I have taken the liberty of inserting punctuation in order to clarify the meaning. However they do not provide witnesses' written statements, nor the summing up of Counsel nor the reasons why the Committee reached its decisions. These two processes appear to have been reached in camera. These typescripts contain several Latin phrases. Suggested translations are:
Puntum saliens: Salient point
Res Integra: With a clean sheet
Salus populi suprema lex: The well-being of the people is the supreme law

House of Commons Select Committee on Railway Bills (Group No2)

HC/CL/PB/2/11/4	Cornwall Railway Bill 1845
HC/CL/PB/2/11/25	Cornwall Railway Bill 1845
HC/CL/PB/2/11/96	West Cornwall Railway Bill 1845
HC/CL/PB/2/12/ 1 and 2	Cornwall Railway Bill 1846
HC/CL/PB/2/12/3	West Cornwall Railway Bill 1846
HC/PO/PB/3/plan 1845/c1	Deposited Plans 1845
HC/PO/PB/3/plan 1846/c30	Deposited Plans 1846

The actual petitions against the bill have been destroyed. Summaries of them are contained in the Journal of the House of Lords.

Government Reports

These relate to Railways in Devon and Cornwall and to Atmospheric Railways both of which were published in 1845 when the first Cornwall Railway Bill was before the Select Committee. There is no doubt that these reports were influential but it is equally clear that the advice that they contain was not always followed.

1) *Report of the Railway Department of the Board of Trade on the Schemes for extending Railway Communication in Cornwall and Devonshire*, 1845. Included as Appendix 1. Henceforward this is referred to as the Board of Trade report.
2) *Report from the Select Committee on Atmospheric Railways with the Minutes of Evidence*, Appendix and Index. 1845 This includes 187 pages of evidence and a 3 page summary which is included as Appendix 2

Bristol University Special Collections:

Brunel's private letterbooks Nos 4, 10 ,11

The Proceedings of the Institution of Civil Engineers.

These provide a repository of expert engineering experience. I have relied, in particular, on the following:

- Description of American Engine 'Philadephia' made by Mr Norris of Philadelphia, North America for the Birmingham and Gloucester Railway, Captain W. S. Moorsom 511 1842/3

- Description of Cast Iron Bridge for carrying the Birmingham and Gloucester Railway over the River Avon near Tewksbury, Captain W. S. Moorsom 611 1844
- The Atmospheric Railway, Jacob Samuda 681 1844
- On the comparative advantages of the Atmospheric Railway System Peter W. Barlow 714 1845
- Railway Incline Planes, Views of Moorsom, Hawkshaw and Vignoles 1855/6
- Description of the Centre Pier of the Saltash Bridge, on the Cornwall Railway, and the means employed for its Construction. Robert Pearson Brereton 1062 1861/62
- Obituary of Capt Moorsom 1863/64
- The Design generally for bridges of very large span for Railway Traffic, Thomas C Clarke 1574 1878
- Reconstruction of the St Pinnock and Moorswater Viaducts on the Cornwall Railway, Peter John Margery 1848 1882
- Obituary of Joseph D Aguilar Samuda 1884/5

RESEARCH RE WILLIAM JOHNSON.
Tracking down the self effacing 'Johnson' who completed the survey for the successful 1846 Cornwall Railway Act required some persistence on the basis of a few clues and substantial help from Nigel Overton of the Plymouth City Museum and Art Gallery, the local history sections of the Manchester City Council and from the Devon Record Office. Johnson is clearly a common name and without the name 'Hornor' on the submitted plan it would not have been possible to trace him or to distinguish him from the Plymouth family of Johnsons. The findings about the Johnson family are set out in Appendix 8.

For other biographical details I have sought out obituaries and used the *Dictionary of National Biography, Modern English Biography,* the *Biographical Dictionary of Civil Engineers, The Law Times* and *The Times*.

There are two topics on which I would have wished to discover more. I have not been able to find Rendel's surveys of either the South Devon or Cornwall Railways. His evidence to the Parliamentary Committee on the Cornwall Railway reveals that he had surveyed lines for both before either Moorsom or Brunel, but neither appears to have survived. In 1845, when asked when he had made the survey, he replied 'I think it was about four or five years ago'.
Another event for which there appears to be little recorded evidence is Brunel's one and only visit to the completed Royal Albert Bridge after his return from convalescence in May 1859. The biography of Brunel by his son, published in 1870 appears to be the only contemporary record. It states that: 'shortly after his return to England he went to Plymouth and over the Saltash bridge ...' He does not give a date or any other detail. Brunel's diary, held at University of Bristol, makes no reference to it and neither do any of the local newspapers. The story appears to have been elaborated in an account published in 1905, some 46 years, after the event, and therefore hardly an original source, by Philip Porter 'Sometime Alderman and one time Mayor of Saltash'. This states:

> Shortly after his return, Brunel went down, and lying on a mattress placed on a carriage truck, saw for the first and last time the bridge in its completed state.

This appears to be the basis of Rolt's seminal biography on Brunel in which the story has been embroidered further. Rolt has not attributed his source. He says;

> He lay on a specially prepared platform truck, while one of Gooch's locomotives drew him very slowly beneath the pier arches and over the great girders. For his railway career was ended. Broken by the last and the most ambitious of all his schemes – his great ship – Brunel was dying

Several authors refer to the event to the effect that he was by this stage so ill that he had to lie on a couch on a train to be taken across the bridge. There is no information about the date that this may have happened. The implication of his lying on a mattress, and this seems to be the first reference to a mattress, suggests that he was very ill. But Brunel was quite active until his stroke on board the Great Eastern on 5 September. Despite the absence of any hard evidence as to when the event may have taken place, various dates have been quoted from 'two days after the opening' to 'the day before he died'. In the absence of any truly contemporary record I have not referred to the event in my text.

I would like to thank the following for their help in enabling me to complete this book:
Patricia Agbarakwe, Network Rail,
Frances Bellis, Archivist, Lincoln's Inn
Angela Broome, The Courteney Library, Royal Institution of Cornwall
Stacey Bullen, Manchester Archives and Local Studies,
Shirley Clarke, Independent Researcher
David Coles, Saltash Heritage,
Kim Cooper, The Cornwall Centre,
Amyas Crump, Great Western Trust at the Didcot Railway Centre
Frank Dumbleton, Great Western Trust at the Didcot Railway Centre,
Simon Gough and staff at the Parliamentary Archive,
Edward Hamer
Ron Hawkins, Falmouth Museum,
Sarah Lloyd-Durrant, Royal Institution of Cornwall,
Anna Monks, Liskeard and District Museum,
Carol Morgan, Institution of Civil Engineers
Nigel Overton, Maritime Heritage Officer, Plymouth City Museum and Art Gallery,
Celia Pilkington, Archivist, Inner Temple,
Peter Rance, Great Western Trust at the Didcot Railway Centre
John Rapson, Recorder for Liskeard Old Cornwall Society
Geof Sheppard, Broad Gauge Society
Candy Smit, Heligan
Howard Somerville
My wife, Monica, for assistance with the text.

Bibliography

The books I have consulted are listed below. Many are specialist in some way: legal, local, engineering or biographical, for example. The three books on Brunel are those by Rolt published in 1957, by Vaughan published in 1991 and by Brindle, published in 2006. Rolt's book performed a valuable service in helping to make industrial history and archaeology accepted as proper subjects. I found it an inspirational book when I first read it at a very impressionable age. It was based partly on published sources and partly on family papers which were not publicly accessible at the time. Vaughan criticises Rolt on the basis that he has produced a hagiography omitting evidence that does not support his preconceived hero worship. Vaughan, on the other hand, portrays Brunel as a man driven on by a ruthless ambition regardless of the interests of contractors, navvies or the companies that employed him: 'This is the first biography to show Brunel as he actually was ... a man who was obstinate, unjust, dictatorial and, in the end, paranoid.' Vaughan seems, however, to come down uncritically on Brunel's side in his arguments with Moorsom.

Baker J. H. *The Order of Serjeants at Law*, Supp Series Vol.5 Selsden Society 1984

Betjeman J. *Summoned by Bells* Readers Union Ltd 1960

Binding, John, *Brunel's Cornish Viaducts* Pendragon 1993

Binding, John, *Brunel's Royal Albert Bridge* Twelveheads Press 1997

Bond M. 'Records of Parliament 2. Private Bill Records' *The Amateur Historian* Spring 1960 Vol 4 No 7

Bourne J. C. *Bourne's London and Birmingham Railway* 1839. Reprinted David and Charles 1970.

Bourne J. C. *Bourne's Great Western Railway* 1846. Reprinted David and Charles 1970.

Brindle S. *Brunel, The Man who Built the World* Weidenfeld and Nicholson 2005

British Railways Board *The Reshaping of British Railways* HMSO 1963

Brunel I. *The Life of Isambard Kingdom Brunel Civil Engineer* 1870. Republished 2006 Nonsuch Publishing.

Cantor, Geoffrey *Quakers, Jews and Science - Religious Responses to Modernity and the Sciences* OUP 2005

Christiansen, Rex *A Regional History of the Railways of Great Britain, Volume 7* David and Charles 1973

Clifford, Frederick *The History of Private Bill Legislation*, 1885 Butterworth, Reprinted Frank Cass 1968

Conder F. R. *The Men who built the Railways,* Hodder and Stoughton 1868. Reprinted 1983 Thomas Telford, edited by Jack Simmons.

Devey J. *Life of Joseph Locke, Civil Engineer MP, FRS, etc*, Richard Bentley, London 1862.

Elvins B. 'Cornwall's Newspaper War; The Political Rivalry between the Royal Cornwall Gazette and the West Briton 1810-55', *Cornish Studies 9 and 11*, The Cornish Studies Unit, University of Exeter Press, 2001.

Elvins B. *The Reform Movement and County Politics in Cornwall* (University of Birmingham thesis) Chapter 9 The Corn Laws and the Protection Issue 1842-52.

Freeman M. *Railways and the Victorian Imagination*, Yale University Press1999

Hadfield, Charles *Atmospheric Railways, A Victorian Venture in Silent Speed* Alan Sutton 1985

Halliday F. E. *A History of Cornwall*, Duckworth 1959
Holborn G. *Sources of Biographical Information on Past Lawyers*
British and Irish Association of Law Librarians 1999
Jenkins S. C. & Langley R. C. *The West Cornwall Railway* Oakwood Press 2002
Keast, John, *The King of Mid Cornwall, The Life of Joseph Treffry (1782-1850)* Dyllansow Truran 1982
Kennedy I. & Treuherz J. *The Railway Art in the Age of Steam*
(Catalogue accompanying an exhibition at the Walker Gallery, Liverpool) 2008
Kittridge, Alan, *Rendel's Floating Bridges* Twelveheads Press 2008
Lane, Michael R. *The Rendel Connection* Quiller Press Ltd 1989
Lewin H.G. *The Railway Mania and its aftermath 1845-1852* 1936.
Reprinted David and Charles 1968
Lewis B, *Brunel's Timber Bridges and Viaducts* Ian Allan Publishing
Long & Awdrey, *Birmingham and Gloucester Railway*, Alan Sutton 1987
Ostler E. *History of the Cornwall Railway*, 1835-1846, Cornwall Gazette Office, 1846.
Parris M. & Maguire K. *Great Parliamentary Scandals* Robson Books 1995
Platt, Alan *The Life and Times of Daniel Gooch* Alan Sutton 1987
Reynolds D. G. *Par Excellence* Par Old Cornwall Society 2008
Rolt L. T. C. *George and Robert Stephenson, The Railway Revolution* Longmans 1960
Rolt L. T. C. *Victorian Engineering* Allen Lane 1970
Rolt L. T. C. *Isambard Kingdom Brunel, A Biography* Longmans, Green and Co 1957
Simmons, Jack, *The Victorian Railway* Thames and Hudson 1991
Simmons, Jack & Biddle Gordon, *Oxford Companion to British Railway History* OUP 1997
Sainty, Sir John *A List of English Law Officers, King's Counsel and Holders of Patents of Precedence*
Supp. Series Vol.7, Selsden Society 1987
Thomas, David StJ. *A Regional History of the Railways of Great Britain, Volume 1*
David and Charles 1960
Vaughan A. *Isambard Kingdom Brunel, Engineering Knight-Errant* John Murray 1991
Walters D. *British Railway Bridges* Ian Allan 1963
Whetter J. *History of Falmouth* Dyllansow Truran 1981
Williams O. C. *History of Private Bill Procedures*, Vol 1 H.M.Stationary Office 1949.
Wilson D. G. *Falmouth Haven* Tempus Publications 2007
Wolmar C. *The Subterranean Railway* Atlantic Books 2005

Appendix One

REPORT of the RAILWAY DEPARTMENT of the BOARD OF TRADE on the Schemes for extending the Railway Communication in Cornwall and Devonshire.

HC 89 (1845) P 1-5

Ordered by the House of Commons to be printed, 4 March 1845

Railway Department, Board of Trade.
Whitehall, 4 March 1845

The Board constituted Minute of the Lords of the Committee of Privy Council for Trade, for the transaction of Railway business, having had under consideration, the following schemes deposited with the Railway Department for extending Railway communication in Cornwall and Devonshire, viz:

The Cornwall Railway (Plymouth to Falmouth);
The Cornwall and Devon Central (Exeter to Falmouth);
The Great Western and Cornwall Junction (Exeter to Falmouth);
The West Cornwall;
The St. Ives Junction;
The Exeter and Crediton;
The North Devon (Crediton to Barnstaple);
The Torquay and Newton:

have determined on submitting the following Report thereon for the consideration of Parliament.

First, as regards the schemes proposed for extending Railway communication to Falmouth.
In this case the question is not so much what is preferable as what is practicable. Had the question of Railway extension to the westward of Exeter been an open one, and had the nature of the country admitted of the construction, at any moderate cost, of a central line through the counties of Devon and Cornwall, combining the traffics of Falmouth and Plymouth, and of both counties over one trunk, we are by no means insensible to the advantages which such a combination would have presented, both as shortening the distance from the extreme points to London and to the rest of England, and as affording better accommodation to the northern and central portions of the two counties.

The question however, assumes a very different aspect when we consider that the Legislature has already sanctioned the South Devon line from Exeter to Plymouth, by which a large proportion of the traffic which was calculated upon to support a central line is irrevocably diverted into another channel; and such an advance is made towards Falmouth that the construction of 66 miles of new Railway as compared with 100½ by the Central line, will be sufficient to complete the communication.

As regards the Central line the question is therefore reduced to this; whether the remaining traffic, that of Plymouth and its vicinity, and probably that of Tavistock in connexion with the Plymouth line, being lost, is sufficient to render at all feasible, as a commercial speculation , the construction of 100½ miles of new Railway from Falmouth to Exeter.

Upon this point we have no hesitation in expressing our opinion, after a careful examination of the traffic tables and other evidence submitted to us, that there would be no probability of such a line being supported in a state of solvency, unless it were one which admitted of being constructed and worked with extreme economy.

The existing through traffic by land between Falmouth and Exeter supports only two coaches, both of which are mails; and the through traffic both of goods and passengers, which now goes by sea, will have to be competed for , with steamboats and sailing vessels. For about two-thirds of its course between Bodmin and Exeter the Central line would traverse a barren thinly-populated country, hardly passing through a single town, and consequently could not expect to command much local traffic.

An examination of the traffic tables prepared by the County committee in 1841, with a view to the Central line then proposed, and which may then be relied upon as erring in excess rather than in deficit, will confirm this result , and show that if, on the one hand, the Plymouth and Tavistock traffic, and on the other, the various sources of local traffic which would have been commanded by the Central line then projected, but not by the present line , be deducted, there will scarcely remain enough to justify the construction of a line 100 miles in length , even if it were of cheap and easy execution.

But the proposed Central Cornwall and Devon Railway would be of a most difficult and expensive character. Throughout its whole length it has hardly a mile running at or near the natural surface of the ground. It has nine tunnels whose united length amounts to 4,820 yards, eight miles of cutting at depths exceeding 50 feet; nine miles of embankment of a height exceeding 70 feet and 1,076 yards of viaduct, at heights of 83 and 45 feet.

The difficulty and expense of such immense works are greatly enhanced by the geological character of the district through which they would have to be constructed. It appears from statements submitted to us, that one tunnel of 700 yards, at a depth of 140 feet below ground, is through granite; a cutting of 1¾ mile, as deep in parts as 70 feet , is through granite and hard greenstone; and, generally speaking, a great part of the line runs through granite, greenstone, silicious slate, and other rocks of a hard description.

The general experience of Railway construction would not warrant us in assuming that a line of this description could be constructed at a less cost than 30,000*l*. or 40,000*l*. per mile; and even if we were to make every allowance for the superior economy of construction which is now expected to prevail, more especially in a district like Cornwall, where mining operations are so well understood , we should be unable to satisfy ourselves that there was any reasonable probability for supposing that the line in question could be completed for anything like the estimate of 1,500,000*l*.

Neither would the result of these immense works be to attain a line with good gradients, admitting of economical and expeditious working. On the contrary, the gradients of the proposed Central line are very severe. At the Falmouth end there is a gradient of 2 miles and 10 chains in length, at an inclination of 1 in 60, terminating in a curve of 20 chains radius. In the central portion of the line there is a continues ascent to the summit on one side of 11 miles, at an average inclination of 1 in 92; and on the other side, of 10 miles at an average inclination of nearly 1 in 100.

It is evident that a line of this description could not be worked with speed and punctuality, as an important passenger locomotive line, without incurring heavy expense for power.

Considering, therefore, the unusually expensive nature of the works upon the Central line, the severity of the gradients, implying additional cost in working, and the comparatively small amount of traffic that could be expected to pass over it, we have had no hesitation in arriving at the opinion that it must be considered under present circumstances, as altogether impracticable as a commercial undertaking.

The plans and sections of another project for a Central line, called the Great Western and Cornwall Junction, have also been deposited with this department; and although it does not appear that the project in question has ever obtained any support, either from the Public or from local interests, as would warrant us in assuming it to be a substantive scheme, likely to be submitted to Parliament; we have thought it right to investigate its engineering circumstances, in order, in order to ascertain whether there was any probability of an easier line than that of the Cornwall and Devon Central being found in a different direction. The result of this investigation has been, however, to satisfy us that the project in question was even more objectionable than that already described. Although the plans and sections deposited with us are in such an imperfect state, that the necessary information is not always to be obtained (the extreme height and depth of the embankment's and cuttings being, for instance, frequently omitted), enough appears upon them to show that the line is one continued succession of cuttings and embankments, many of which are of enormous dimensions. There are 31 cuttings, whose depth exceeds 50 feet, some of them reaching the depth of 90 and 100 feet; 11 embankments, exceeding 70 feet in height; 4,880 yards of tunnels; and nine viaducts, of the length of 3,980 yards.

We therefore, are compelled to abandon the idea of a Central line, as altogether impracticable, and to confine ourselves to the sole question of the Coast line from Plymouth to Falmouth. This line is only 60 miles in length, and the works are not, on the whole, of a very heavy character.

The total length of cutting exceeding 30 feet in depth, is only four miles, and it has only one cutting of half a mile, at a depth exceeding 50 feet, at and beyond which depth the Central line had eight miles in cutting. It has only 2¼ miles of embankment at a height exceeding 40 feet, and only half a mile as compared to nine miles on the Central line, at a height exceeding 70 feet. There is but one tunnel of 580 yards, and 739 yards of viaduct, at heights varying from 20 to 100 feet.

There does not appear, therefore, to be any material difficulty in the way of the Coast line as regards the expense of construction. The probability of a sufficient traffic is also greater upon this line than upon the Central line; since in the event of the latter not being constructed, it will command the greater part of the same through traffic, while it will probably obtain a much larger local traffic in proportion to its length, passing as it does through more populous district, and connecting Cornwall with the large and important towns of Plymouth and Devonport.

We are of the opinion, therefore, that the extension of the Coast line from Plymouth to Falmouth may fairly be sanctioned as a commercial speculation, and that, in this point of view, it affords the only practicable means at present of extending Railway communication to the county of Cornwall.

The principal objections to the line arise in the nature of its curves and gradients. The ruling gradient of the line is 1 in 60, at which high inclination there are no fewer than 28 planes, whose united length amounts to very nearly 26 miles. There are four planes even steeper than this; one of a mile in length being 1 in 45 , and three at others at 1 in 50. Generally speaking, these steep inclines are for short lengths, and undulating, the longest being an incline of 1 in 60 for two miles six chains.

The curves of the line are also very severe, there being about 60 curves, of 15 chains radius, and several others approaching the same degree of curvature, and many of these curves are on steep gradients.

The promoters state that the line has been laid out with a view to the adoption of the atmospheric system, upon which system the gradients and curves might not be objectionable.

In our Report upon the Newcastle and Berwick schemes, to which we must here refer, we have fully stated our views with regard to the atmospheric system, and the reasons which make it impossible at present to assume its complete success in making a comparison between competing schemes. In the present instance, these considerations might be somewhat modified by the circumstance that, in our opinion, the Central scheme cannot be considered as practicable, and therefore not as entering into competition with the Coast line. Also the comparison is not with a line which offers good locomotive gradients, those of the Central line being also severe as we have already seen.

At the same time we feel that these circumstances do not obviate the objections which may be urged against sanctioning the line which, in the present state of experience, cannot be considered as practicable for the locomotive engine.

Upon this point we have fully stated our views and the conclusion which experience appears to justify, in our Report on the Manchester and Leeds district to which we beg to refer.

From these facts it does not appear that experience would warrant us in pronouncing the gradients proposed upon the Cornwall line to be absolutely impracticable or dangerous for the ordinary locomotive engine; and nothing short of this would, as we conceive, justify us in reporting to Parliament an opinion adverse to a line which affords, in our belief , the only practicable means of attaining such an important object as the connexion of the county of Cornwall by railway with the rest of the kingdom.

The necessity of a passage of the Hamoaze, involved by this line, has been strongly objected to, as calculated to create delay and inconvenience. Undoubtedly, if the comparison had lain between this line and one equally practicable in another direction, the interruption occasioned by the ferry would have been a strong argument in favour of the competing project. It does not appear, however, that this passage is in itself so objectionable as to weigh materially in a consideration of the sole practicable line proposed into Cornwall. The ferry at the Hamoaze is in a situation sheltered from the sea and comparatively little affected by the tides; and there appears to be no insurmountable impediment in the way of transporting the carriages and waggons of railway trains across it, by a moveable bridge worked by machinery, in the same manner as the ordinary traffic passing the ferry is now transported. It is certified to us by the treasurer of the Torpoint Steam Ferry Company, that the present bridge has been in operation for the last ten years, and has never on any occasion experienced interruption from the weather. Also, that the bridge crosses every quarter of an hour for 15 hours a day, and that the actual average time of crossing is only about six or seven minutes.

It appears to us, therefore, that independently of the improvements in the present mode of transit which the promoters of the Cornwall Railway, in conjunction with the South Devon Railway Company, look forward to introducing, there is no such objection to the crossing as should weigh materially in a consideration of the line.

On the whole, therefore, considering that the proposed Cornwall Railway from Plymouth to Falmouth affords the only practicable means of extending Railway communication to Cornwall; that it will thus afford great benefits to a large and important district; and that although bad in respect of curves and gradients, it is not absolutely impracticable as a locomotive line, and not inferior to any other line that is likely to be obtained at any moderate expense;- we have to report our opinion that there no sufficient public grounds why it should not receive the sanction of Parliament.

The West Cornwall Railway is an unopposed local scheme in connexion with the above, and with the Hayle Railway, extending Railway communication through the populous mining districts west of Truro as far as Penzance. There seems no reason to doubt that it will be productive of a considerable local benefit, and will command a large local traffic, sufficient to warrant its construction, besides affording a prolongation of the trunk line almost to the Land's End. The gradients are in part steep, but not impracticable and the works are generally easy, the total estimated capital for a single line of 23 miles being only 180,000*l*.

Plans have been deposited for a portion of the line up to Truro, common to the Cornwall Railway; but of course this portion ought to be in the hands of the more important company, and the West Cornwall line should be considered as commencing at the junction.

The St, Ives Railway is a short branch, in connexion with the above, of three miles in length, from Hayle to St Ives, intended to afford access to that port.

We are aware of no public reasons why this and the West Cornwall scheme should not receive the sanction of Parliament.

In conclusion, we beg to draw attention to the passage of the Fifth Report of the Select Committee of last year, in which it is stated, in recommending that Reports should be made to Parliament by this department upon Railway schemes, That no such Report should be held to prejudice the claims of private persons, the examination of which should be altogether reserved to the House of the Legislature.

In submitting to Parliament, in conformity with the recommendations of that Committee, the results at which we have arrived, with a view to the information and assistance of Parliament in forming a judgement upon the schemes in question, in so far as our Report may be available for that purpose, we are anxious that it should be distinctly understood that we have arrived at these results solely upon public grounds, and to the exclusion of all considerations how far such results might require to be modified by a due regard for private rights and interests.

DALHOUSIE
D. O BRIEN G. R. PORTER
T. CODDINGTON S. LAING

APPENDIX TWO

REPORT

FROM THE

SELECT COMMITTEE

ON

ATMOSPHERIC RAILWAYS

Ordered, by the House of commons to be Printed,

24 April 1845

HC 252 (1845) p iii-v

THE SELECT COMMITTEE appointed to Inquire into the Merits of the ATMOSPHERIC SYSTEM OF RAILWAY; Have examined the Matters to them referred, and have agreed to the following REPORT:

OUR Committee have given their best attention to this interesting subject.

Adverting to the great number of Railway Bills now in progress, they consider that one of the most practical results of this inquiry would be lost if their Report were delayed until after these Bills had passed through Committee and a decision had made on their comparative merits.

Your Committee have endeavoured therefore to present to The House, with as little delay as is consistent with the due discharge of their duty, the Evidence which they have taken and the Opinions to which they have come, and they trust that their labour may not prove altogether useless to the committee that have decided on the schemes now pending.

The House are aware that a Railway on the Atmospheric principle is already in operation between Kingstown and Dalkey in Ireland.

The first object of Your Committee was to make a full inquiry into the results of this experiment. From Mr Gibbons, Mr Bergin and Mr Vignoles, gentlemen officially connected with the Kingstown and Dublin and Kingstown and Dalkey Railways, they have received the fullest and frankest evidence on all the points connected with their management. Your Committee had also the advantage of the opinion of Dr Robinson, of Armagh, whose scientific knowledge and acquirements render his testimony particularly valuable on the theoretical merits of such an invention.

From this evidence, and from that of Mr Samuda it appears that the Dalkey Line has been open for 19 months, that it has worked with regularity and safety throughout all the vicissitudes of temperature, and that the few interruptions which have occurred have arisen rather from the inexperience of the attendants, than from any material defect in the system.

Your Committee find moreover that high velocities have been attained with proportional loads on an incline averaging 1 in 115, within a course in which the power is applied only during one mile and an eighth.

These results have been displayed under circumstances which afford no fair criterion of what may be expected elsewhere; for, in addition to the curves on the line, which would have been considered objectionable, if not impracticable, for Locomotive engines, there are alleged to exist deficiencies in the machinery and apparatus, occasioned partly by the difficulties of the situation, partly by mistakes inseparable from a first attempt, which very seriously detract from the efficiency of the power employed for the remedy of which provision has been made in the experiments now in progress.

These are important facts. They establish the mechanical efficiency of the Atmospheric power to convey with regularity, speed, and security the traffic upon one section of the pipe between two termini; and Your Committee have since been satisfied by the evidence of Messrs Brunel, Cubitt, and Vignoles, that there is no mechanical difficulty which will oppose the working of the same system on a line of any length. They are further confirmed in this opinion by the conduct of the Dalkey and Kingstown directors, who have at this moment before parliament a proposition to extend their Atmospheric Line to Bray.

In addition to the witnesses already mentioned, Your Committee have had the advantage of hearing the objections urged by Messrs. Nicholson, Stephenson, and Locke against the adoption of the Atmospheric principle and the grounds of their preference of the locomotive now in use.

Your Committee must refer The House to the valuable evidence given by these gentlemen. It will be seen that great differences of opinion exists between them and the other witnesses to whom Your Committee have before referred both in their estimation of what has already been effected, and in their calculations for future improvement.

But without entering upon all the controverted points, Your Committee have no hesitation in stating that a single Atmospheric line is superior to a double locomotive line both in regularity and safety, in as much as it makes collisions impossible except at crossing places, and excludes all the danger and irregularity arising from the casualties to engines or their tenders. Now the importance of these considerations will be best estimated by a reference to the return of accidents for 15 months appended to this Report. It will there be seen that there have been during that period 14 collisions upon the road and 13 accidents to engines to engines, which would altogether have been avoided on the Atmospheric system, and that these casualties entailed the loss of 11 lives, as well as the serious injury of 45 persons. From the other 20 accidents, common to both systems, resulted in only four deaths, and two persons injured. There is certainly one case in which the engine passed uninjured over cattle lying upon the road together with its entire train: but then against this security derived from the advantage of weight in surmounting obstacles, must be set the great danger to which the engine driver and stoker are exposed, standing as they do upon an open platform.

Your Committee desire also to bring to the attention of The House a peculiarity of the Atmospheric system which has been adduced by the objectors to prove how unsuited it must be profitably to carry on a small and irregular traffic: namely, that the greatest proportion of the expenses of haulage on the Atmospheric principle are constant and cannot be materially reduced, however small the amount of traffic may be. This is, no doubt, a serious objection to the economy of the Atmospheric system under the circumstances above alluded to. But, on the other hand, as the expenses do not increase in proportion to the frequency of the trains, it is to the interests of the Companies adopting the Atmospheric principle to increase the amount of their traffic by running frequent light trains, at low rates of fares; by which the convenience of the public must be greatly promoted. Upon an Atmospheric Railway the moving power is most economically applied by dividing the weight to be carried into a considerable number of light trains. By Locomotive engines on the contrary, the power is most conveniently applied by concentrating the traffic in a smaller number of heavier trains. The rate of speed at which trains of moderate weight can be conveyed on an Atmospheric line, makes comparatively little difference in the cost of conveyance; while the cost of moving trains by Locomotive engines increases rapidly with the speed.

Now when it is considered that we surrender to great monopolies the regulation of all the arteries of communication throughout the kingdom, that it depends in a great measure upon their view of their interest when we shall travel, at what speed we shall travel, and what we shall pay, it becomes a material consideration, in balancing the advantages ensured to the public by rival systems, to estimate not so much what they respectively can do, but what, in the pursuit of their own emolument, they will do.

The main objections of the opponents of the Atmospheric system seem to rest, 1st, on the supposed increased expense of the Atmospheric apparatus over and above the saving made in the construction of the road; 2nd, on the inconvenience and irregularity attending upon a single line. With reference to the last point, Your Committee felt it their duty to direct their first attention to the question of security, and they have already stated that there is more security in a single Atmospheric line than in a double Locomotive. They may further observe, that they find the majority of the engineers who have been examined are decidedly of opinion that any ordinary traffic might be carried on with regularity and convenience by a single Atmospheric line.

Mr Brunel has proposed to double the line in those places where trains are intended to meet; and he has further shown that in a hilly country, with long planes of sufficient inclination to allow of the descent of trains by the unaided power of gravity, it might be possible to effect this object without the expense of the tube.

With respect to expense, and to some other contested points, Your Committee do not feel themselves competent to report a decided opinion. It would scarcely be possible at the present time to institute a fair comparison of a system which has had 15 years of growth and development, with another which is as yet in its infancy. That comparison would, after all, be very uncertain: it must depend much on details of which we are ignorant: much on scientific knowledge which we do not possess.

There are, however, questions of practical importance, having reference to the present state of the Railway Bills before the House, to which Your Committee consider themselves bound to advert.

There is a doubt raised in the Reports of the Board of Trade, whether the Atmospheric system has been sufficiently tested to justify the preference of a line which can only be worked on the Atmospheric system, or which presents gradients less favourable than a competing line for the use of the Locomotive engine.

If it were practicable to suspend all railway legislation until the result of the Devon and Cornwall, and of the Epsom and Croydon Atmospheric lines were know, it would be perhaps the most cautious and prudent course to wait that result; but such a course, independent of all considerations of expediency, is evidently impracticable. Your Committee venture therefore to express their opinion to The House, that in deciding between competing lines of railway, those which have been set out to suit the Atmospheric principle ought not to be considered as open to valid objection merely on account of their having gradients too severe for the Locomotive, nor should they be tested in comparison with other lines solely by the degree of their suitableness to the use of the Locomotive.

No doubt in matters like these, experience alone can decide the ultimate result, but Your Committee think that there is ample evidence which would justify the adoption of an Atmospheric line at the present time. All the witnesses they have examined concur in its mechanical success. Mr Bidder says, 'I consider the mechanical problem as solved, whether the Atmosphere could be made an efficient tractive agent. There can be no question about that: and the apparatus worked, as far as I observed it, very well. The only question in my mind was as to the commercial application of it.' Mr. Stephenson admits that under certain circumstances of gradients, and under certain circumstances of traffic without reference to gradients , the Atmospheric system would be preferable.

While your Committee have thus expressed a strong opinion in favour of the general merits of the Atmospheric principle, they feel that experience can alone determine under what circumstances of traffic or of country the preference to either system should be given.

22 April 1845

APPENDIX THREE

CORNWALL RAILWAY

Provisional Committee

(All of whom are Shareholders)

JOSEPH THOMAS TREFFRY Esq, Place, Chairman
THE RIGHT HONOURABLE THE EARL OF FALMOUTH
THE RIGHT HONOURABLE THE EARL OF ST GERMANS
THE RIGHT HONOURABLE THE EARL OF MORLEY
THE RIGHT HONOURABLE THE LORD FORTESCUE
THE RIGHT HONOURABLE LORD CLINTON
THE RIGHT HONOURABLE THE LORD WODEHOUSE
THE HONOURABLE GEORGE MATHEW FORTESCUE, Boconnoc, Cornwall
SIR WILLIAM MOLESWORTH, Bart, MP, Pencarrow, Cornwall
SIR CHARLES LEMON, Bart, MP, Carclew, Cornwall
SIR ANTONY BUTLER, Pound, Devon, Member of the Provisional Committee of the North Devon Railway Company.
WILLIAM TYRINGHAM PRAED Esq. MP., Trevethon, Cornwall
CHARLES RUSSELL Esq. M.P. Chairman of the Great Western Railway Company
THOMAS GILL Esq, M.P. Chairman of the South Devon Railway Company
MONTAGUE GORE Esq M.P. for Barnstable, Member of the Provisional Committee of the North Devon Railway Co
WILLIAM HAYTER Esq. M.P., Director of the Great Western Railway Company
JOHN ALLEN Esq., Liskeard
WILLIAM AVERY Esq., Member of the Provisional Committee of the North Devon Railway Company.
FREDERICK PRATT BARLOW Esq., Director of the Great Western Railway Company
DEEBLE BOGER Esq, Plympton
SAMUEL BORLASE Esq, Castle Horneck, Penzance, Cornwall
JOHN BROWN,Esq., Director of the Bristol and Exeter Railway Company
JOHN BATTEN Esq., Penzance
WILLIAM BROWN,Esq Director of the Bristol and Exeter Railway Company
GEORGE BRAGINTON Esq., Member of the Provisional Committee of the North Devon Railway Co.
ROBERT RICHARDS BROAD Esq., Falmouth
RICHARD BASTARD Esq., Member of the Provisional Committee of the North Devon Railway Company
WILLIAM RICHARDS BROAD Mayor of Falmouth
JAMES WENTWORTH BULLER ESQ., Downes, Crediton, Devon
JOSEPH BROKENSHIR Esq Mayor of Penryn
JOHN BEAVIS BIGNELL MD Barnstable, Member of the Provisional Committee of the North Devon Railway Company

CLEMENT CARLYON MD Mayor of Truro
WILLIAM CARNE Esq., Rosemundy, Cornwall
EDWARD CLIFTON CARNE, Esq./ Falmouth
RALPH COLE, Esq., Director of the South Devon Railway Company
JOHN CHING Esq., Launceston
JOHN KNILL COTTON Esq., Member of the Provisional Committee of the North Devon Railway Company
ROBERT COTESWORTH Esq., St Helen's Place, London, Director of the Royal West India Mail Steam Packet Co.
THOMAS BURNARD CHANTER Esq., Mayor of Bideford
WILLIAM DAUBUZ Esq, Killiow, Cornwall
RICHARD DINGLEY Esq Launceston
CHARLES B TRIPP Esq Director of the Bristol and Exeter Railway Company
ROBERT WERE FOX Esq., Falmouth
ALFRED FOX Esq., Falmouth
CHARLES FOX Esq., Perranarworthal, Cornwall
THOMAS WERE FOX Esq Plymouth
WILLIAM FOX Esq, Director of the South Devon Railway
JAMES GIBBS, Esq., Chairman of the Bristol and Exeter Railway Company
MAJOR GULLY, Trevenon Cornwall
JOHN G WATKIN Esq., Parc-Behan Cornwall
COLONEL HARRIS, of Radford Devon
JAMES HARTLEY Esq., Director of the Oriental and Peninsular Steam Navigation Company
WILLIAM HENRY HAWKER Esq., Director of the South Devon Railway Company
HENRY HOOPER Esq., Member of the Provisional Committee of the North Devon Railway Company
FRANCIS HOWELL, Esq., Ethy, Colrnwall
EDWARD JOHN HUTCHINS Esq., Llansainthead House Abergaveney
T. GOLDIE HARDING Esq., Monkleigh, Devon, Member of the Provisional Committee of the North Devon Railway Co
WILLIAM JOPE Esq., Tremedon, Cornwall
GEORGE JONES Esq., Redland, Bristol, Chairman of the Bristol and Gloucester Railway Company
SAMUEL TREHAWKE KEKEWICH Esq., Penmore, Devon
STEPHEN KNOWLES Esq., Exeter
HENRY LAMBE Esq., Truro
PHILIP EDWARD LYNE, Esq., Boscarrock, Mayor of Plymouth
WILLIAM MORGAN Esq., Director of Bristol and Exeter Railway Company
WILLIAM MICHELL Esq., Truro
PATRICK MILLER MD Director of the Bristol and Exeter Railway company
JAMES MARSH Esq., Rock House, Alphington Devon
JOHN NELSON Esq., Doctors Commons
THOMAS JOHN PHILLIPS Esq., Landue Cornwall
JOHN PAYNTER Esq., Boskenna Cornwall
HENRY PETHICK M.D. Launceston
THOMAS JAMES AGAR ROBARTES Esq., Lanhydrock Cornwall
JOHN CORYTON ROBERTS Esq., Trevol Cornwall
WILLIAM RASHLEIGH, Esq., Menabilly, Cornwall

PHILIP VYVYAN ROBINSON Esq., Rectory Redruth
THE REV. CANON ROGERS R.N. Mawnan, Cornwall
ROBERT RUNDLE Esq., Mayor of Devonport
JOHN RUNDLE Esq., Member of the provisional Committee of the North Devon Railway Company
THE REV. HENDER MOLESWORTH ST AUBYN, Clowance Cornwall
EDWARD ST AUBYN, Esq., Member of the Provisional Committee of the North Devon Railway Company
GEORGE SMITH, Esq., Camborne
CHRISTOPHER SHAPLAND Esq., Director of the Bristol and Gloucester Railway Company
THOMAS SYMONS Esq., Little Falmouth House Cornwall
WILLIAM TOTHILL Esq., Director of the Great Western Railway Company
SEYMOUR TREMENHEERE, Esq., Pall Mall, London
WILLIAM TWEEDY Esq., Truro Vean, Cornwall
WILLIAM MANSEL TWEEDY Esq., Alverton, Cornwall
THE REV. ROBERT MICHAEL NOWELL USTICKE, Penwarne, Falmouth
MICHAEL WILLIAMS Esq., Trevince, Cornwall
WILLIAM WILLIAMS Esq., Tregullow
JOHN MICHAEL WILLIAMS Esq., Scorrier House, Cornwall
THOMAS WOOLLCOMBE Esq., Director of the South Devon Railway Company
WILLIAM D. WILLS, Esq., Director of the Bristol and Exeter Railway Company
WILLIAM WATSON, Esq., Director of the Bristol and Exeter Railway Company
JAMES C WILLCOCKS, Esq., Member of the Provisional Committee of the North Devon Railway Company

Committee of Management

JOSEPH THOMAS TREFFRY CHAIRMAN
JAMES GIBBS
FREDERICK PRATT BARLOW ESQ
PATRICK MILLER
CLEMENT CARLYON
THOMAS JAMES AGAR ROBARTES
WILLIAM CARNE
CHRISTOPHER SHAPLAND Esq
RALPH COLE
GEORGE SMITH
ROBERT WERE FOX
WILLIAM MANSEL TWEEDY
WILLIAM FOX
JOHN VIVIAN
THOMAS GILL
MICHAEL WILLIAMS
JOHN G WATKIN
THOMAS WOOLLCOMBE

Source Devon Record Office 1262M/E/24/10

Appendix four

CORNWALL AND DEVON CENTRAL RAILWAY

FROM

EXETER TO FALMOUTH AND PENZANCE

WITH BRANCHES TO

Plymouth, Tavistock, Bideford, Barnstaple and St. Austell

FORMING, IN CONTINUATION OF THE

LONDON AND SOUTH WESTERN, - LONDON, SALISBURY AND YEOVIL, - AND YEOVIL, DORCHESTER, AND EXETER RAILWAYS

A DIRECT LINE FROM

LONDON TO EXETER, FALMOUTH, AND PENZANCE

Capital £3,000,000 in 120,000 Shares of £25. each

Deposit £2. 12s. 6d per Share

With power to decrease the Capital to £2,000,000 should the branches be carried out by Auxilliary Companies.

PROSPECTUS

The Bill for making a Railway from PLYMOUTH to FALMOUTH, and the WEST CORNWALL RAILWAY BILL, having been both rejected by Parliament, and the projected SOUTH DEVON RAILWAY from EXETER to PLYMOUTH pursuing only a winding and precarious course along the margin of the Southern Channel, the great area of Devonshire West of Exeter, and the whole of the County of Cornwall, are now destitute of Railway accommodation.

The object of the present undertaking is to provide an efficient system of Railway communication for the whole of the Western Peninsula; and as the waste of capital and time, involved in the circuitous route by BRISTOL, is greatly complained of, the leading and indispensable feature of the project will be to obtain the most direct, punctual and economical line between LONDON, FALMOUTH and PENZANCE. As far as EXETER, that project is already in the hands of the "*London and South Western*," the "*London Salisbury, and Yeovil Junction*" and the "*Yeovil, Dorchester and Exeter*" Companies. It was this Central Line, Westward, which the Committee of the House of Lords, in the WILTS AND SOMERSET RAILWAY Bill, in the present Session, obliged the GREAT WESTERN RAILWAY COMPANY to pledge themselves not to oppose; and which they speak of in their report "*as the Line which the best interest of the Country require, and which must eventually be carried direct to Falmouth, the most Westerly Port in the Channel.*"

Under these auspices, and with this strong expression from the Legislature, it may be considered that a continuous Line of Railway, from LONDON through SALISBURY, to YEOVIL and EXETER, no less than 30 Miles shorter than the devious course of the GREAT WESTERN RAILWAY is already morally secured. In order, therefore, to complete this great national project thus suggested by the House of Lords, it remains only to extend this direct EXETER LINE, without change of Gauge or Terminus, direct to FALMOUTH and PENZANCE.

The saving in actual distance thus effected between LONDON and FALMOUTH, as compared with the GREAT WESTERN and its extensions amounts to more than 50 Miles; whilst the time also saved by avoiding the passage of the Hamoaze, to say nothing of all other difficulties involved in that project, was estimated, in the recent enquiry before Parliament as equal to a saving of 15 or 20 Miles more.

Bearing in mind, therefore, the geographical position of FALMOUTH and PENZANCE, especially the great advantage of the former, as the most Westernly Station for our Naval and Packet Service, and as affording a most secure refuge in the event of War; and remembering, too, that this must eventually become the Highway to the Mediterranean, the East and West Indies, and America, the importance to the Admiralty and Lloyds of such a direct Railway, with a continuous and efficient Electric Telegraph, can hardly be over-rated.

The Central District from Exeter, Westward, has been recently re-surveyed, and has been found to afford a Main Trunk Line, with good locomotive gradients, attainable without engineering difficulties, and at a reasonable expense; the general course being near or through CREDITON, BOW, HATHERLEIGH, NORTH TAWTON, OKEHAMPTON, LAUNCESTON, CAMELFORD, BODMIN, ST. COLUMB, ST. AUSTELL (by means of a branch), TRURO, and PENRYN;- at TRURO, an extension Line through West Cornwall will diverge to CHACEWATER, REDRUTH, CAMBORNE, HAYLE, (with a Branch to ST. IVES,) MARAZION AND PENZANCE.

This extension runs for more than 30 Miles through the most populous and flourishing part of Cornwall; the Tables of the recently rejected WEST CORNWALL Bill shewed an existing traffic, through that district, of £10. per Cent after deducting working expenses. But as the constructing and working this Line by a separate Company would be productive of unnecessary expense and inconvenience to the public, the Line to PENZANCE, as well as FALMOUTH, will form an integral portion of the main work under one and the same management.

From TRURO, Eastward, the Main Line will pass several important Mines; and near BODMIN will throw out a Branch through the China Clay District to ST. AUSTELL, and its populous Mining neighbourhood. It will also avail itself of the Railways now in process of construction from NEW QUAY on the North, and PAR on the Southern Channel.; whilst a connexion with the already constructed Railway from BODMIN to WADEBRIDGE, will open, through to the PORT of PADSTOW, the best communication between CORK, the South of IRELAND, and LONDON. Advancing further, an opportunity will occur of establishing a traffic with the well known DELABOLE SLATE QUARRIES on the one hand and the flourishing CARADON MINES on the other; whilst the Sand supplied by the BUDE CANAL and the Lime which abounds in the Neighbourhood of LAUNCESTON, will be the subject of most considerable transport into the highly improvable Agricultural Districts Westward and Eastward.

Passing onward into DEVONSHIRE, a Branch will be thrown out from the Main Line to the PORT of BIDEFORD, thus opening, for the second mineral produce of WALES, a Market in CENTRAL DEVON and CORNWALL which are destitute of Coal; and another Branch will diverge Southward by TAVISTOCK to PLYMOUTH, thus affording the most direct communication between those Towns and EXETER. This Branch being also accessible from LAUNCESTON, will open for the North and West of Cornwall, and for FALMOUTH, a Line to PLYMOUTH, in point of time shorter than the lately projected Line across the Hamoaze from PLYMOUTH to FALMOUTH. Should the traffic, nevertheless, be found to justify another Branch from a point near BODMIN, through LISKEARD to PLYMOUTH, such a Branch may and will be constructed.

Arriving within 14 Miles of EXETER, the Main Line will be joined from the North by a Direct

Line from ILFRACOMBE and BARNSTAPLE to EXETER, and about 7 Miles further on by the DARTMOUTH, BRIXHAM, TORBAY and EXETER LINE an amalgamation of which two Lines is now under consideration, thus affording to these two friendly companies a direct communication from North to South, from the Bristol to the English Channel, and carrying their traffic on one common trunk, on to one common terminus, with the YEOVIL LINE at EXETER.

The inspection of a Map will better shew the importance of this comprehensive scheme, which overspreads the surface of DEVON and CORNWALL and leaves little to be desired to give full value and effect to objects of such importance.

The supply and demand created by this large area,- its Population, amounting to more than 600,000,- its Ports, situate on both Channels,- its Fishing, Mining, Commercial, and Agricultural advantages,- its exports of Corn, Wool, and Cattle - its probable consumption of Coal, Manure, Mining and general supplies - were fully gone into in a recent enquiry before the House of Lords, and forcible require increased facilities, and diminished costs of transport. The general evidence, also, given in that House, shewed a good remunerative existing traffic, without any such increase as may be reasonably be expected from a well digested system of Branches: and when the further increase in passenger and general traffic, East and West, is taken into consideration, which means must necessarily arise from bringing FALMOUTH, its harbour and foreign relations, and PENZANCE, with its much sought after climate and early markets, so much nearer to the Metropolis and the Northern and Eastern parts of England than can possibly be accomplished by any other devisable Railway communication; and when it is also borne in mind, that from the Peninsular form of the County of Cornwall this Line when established, can have no competitor;- it is not too much to assert that this project offers a very eligible opportunity for the Investment of Capital.

The strong feeling in favour of a CENTRAL LINE, evinced by Public Meetings and Petitions from every part of the County of Cornwall and West Devon; the support of Noblemen, Magistrates, Merchants, Mine Owners and Agriculturalists, in the recent struggle; the numerous and strong assurances of support already received from the Land-owners and general interests along the Line; and the hearty concurrence and co-operation of the Associated Companies, whose names will appear in the Provisional Committee;-leave no doubt of the successful issue of the application which will be made to Parliament in the next Session.

The Act to be applied for will contain the usual Clauses for limiting the liabilities of Shareholders to the amount of their Subscriptions, and for allowing Interest at £4. per Cent. Per Annum, on all Calls, from the time of payment until the opening of the Line

The Provisional Committee reserve to themselves the power of making such alterations in the Main Line, or Branches, and also of entering into such arrangements for the construction of those Branches, by Auxilliary Companies, as may be deemed advisable.

The Deposit will be payable on the allotment of the Shares. It is intended to proceed to an early allotment giving a preference to local applicants, and to the Shareholders in the above-named Associated Companies.

The usual Subscribers' Agreement and Parliamentary Contract must be executed by the Shareholders when called upon.

Applications for Shares, in the Form annexed, (accompanied by a satisfactory reference,) should be addressed to T. H. TILLEY, Esq. Solicitor, Falmouth; or to LEWIS CROMBIE, Esq. Interim Secretary, 63 Moorgate Street, London; or to the following Brokers;- Messrs TUCKER, BARNET, and Co. Birchin Lane, or H.TUDOR Esq. Hatton Court, London; or to Messrs. NEILSON and Co. Liverpool; and Messrs. CARDWELL and SONS, Manchester; of whom, and at the above-mentioned Banks, Copies of the Prospectus may be obtained.

Appendix five

Cornwall Central Railway versus Cornwall Railway
To the Editor of *The Times* Nov 12 1844

Sir,
The reply to my letter of 28th ult. from Mr Turner which is addressed to you and was published yesterday in the Cornwall papers, although it has not yet appeared in your columns, requires an answer. I shall endeavour to give it in few words. First, in reference to the quotations from various reports of the Devon and Cornwall Railway committee in which Mr Turner assumes that I concurred, I am most ready to admit that I have frequently asserted and am still of opinion that the north (or central) line surveyed by Captain Moorsom in 1841 viz "A trunk line of about 31 miles out of Exeter by way of Okehampton, under the northern face of Dartmoor to Lydford, in the neighbourhood of Tavistock, on to Plymouth and from Lydford through Launceston, near Bodmin, and by St Austell and Truro to Falmouth" might be fairly expected to remunerate those who would invest their capital in the undertaking but of the central line proposed and surveyed by Mr Richard Thomas which is laid down on such different principles and respecting which the traffic taken by Mr F. Fox in 1839 and 1840 does not apply, I have never offered a favourable opinion.

The county committee in 1841 calculated upon three distinct branches of traffic – that between Plymouth and Exeter by way of Tavistock; second between Plymouth and Falmouth; and third, between Falmouth and Exeter.

Of these the two first have been cut off by the adoption of a south line through Devon and by the determination to connect Tavistock with Plymouth. The third branch alone is left, and from that the traffic from Crediton to Exeter, which was estimated highly, is also gone, the Bristol and Exeter having determined to go to Parliament for a branch to that place and which will no doubt be extended to Barnstaple thereby taking the traffic of North Devon to Exeter.

Of the traffic remaining for the central line, anyone who has travelled from Exeter over the moors to Truro will bear me out in the assertion of my "honest conviction" – a conviction founded upon documentary evidence – "that there is not now sufficient traffic to warrant the construction of a north or central line through Cornwall". I must next advert to the change of opinion which Mr Turner attributes to me, and to the noblemen and gentlemen who compose the Provisional Committee of the Cornwall Railway. In August this year a meeting was held at Redruth over which Mr Pendarves presided, at which the position of the county, in reference to a railway, was considered. At this meeting it was determined that Mr Tweedy and myself should proceed to Bristol, and, if possible, induce the directors of the Great Western Railway, then about to assemble there, to extend the contemplated South Devon line through Cornwall. We had an interview with the chairman, secretary and engineer of the Company which led to us receiving an assurance of essential aid at the proper moment, and if I have any pleasure in penning this letter, it is in bearing my most unqualified testimony to the liberal, courteous and honourable manner in which Mr Saunders, the Secretary and the Board of Directors of the Great Western Company, have fulfilled every engagement in which they have entered. When the present committee, therefore, commenced their labours they considered the interests and prospects of the county. They had gone to the trouble and expense of taking the traffic and of surveying a central line; they had before them the results of the previous inquiries and therefore all the data were before them upon which they could determine and they finally abandoned the central line and diverted their attention to a south line.

At the meeting referred to Mr Pendarves, with a liberality which has ever distinguished the honourable gentleman in everything connected with the county, offered 5,000*l* which was followed by the offers of an equally liberal amount. Thus the change of opinion to which Mr Turner so frequently adverts was brought about, and in this change Mr Turner fully concurred and participated. Throughout the whole of the inquiries on this subject by the leading gentlemen of Cornwall, I think I am justified in stating that whenever the question of raising the funds for the construction of the line was mooted it had especial reference to "the prospect of a fair return upon the capital invested" upon which consideration alone could honourable men afford it their support, or give it the countenance of their names. Certainly Mr Turner might procure the aid of a banking company to any line of railway without an investigation of such an important particular as I have referred to but bankers generally require the clearest evidence of security before they adventure themselves or their clients in a financial speculation of so much moment.

In consequence of the inquiries which have been made, a public meeting was held in January last at Truro which persons from all parts of the county assembled, and the committee and officers were unanimously appointed with full powers to carry out the great undertaking.

On that occasion Sir Charles Lemon and others expressed a strong opinion in favour of a connexion with the Plymouth Railway, and Mr Turner spoke as follows:- I think I shall show that Mr Thomas's, the present engineer of the central line, statistics are ill based; and I think I shall be able to show the contrary in every respect will be the result of the figures I shall bring before your Lordship on this occasion. But, my Lord, there is another point we cannot get over by our speeches or our arguments and it is of no use to hold out to this meeting that there is a prospect of such a sum of money as would carry out the line from hence to Exeter. I think it is the only way to come to a safe and honourable conclusion, having so often called the county together, at once to state, that unless we avail ourselves of that capital which is to be had from the great railroad companies now formed, it will be impossible for us to have a railroad at all. I have come to the conclusion, after all that has passed, that my judgment, my individual judgment is perfectly correct – that you are arrived at a period when you must join the Plymouth company, or you will not have this railroad at all. But, my Lord, is it not of some importance that we should keep within our range an easy access to Plymouth – the great arsenal of the empire – with its vast population?

I think it important in this very point – that it will give us a reasonable return for the capital we invest. I hope the meeting will be of the opinion that the population of the county of Cornwall is best served by a South Devon line and, more than this, that it is best served by our acting at once. For your committee but without you give them unlimited powers, you will fail in your object . I am disposed to place entire confidence in the committee. I hope that the committee will have power to carry out the formation of a company and, as far as the expenditure of money goes, it could not be in better hands. In this opinion so well and so ably expressed, Mr Turner continued until after the survey of the south line had been made and the traffic taken, for on 2nd August last at a meeting of the shareholders held at Truro Mr Turner said - "He thought that the time would come when they should carry out this project or abandon it and that even another meeting without their showing their determination to proceed would place them in a position from which they would never recover (hear, hear). The time was past when they could have carried a railroad through the 'backbone' of Cornwall; the South Devon Railway was established and, although with no better prospects than our own, it was so high in public estimation that shares were selling at a premium of 10*l*. He had looked at the sources of income of the Cornish line, and he thought that the anticipations of the committee would in the long run be fully realized (Cheers). As the atmospheric principle might be adopted at an expense of only 40,000*l* extra he was extremely desirous that it should be applied. He thought that Falmouth especially would be benefited by the railway – much more than Truro – and beyond all the anticipations of the inhabitants. It was their duty to endeavour to obtain the restoration of the packets to Falmouth but even if they came to Plymouth, this county would be benefited, especially in the sale of its agricultural produce. Mr Turner then referred to the amount of capital required for this undertaking and expressed his opinion that no great difficulty would be experienced in obtaining it, especially as the Great Western Company were holding out the hand of friendship to them, which they should receive with gratitude."

Under the influence of these opinions Mr Turner acted in approving the prospectus as placed before the public, in accepting the office of a representative of the Cornwall Railway at the Admiralty and at the Board of Trade conjointly with the Earl of Falmouth and myself most strenuously advocated the superior claims of a south line before Lord Dalhousie and Captain Beecher, and others; and gave no notice of his altered opinion until after the prospectus had been long before the public, and the shares in the course of allotment . Whatever opinion may have been entertained formerly by Captain Moorsom or myself of the engineering difficulties to be encountered on the south line, it must be remembered that no survey had been made nor had the traffic been ascertained. Now the report of his survey is before the county in which the cost of construction and the expense of working had been plainly stated – not pledging the county to an atmospheric experiment, as is estimated by Mr Turner, nor confining the undertaking to a single line.

The following extract from the report will show on what ground the committee will form their decision respecting the sort of line they will recommend to their shareholders for adoption:- "Assuming that an atmospheric line is adopted, Captain Moorsom estimated the working expenses at 38,000*l*. This would leave $7^{1}/_{2}$ per cent profit for the shareholders. If worked as a locomotive line the annual expenses would be 45,000*l*, which would leave, if a double line be adopted $6\ ^{1}/_{4}$ per cent, and if a single $8\ ^{1}/_{4}$ per cent." Based on these statements the prospectus was issued; the Provisional Committee was formed of noblemen and gentlemen who had taken shares some to the amount of 5,000*l* ... and none less than 500*l*. The undertaking was supported by the leading landholders of the county; and it was responded to so liberally that 67,000 shares were applied for before one was issued although only 13,000 were to be distributed. The allotment has been made and the deposits received, and therefore, let the consequences be what they may, the undertaking must go forward.

I shall not condescend to notice any personal attacks upon myself, the object is too momentous - nothing less than the restoration to Falmouth of that prosperity in which I once participated and which I would not take a single step to damage: if therefore , my judgement is erroneous or in the estimation of others it is because I conscientiously believe that the Cornwall Central Railway can never be carried out.

I am etc William Henry Bond
London Nov 8

Appendix six

Extracts from *Royal Cornwall Gazette* 15 November 1844

THE GREAT ADVANTAGES OF

A RAILWAY

FROM FALMOUTH TO PLYMOUTH

OVER ANY OTHER LINE WHICH AT THE PRESENT TIME
CAN BE CONSTRUCTED THROUGH CORNWALL

I. This line has been carefully surveyed, and the traffic on it calculated from data presented by actual observation at a very great sacrifice of labour and expense to the County; while no other line which can at present be recommended has been surveyed by any practical Railway Engineer, or the traffic applicable to it ascertained by a competent person

II. The South Line not only completes the communication between Falmouth and Exeter, but it also places Plymouth, Stonehouse, and Devonport with their 100,000 inhabitants, in direct connection with Cornwall, which no other line can do.

III. It passes through or comes into direct contact with 500,819 inhabitants out of 341,323, thus affording demonstrative evidence, that both in regard to public convenience and the interests of shareholders, it can have no successful competitor.

IV. It must have the largest amount of traffic per mile of any Line that can be constructed in a parallel direction; the minimum traffic on this Line being £93,904 for sixty six miles or about £1423 per mile while, deducting the traffic from Plymouth to Falmouth, and from Plymouth to Exeter from the amount stated in the Traffic Table which accompanies CAPTAIN MOORSOM'S Report for a North Line, there will remain but 100,000*l* traffic for 100 miles or about 1000 per mile.

V. It certainly secures the approbation of the Government, which has been unequivocally expressed in favour of the coast line, and which in the event of War would be immense importance, as with the advantage of the electric telegraph, it would place the resources of the great military Arsenal at Plymouth within a few hours of the entire coast from thence to Penzance, an object which could in nowise be embraced by any other Line.

VI. It has obtained the powerful support and substantial aid of the Great Western, Bristol and Exeter, Bristol and Gloucester, and South Devon Companies, who have subscribed 250,000*l* towards its capital; whilst any other Line must not only be destitute of such support (for no other railway company has yet formed a connexion with Exeter) but must, on the contrary, encounter the opposition of those powerful bodies

VII. It will provide the best and largest amount of accommodation for the public, enabling passengers to pass from Falmouth to Liverpool in *fourteen* hours. For although by a central line passengers might possibly reach London in twenty minutes less time, the obstruction and delay to which persons travelling to Bristol and the North would be liable will much more than counterbalance this trifling advantage

VIII. This line is not only the best for Cornwall traffic, but it can certainly and without delay be secured. It has the support of all the Nobility, and nearly all the leading Landholders of the County; and the Capital has been raised, and the applications have been so numerous that very many thousands have been rejected. The North or Central Line is destitute of such support, and has only been presented to the public as the project of individuals, who themselves have not announced any subscription of capital towards it.

IX. The arrangements for the construction of this Line are in such a state of forwardness that it can be finished in two years from the passing of the Act- thus completing the Grand Chain of Railways from Scotland to Penzance.

X. It will with the Port of Falmouth and its contemplated improvements, afford the Mail Department such superior advantages, that Her Majesty's Government, it is presumed, cannot refuse the restoration of the packet establishment to that place.

CORNWALL CENTRAL RAILWAY

At a Meeting of the Inhabitants of the Town and Neighbourhood of Penzance, (held pursuant to requisition) in the GUILDHALL, on Friday the 8th day of November 1844
John Batten, Esq., Mayor
IN THE CHAIR
The following resolutions were unanimously adopted:

1st Resolution - Moved by RICHARD PEARCE, Esq., seconded by CAPT TAYLOR, R.N.
That it is the decided opinion of that the Central Railway is the only one calculated to meet the requirements of this town and neighbourhood, and the county in general.

2nd Resolution – Moved by the REV M. N. PETERS, seconded by R. BRANWELL Esq.,
That this meeting is quite convinced that in a National point of view, the Central line will ensure greater facility of intercourse, and certainty of communication, than any line which should depend on the doubtful passage across the Hamoaze

3rd Resolution – Moved by Lieutenant ROBYNS, seconded by A. DALBY; Esq., R.N.
That a Memorial in support of the Central line be prepared for presentation to the Board of Trade.

4th Resolution – Moved by B. P. BATTEN Esq., seconded by R. MILLETT, Esq.,
That a committee be formed for the purpose of conferring with the Committee of the Coast line, with the view of inducing them to co-operate in carrying out a measure which they have so repeatedly stated to be of such vital importance to the County.

5th Resolution, - Moved by R. V. DAVY, Esq., seconded by R. MOYLE. Esq.,
That the cordial thanks of this meeting be given to Edward W. W. Pendarves, Esq., and Edmund Turner Esq., for their generous determination to maintain the interests of the County by withdrawing their support from the Plymouth and Falmouth Line, when they found that a Central Line was attainable.

6th Resolution, - Moved by S. HIGGS, Esq., seconded by R. EDMONDS, Esq.,
That the Members of the County be requested to promote, by every means in their power, the Central Line which is of such essential importance to the welfare of this County.

7th Resolution, - Move by J. J. A. BOASE, Esq., seconded by J. N. R. MILLETT, Esq.,
That the Mayor and Corporation be requested to cooperate in carrying out so important an object to this Town and Neighbourhood.

8th Resolution, - Moved by M. COLLIVER, Esq., seconded by E. PEARCE .
That the thanks, of this meeting be given to Mr Tilly for his clear, lucid, and satisfactory statement; one which cannot fail to convince every one who has heard it of the great value of a Central Line over all others.

JOHN BATTEN, MAYOR.

Appendix Seven

At a General Meeting of Shareholders

Held at the Assembly Room, Truro, on Tuesday the 26th day of August 1845 pursuant to public advertisement

J. T. Treffry, Esquire of Place in the chair

The following report was read:-

Report

The Committee have deemed it their duty to convene the present Meeting at the earliest possible period, for the purpose of laying before the Proprietors a Report of their past proceedings, and the course which they recommend for adoption under the circumstances in which the Company is placed.

In discharge of the trust reposed in them and encouraged by the cordial co-operation of the Great Western – the Bristol and Exeter – the Bristol and Gloucester – and South Devon Associated Companies who converted to become shareholders to the extent of £250,000 by an unusually large and influential local interest, amounting to nearly £300,000, and by the support of a highly respectable Proprietary, your Committee proceeded to take the necessary steps to bring a Bill before Parliament for the construction of the Cornwall Railway.

In laying their case before the Board of Trade the Company had to contend with two rival and competing schemes, but after an examination into their merits the Board decided on reporting to Parliament in favour of the Cornwall Railway, and against the competing projects.

The favourable opinion of the Board of Trade was afterwards fully confirmed by the deliberate judgment of the Select Committee of the House of Commons.

That Committee over which the Right Honourable Mr Macauley presided, after a most laborious investigation, which was rendered the more searching by an unusually severe opposition, came to a unanimous decision in favour of your line and reported accordingly to the House.

Their Report, and the discussion which arose upon it, gave an opportunity to Mr Macauley and other Members, to hear their testimony to the merits and importance of the income, and after a debate in which very valuable and favourable expressions of opinion were elicited, the Report of the Committee received the approval of the House.

The undertaking being thus sanctioned by the Board of Trade and the House of Commons, the Bill was introduced into the House of Lords and after an unsuccessful opposition in the Committee on Standing Orders, was referred to a Select Committee of their Lordships' House.

To the proceedings and decision of that Tribunal your Committee would beg to draw your particular attention – after a protracted investigation – after an almost unexampled opposition - after having heard a mass of evidence in favour of other lines, and against the Cornwall Railway , the Committee, notwithstanding all that had been said and urged on behalf of the other lines, came to a special and unanimous resolution, affirming the advantages of the line selected by the Promoters of the Cornwall Railway - adopting in the declaratory part of their resolution the very terms of the preamble of the Bill , although at the same time expressing an opinion that it would not be advisable to adopt definitively the plan of Railway communication which was intended to be carried out by the bill without a further and most accurate survey of the whole line of country traversed between Plymouth and Falmouth, with a view of obtaining gradients and curves more favourable, and avoiding the passage of the Hamoaze and of the Penryn River below Penryn, if these last objects could be effected without any great countervailing cost and disadvantage. The Committee were therefore of opinion, that the Bill should not be then further proceeded with.

The effect of this resolution, although it gave cause for regret and disappointment at the postponement of a measure so important to the County and to the Public, cannot fail to inspire confidence and insure success.

The principle of the measure is recognised and established, its completion only is delayed and the sole requirement is that a further and most accurate shall be made.
The Proprietors will also have observed with satisfaction that on bringing up the report of the Committee to the House of Lords, Lord Wenborough spoke of the great importance of obtaining a line of Railway from Plymouth to Falmouth

Your Committee acting in conformity with the recommendation thus given to them, proceeded to take such course as appeared to them to be necessary and at a meeting, which was attended by Members of the Cornwall and West Cornwall Committees, and by Directors of the Great Western, Bristol and Exeter, Bristol and Gloucester and South Devon Companies, the following resolutions were unanimously passed:-

> "That it is important for the interests of the Cornwall Railway Company that immediate steps should be taken to give full effect to the said resolution
> "That in the opinion of the Gentlemen present the cordial cooperation of all Parties connected with the Provisional Committee and with the several Associated companies, is essential for such object and that each individual will recommend to their respective boards to continue their best assistance to carry the bill in the coming session.
> "That Mr Brunel be requested carefully to survey the Country, for the purpose of recommending such improvements or alterations in the line of Railway as may seem to him expedient.
> That each of the Associated Companies as well as the Provisional Committee of the Cornwall Railway Company and also the West Cornwall Railway Company be requested to delegate to two members the power of assisting in the deliberation as to the proper steps to be taken, and as to the course of the improved line, upon receiving Mr Brunel's report and that such meeting be held in London with the least possible delay".

Your Committee have confirmed and adopted the above resolutions and appointed Mr Brunel to be the Engineer of the Cornwall Railway Company.

At a meeting of the Gentlemen appointed in pursuance of the above resolutions Mr Brunel stated that in his opinion he should be able to lay out such a line as he believes would be satisfactory to all parties and would meet the approval of Parliament and the Public and with a view of attending to the County of Cornwall more extensive railway accommodation, Mr Brunel suggests the expediency of a junction with the proposed North Devon line for a period not exceeding 3 months.

Moved by Mr W. M. Tweedy – seconded by Mr Wm Carne
Resolved that the South Devon Board be thanked for their offer and that the Finance Committee be requested to arrange with them for a loan.

Capt Moorsom's account amounting to £369.7/- having been submitted to this Board.
Moved by Mr Gill - Seconded by Mr Tweedy.
Resolved that the Secretary be instructed to ask Captain Moorsom by whose authority and at what dates he undertook the journeys and rendered the services referred to in his account.

Source PRO RAIL 134/1

Appendix eight

Identity of William Johnson

The plan and sections for Cornwall Railway Bill submitted to Parliament in November 1845 was carried out by Messrs William Johnson and Henry Hornor Johnson immediately after the failure of the previous Bill. The name Hornor, is the maiden name of Elizabeth (1776-1820), first wife of William Johnson I, on the survey for the Cornwall Railway. The biographical details of the Johnsons come from several sources. Sarah Bendall's *The Dictionary of Land Surveyors and Map Makers* identifies William Johnson I and William Johnson II. It also identifies the brother in law Thomas Hornor (1785-1844) who was trained as a land surveyor by William I and became renowned for his topographic artwork.

In the 1841 Census, William I and his second wife Elizabeth (nee Waterhouse) and Henry Hornor Johnson are resident together in Manchester. William II is also Manchester based. A letter held in the local studies section of the Manchester Archive provided the link with Cornwall. It is from Henry H. Johnson dated 20 September 1845 from the White Hart Hotel in Hayle, to the Lancashire and Cheshire Working Men's Singing Club concerning the renewal of his subscription. This would have been exactly at the time he would have been surveying the Cornwall, or possibly West Cornwall, Railway. William Johnson senior belonged to a Quaker family. He was born in 1771 and died in February 1845. He along with other members of the family were buried in the graveyard of the Society of Friends at Mount Street, Manchester. His date of death clarifies that it must have been William Johnson II with his younger brother Henry Hornor Johnson who carried out the survey for Brunel later that year.

William Johnson I set up a land surveying practice in Manchester which his son duly joined. He carried out a survey of 'The Parish of Manchester' in 1818/19. He updated it in 1836/7 to take account of the rapid growth of the city. The *Manchester Guardian* (13 June 1840) records that it is to be published: *Altogether the plan deserves a place in every public institution of the town, and in the libraries of all who take an interest in the geological, botanical, and other features of this remarkable district.* The work included canals and railways. One example was the survey and levels for a map of the canals of Lancaster, York, Derby and Chester. The Manchester Archive and Local Studies have provided the details of the marriage on William Johnson I to Elizabeth Hornor in 1798, and the dates of the birth of their six children particularly William (born 1801 at Yealand Conyers, near Carnforth, Lancs) and Henry (born 1817). There are several letters in the Brunel letterbooks at Bristol University addressed to both 'William Johnson' and 'William Johnson Jn' which give an indication of some of the surveys that they carried out for Brunel. These included the Sheffield Railway, the Stroud Valley and Taff Vale line. Brunel approached William Johnson junior with a view to surveying the Genoa/Milan line in 1842. Brunel also wrote to him in 1844 asking if he could possibly lend any surveyors to work on the Wexford /Waterford railway in Ireland.

Bendall records that, by the mid 1840s, the Johnson's were also involved in a land surveying business in Westminster, London as Martin, Johnsons and Fox - a given address is 24 Great George Street. The Lancashire Record Office hold a document which confirms that in June 1847 Henry

Horner [*sic*] was describing himself as an 'engineering surveyor' of Westminster, London.

It has not been possible to establish the dates of their deaths. By 1851, William junior and his family are living at Woodlands, Cottington, Sidmouth, Devon and Henry Horner is resident in Newport, South Wales. By 1857 it appears Henry too was residing in Sidmouth. In the 1871 Census they have moved to Walcot, Bath. However there is no record of them in the Quaker cemetery at Clarendon Road, Widcombe, Bath.

The 'Manchester Johnsons' are not to be confused with the 'Plymouth Johnsons'; the brothers William and John who had interests in granite quarrying in South Devon, the Plymouth or Haytor Granite Works, Plymouth, the Plymouth and Dartmoor Railway and Plymouth wharves for the shipment of their stone and masonry. Amongst other contracts the Plymouth Johnsons supplied granite for the Plymouth breakwater and constructed the masonry for Rendel's Laira Bridge. John and his family lived at Laira House, situated close to Laira Bridge and the Plymouth Granite Works. A William Johnson, possibly his brother, applied to the Institution of Civil Engineers, for membership in 1840, giving both Laira House and Grosvenor Wharf, Westminster as his addresses, on *'account of his pursuits being connected with branches of civil engineering'*. He was elected as an associate presumably on the basis that he was not a fully trained civil engineer but was intimately involved in construction projects.

A.1 *From the plans accompanying the 1846 Cornwall Railway Bill.*

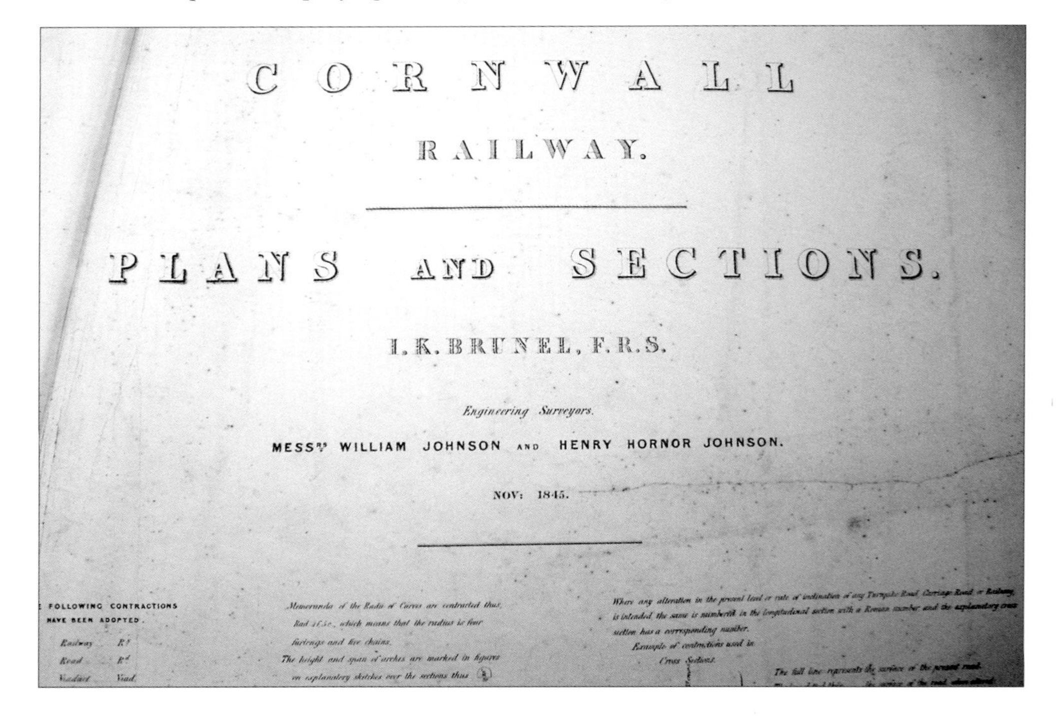
CORNWALL

RAILWAY.

PLANS AND SECTIONS.

I. K. BRUNEL, F.R.S.

Engineering Surveyors.

MESSRS WILLIAM JOHNSON AND HENRY HORNOR JOHNSON.

NOV: 1845.

[THE] FOLLOWING CONTRACTIONS HAVE BEEN ADOPTED.

Railway Ry

Road Rd

Viaduct Viad.

Memoranda of the Radii of Curves are contracted thus, Rad 4f.5c., which means that the radius is four furlongs and five chains.

The height and span of arches are marked in figures on explanatory sketches over the sections thus

Where any alteration in the present level or rate of inclination of any Turnpike Road, Carriage Road or Railway, is intended the same is numbered in the longitudinal section with a Roman number and the explanatory cross section has a corresponding number.

Example of contractions used in Cross Sections.

The full line represents the surface of the present road.

Appendix nine

Extract from *West Briton* and *Cornwall Advertiser* Friday May 13 1859

DEPLORABLE ACCIDENT ON THE CORNWALL RAILWAY THREE LIVES LOST

An accident occurred on this railway on Friday evening last, near to St Germans which produced a feeling of consternation and dismay throughout the entire county. The line had been opened to the public on the previous Wednesday, under the most auspicious circumstances; every one travelling on it appeared thoroughly to appreciate and to enjoy the accommodation which it afforded, and pass which way you would you heard only one general feeling of gratification expressed with the improved means of locomotion that had been provided, when this melancholy event occurred to shock the public mind and cast a gloom over the county. The train to which this accident occurred was the one which leaves London at six o'clock in the morning performing the entire distance between the metropolis and Truro in one day, and arriving at the latter at the latter at ten minutes after ten at night. The train reached Plymouth shortly after seven o'clock on Friday, and at 7.25 started on its way for Truro. It consisted of a second class carriage, then a first class carriage, next another second class, and lastly a goods truck. The engine was a new one, named the "Elk." and was driven by Henry Biscombe, a man named Davis Hannaford being the stoker. Two guards attended the train, the head guard, William Hoskins, being in the first compartment of the second class carriage next to the engine, and the second guard, Richard Paddon, occupying the break compartment in the other second class carriage which stood third in the train. It was four minutes after its time when it started from Plymouth, and it then contained about 100 passengers. But nearly half of this number were only going to Devonport, and on arriving there it was found that three of the four minutes had been made up. The train proceeded onwards to Saltash, which it reached in fourteen minutes from Plymouth, nothing unusual occurring calculating to excite uneasiness. After leaving Saltash the train passed down an incline of about a quarter of a mile in length, the gradient of which is one in eighty; then up a gradient, until approaching the bridge which crosses the line about a quarter or a third of a mile from a slight incline from the Grove lake, an inlet of the Lynher, when there is another slight incline, and then onto the level. It ran along this with perfect steadiness until arriving within a distance of 148 feet of the Grove viaduct, when without any perceptible cause, there was a sudden jerk, which was followed by several more, and it was found that the engine was off the rails. The left side driving wheel appears to have the been the first to get out of position, and it ran for some distance on the wooden sleeper, being kept there by the flange of the opposite wheel pressing against the rail, and such was the force of this pressure that one of the strong rails was forced from its fastenings and bent considerably outwards. The engine seems to have run in this way for about 39 yards, the flange of the wheel making considerable indentations in the heads of the bolts which fasten down the rails, as it proceeded, when it left the line, and gradually converged towards the right, the left side wheel cutting through the strong wooden transoms of the permanent way, and destroying everything that its progress. Shortly after passing the end of the viaduct, the engine came into contact with the parapet, the timbers of which to look at them, seem strong enough almost to resist a cannon ball, but it cut through and completely shattered one of the thick diagonal supports against which it struck, destroyed 56 feet of the framework and flew over the embankment, traversing a space of 71 feet while falling the distance of

28 feet perpendicularly from the rails to the mud at the bottom of the viaduct. In its passage it turned over and fell parallel with the rails, burying itself in the mud, to the depth of nine or ten feet. The engine also dragged the second class carriage, which followed it, and the first class carriage behind that, after it. The former fell diagonally to the engine, the end just touching it, and fortunately it was not upset in its descent. The first class carriage fell upon the fore part of the second class carriage, crushing the first two compartments, in one of which was the unfortunate guard, and it is supposed that he then met with his death, as his body was found there afterwards. It then rolled over, falling outside the other carriage. Paddon, the second guard, who was in the third carriage, on first suspecting that the engine was off the line, with great presence of mind and promptitude, instantly screwed on his break to its utmost force and to this circumstance is in all probability, owing the preservation of his own life and the lives of the passengers in that and other carriages, as had his carriage and the goods truck been dragged over the viaduct and on to the other carriages below, the loss of life would doubtless have been frightful. Notwithstanding the awful position in which he found himself and others placed he held his break [*sic*] screwed down to its utmost force, with the firmness of a hero, and he thus succeeded in giving such a check to the carriage that, on the engine taking its fearful plunge, the coupling chains broke and the connection was severed. On getting out of the carriage instantly after, he found that the peril had had been most imminent. Had the coupling chains held a moment longer the third carriage and the truck must have followed the others in their tremendous descent, the two front wheels of the former and the two hind wheels of the latter having been dragged of the rails. A glance over the viaduct revealed the fearful nature of the accident. There lay the engine overturned and embedded in mud; beside it was the second class carriage, the water reaching half way up it: and beyond that the first class carriage, with its wheels in the air, also half covered with water. Paddon immediately proceeded to extricate the passengers from their perilous position, a work in which he was assisted by those who had been so providentially preserved. The noise of the crash and of the steam from the engine fire were heard at St Germans, and attracted a pilot of the St German's river and several other persons to the spot, all of whom promptly rendered every assistance in their power . . .

It has been found impossible to give any satisfactory explanation as to the cause of the accident. The embankment was found to be perfectly sound and firm, and the permanent way even in good order; there was no incline or curve at the place, and at present all is conjecture as to what caused the engine to jump from the rails, none of the engineers on the line being able to throw any light upon the subject. Neither can the extent of the damage at present be estimated; as this will depend upon how far the injured materials can be made available. The engine cost £3000 in its construction, but it is expected that it can be put in serviceable order again for a comparatively small outlay. The first class carriage appears not to have received serious injury beyond the damage to the lining by the mud and dirty water. The second class carriage appears to have sustained the greatest amount of damage, two of the end compartments having been completely smashed by the fall of the first class carriage upon it. The parapet of the viaduct was considerably damaged, but this has been easily repaired. With respect to the permanent way, the injury was confined to the destruction of some of the transoms, and the breaking of one of the rails, a matter of no serious moment . . .

After the accident, the trains only ran from Truro to Liskeard. Workmen were set to work to repair the damage to the permanent way and the viaduct, and to take the engine to pieces, and remove it from the debris of the carriage. By Monday, the work was completed, and on Tuesday the line was again opened to the public through to Plymouth. In order to give greater confidence to the public, it has been determined to allow ten minutes or a quarter of an hour more time to each train on its passage to and from Truro and Plymouth.

Appendix ten

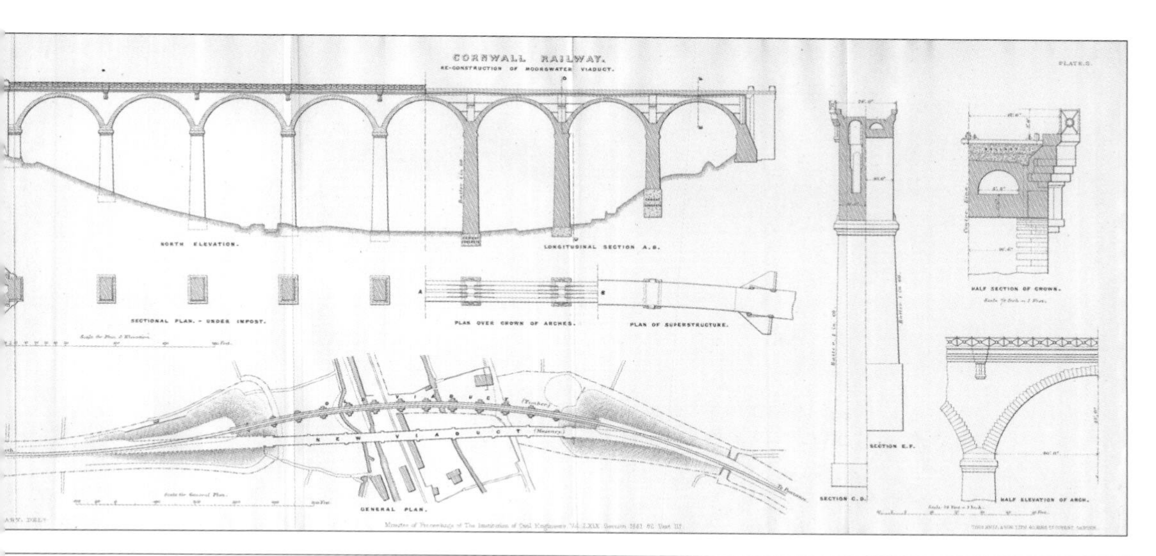

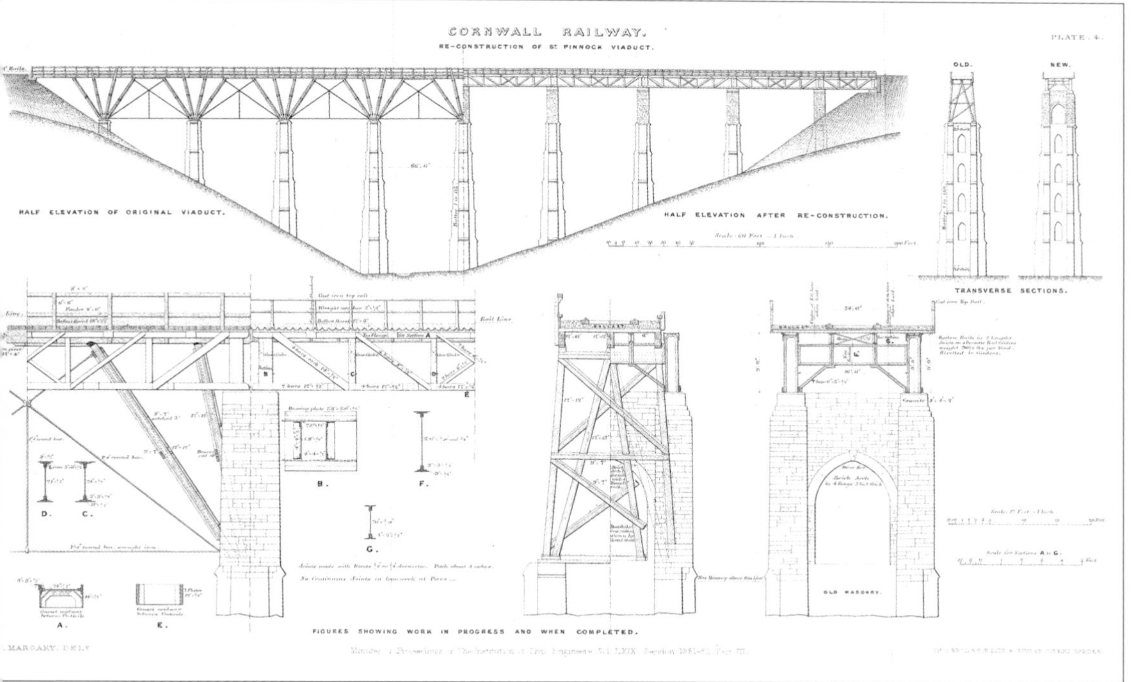

and A3 *Plans and elevations for the reconstruction of Moorswater and St Pinnock viaducts*

Index

INDEX OF PERSONAL NAMES